Well — I could fill this
McCahons and be happy
and which one do you
I was tempted to make a point
by having no image here at all —
just talk about them — Colin's
uncanny sense of proportion — how
little he needed to make his
point — how the positive spaces &
the negative spaces somehow
swell into each other! How the same
line ~~could~~ can ~~[illegible]~~ describe a line — or
describe a mass — & how the
masses seem to hover in so much
space + vice versa. The truth in a McCahon
glows through the work unimpeded
by ~~fear of failure~~ — like the wind
through the back ~~porch~~
[illegible] through

IT'S ALL ABOUT THE IMAGE

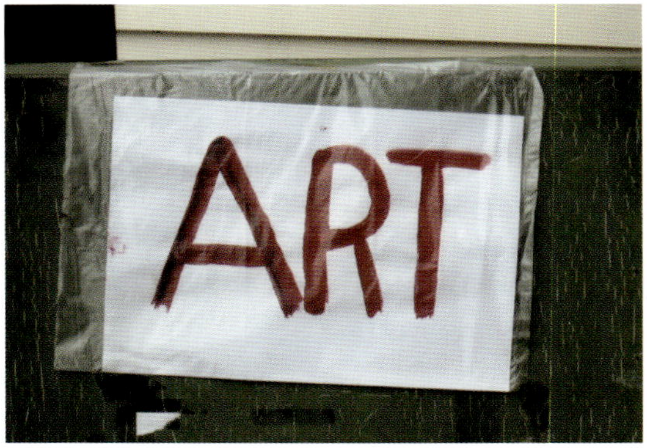
ART

IT'S ALL ABOUT THE IMAGE

GODWIT

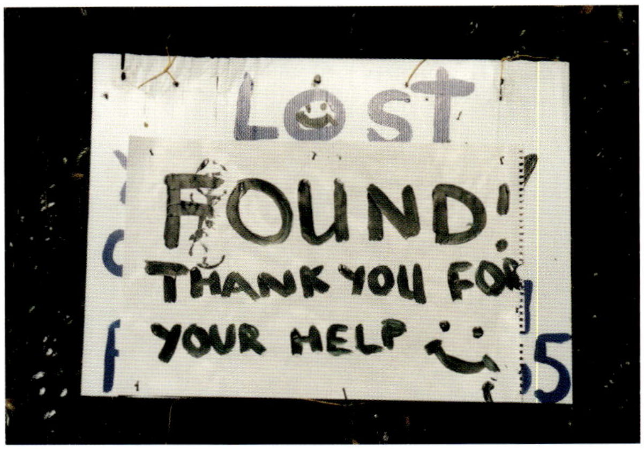
LOST
FOUND!
THANK YOU FOR
YOUR HELP

For Tom Kreisler and Julian Dashper

To learn more about Dick Frizzell, read *Dick Frizzell: The Painter*, Godwit, 2009

A GODWIT BOOK published by Random House New Zealand
18 Poland Road, Glenfield, Auckland, New Zealand

For more information about our titles go to www.randomhouse.co.nz

A catalogue record for this book is available from the National Library of New Zealand

Random House New Zealand is part of the Random House Group
New York London Sydney Auckland Delhi Johannesburg

First published 2011

ISBN 978 1 86979 707 2

Design: Saskia Nicol and Dick Frizzell
Printed in China by Everbest Printing Co Ltd

Contents

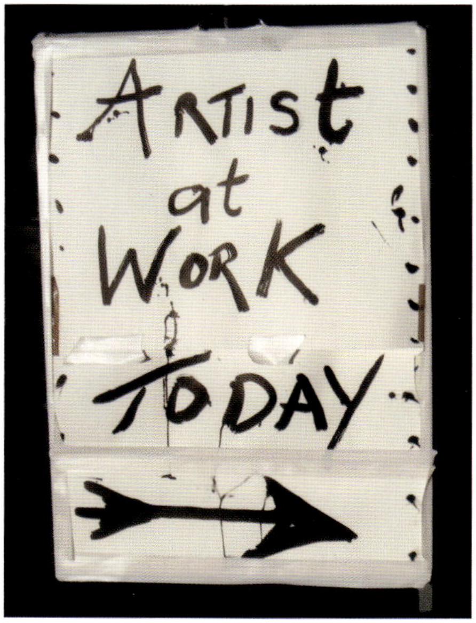
Artist
at
WORK
TODAY

The contemplation of extreme novelty [newness] cannot please a man whose taste is already formed, because he sees in it signs of an evolution that no longer depends on him, something like an announcement of death.

Robert Rey (c. 1913)

To give yourself completely to what you're doing while simultaneously watching yourself do it — that's the hardest of all . . .

Henri Matisse

Introduction

In 1978 I got a QE II Arts Council grant to travel to America. The plan was to drive from coast to coast and take in as much of the culture – the good, the bad and the ugly – as possible.

We bought a large station wagon in LA, loaded it with family, food and shelter, and set off with our list of art galleries to visit and camping grounds to stay at.

This was my first OE, at 35, having till then picked up what art history I had from reproductions, and local variants of international movements.

The shock of actually seeing the originals of the paintings that had inspired and influenced me was overwhelming and every museum in America seemed to have more than its fair share of these significant milestones. I couldn't believe I could stand right there in front of Matisse's *Red Studio* in the Museum of Modern Art (MOMA)!

A few thousand miles further on we arrived in Washington DC and, after pitching the tent and unpacking the chilly bin and the Coleman, we rolled up to the Smithsonian for the ritual visit. We walked into the first gallery and there was Gauguin's self-portrait with the halo, snake and apples on a red and yellow background. I let out a gasp and shouted,

Colin McCahon
Here I Give Thanks to Mondrian
1961, enamel on board
1215 x 915 mm

And here I give thanks to McCahon. A revelation for a teenage art student back in 1962.

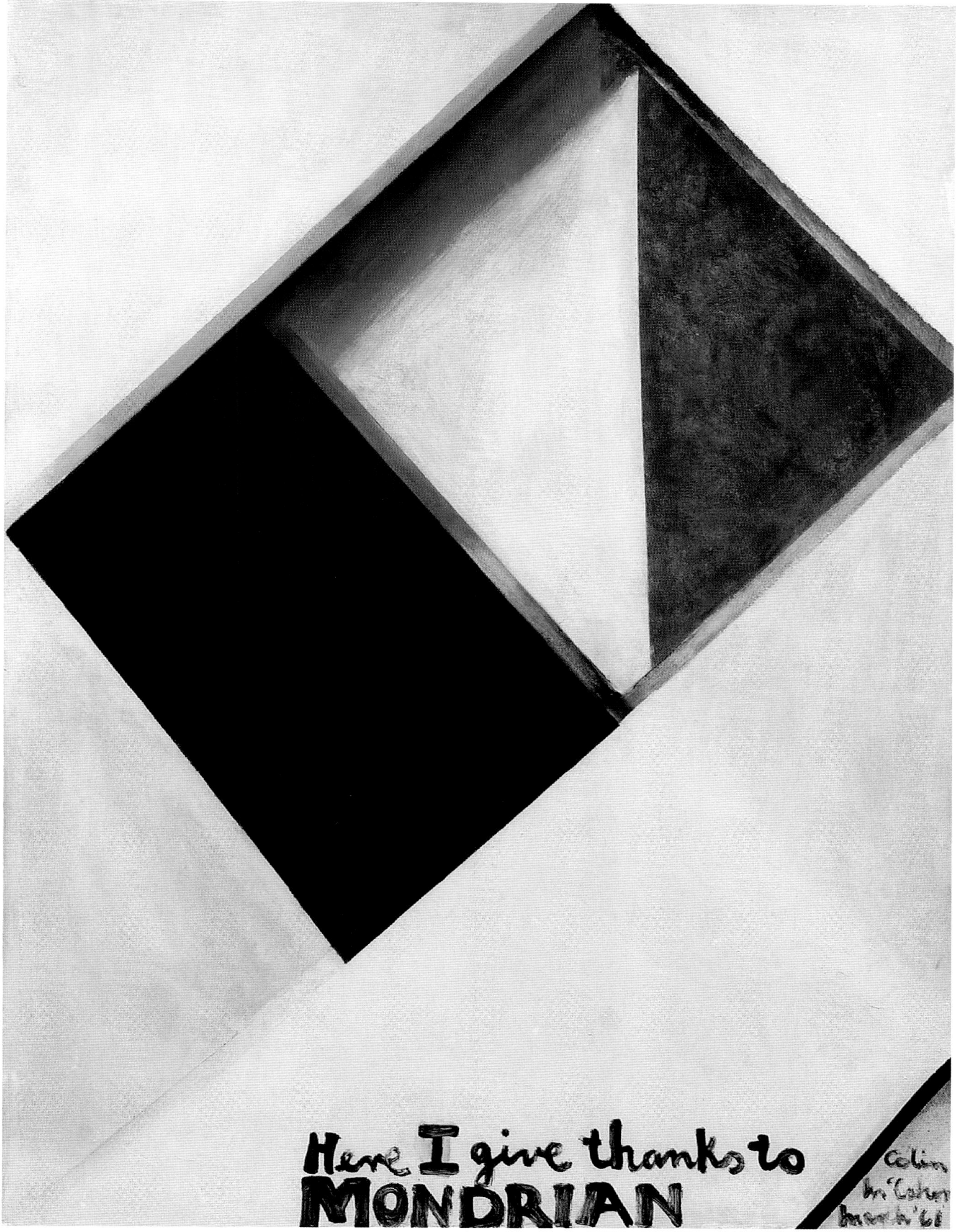
Here I give thanks to
MONDRIAN
Colin
McCahon
March '61

'There's my favourite painting!' And Josh, 11 years old, looked up at me with a weary tilt of his head and said, 'How many favourite paintings have you got, Dad?'

And that's more or less the organising principle behind this book – a list of my favourite New Zealand paintings.

When Jenny Hellen at Random House approached me with this project, 'my' history of New Zealand art, I found myself jotting down names before I'd hung up the phone. What a fantastic idea, I thought; shine a light on some of the works I've always loved that always seem to miss muster in the usual round-ups. (Like Bill Sutton's portrait of his shirt-sleeved dad in Te Papa – a New Zealand masterpiece in my mind.)

And of course that got me to thinking why this should be so, why I should even have a point of view worth bothering about, and when I eventually sat down to write the introduction to the book, how would I explain this solipsistic exercise?

Maybe it would be interesting to try to explain it to myself!

So I got to thinking about the images I was drawn to (because that's what it's all about – images) back before I was told what I'd be better off looking at. What formed the formative thinking?

Given the almost total lack of anything even vaguely representing 'art' in Hastings and Hawke's Bay in the early 1950s, or none that I was likely to gain access to, I had ample opportunity to exercise my innocent eye. I developed a fascination with anything – outside of comics which were something else entirely – that held technical or narrative intrigue. I'm not alone in this – it seems to be the universal default position – but it has stuck with me on some deep level that even years of an intense modernist art education couldn't erode.

The first piece of 'real' art that I can remember seeing and identifying as art (because it was in a frame, which was the way art was always depicted in my *Beano* comics – it's funny where the information comes from now that I think about it) was a reproduction of Vladimir Tretchikoff's *Lost Orchid*, a painting of an orchid on stone steps, with a dewdrop, propped up in a furniture shop window in Heretaunga Street, Hastings. I passed this rapidly fading artefact on my way to and from school, and would always pause to stare into that dewdrop. The idea that it was possible to paint anything as unfathomably infinite as that seemed absolutely magic to me.

I saw a similar conjuring trick happen right in front of my eyes a few months later when Peter McIntyre invited me (I'd been staring again)

Mollie Miller Atkinson
Richard Bird in the Bush
AH & AW Reed,
Wellington 1944

Richard Frizzell was pretty happy too.

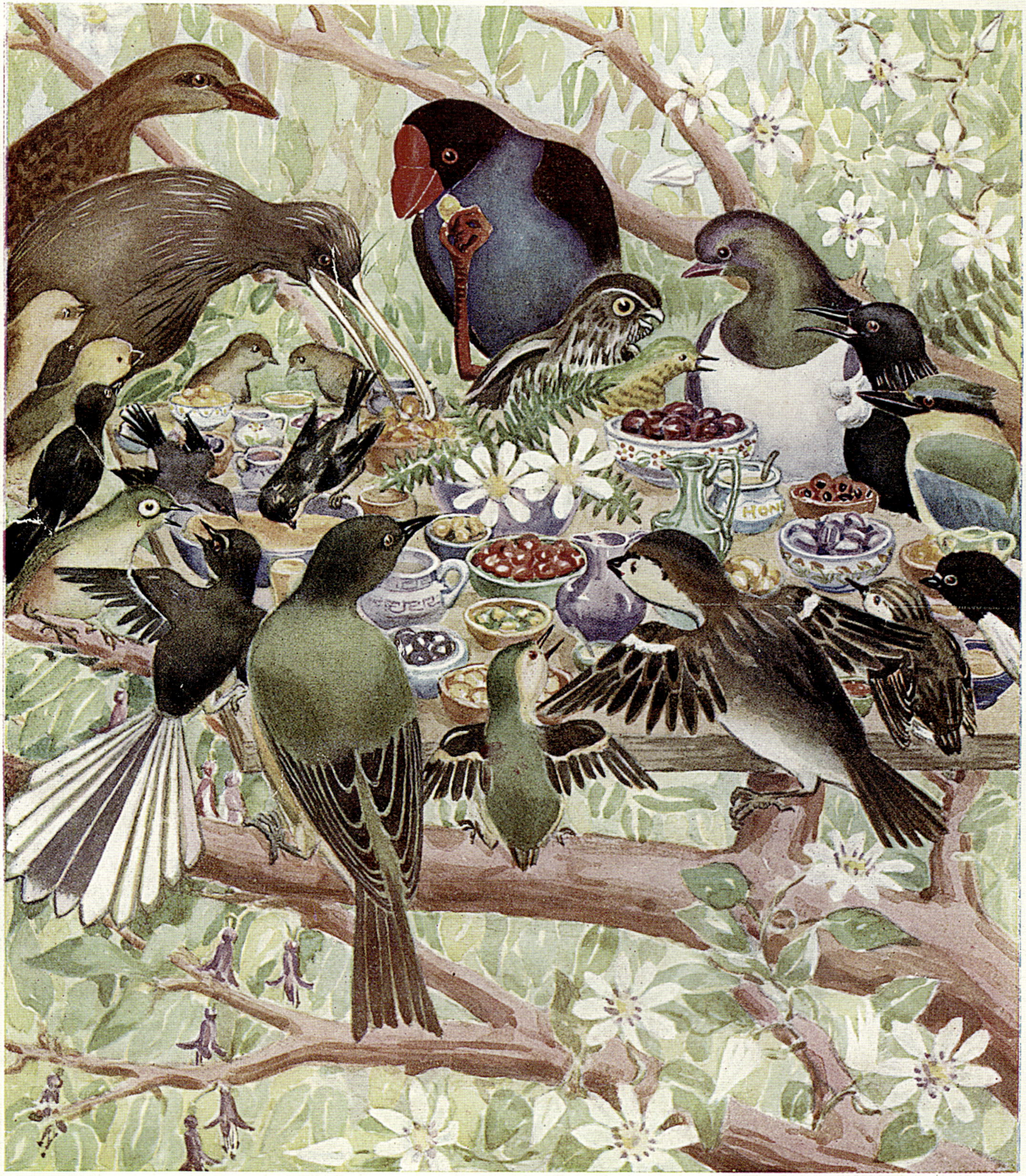

RICHARD BIRD NEARLY BURST WITH PRIDE

onto the scaffolding to watch him painting the World War Two mural in the Hastings War Memorial Library. He painted some small rocks on the desert sand at the feet of the soldiers and with what seemed like just a couple of brushstrokes he rendered the texture of the rock, the sun on the rock, the reflected light on the shady side of the rock, and the shadow of the rock on the sand! The entire Universe right there! With a brush and some paint. I've been trying to be that clever ever since.

Things had moved on, of course, by the time I was at art school, where I enthusiastically embraced the whole social and political notion of Modern Art, what it was saying and why it was saying it. But I still kept an eye on what I guess was the popular culture of the time, things like the Kelliher Prize. I knew what the 'correct' art rules were but I still found it weird on some level that such rendering skills and the obvious delight in being able to 'picture' the world like that had such zero credibility. One of the things that fascinated me about those oily landscapes was that it all looked so learnt, displaying a depth of technical know-how that could only have been accumulated by experience, or passed on – learnt. Where did they learn it?!?

Meanwhile, at art school we seemed to be making it up as we went along ('moving it on by getting it wrong' indeed!), clumsily discovering that there is in fact a limit to what a surface slick of technical prowess can provide. So we plunged into a mess of socio-political commentary, fashion, formal contrast, concept, self-expression – all of this dovetailing in a convenient and punkish way with a sort of ANTI-technique. The virtual obligation to be anti-bourgeois coincided rather nicely with the fact that none of us could afford to join the bourgeois even if we wanted to. (Andy Warhol said that there is nothing more bourgeois than being anti-bourgeois, but I read that much later.)

It's all rather peculiar, when I look back, that we had to jettison so much of what I'd previously believed in: detail, finish, narrative, the pictorial and so on. I should say I wasn't too conflicted about this because as youthful adventures go the modern art movement ticked all the boxes, or nearly all of them.

I think the thing that finally got to me, and prompted the beginning of my own resistance to all this received wisdom, was the growing awareness that there was something missing, that all those years of ruthless 'artopsy' had left a large hole at the centre and that the baby might have been thrown out with the dirty turps.

My breakthrough was to decide to start putting back all the bits I was

Peter McIntyre
Major General Sir Bernard Freyberg, V.C.
1943, oil
900 x 800 mm

Early McIntyre – before the signature went modern.

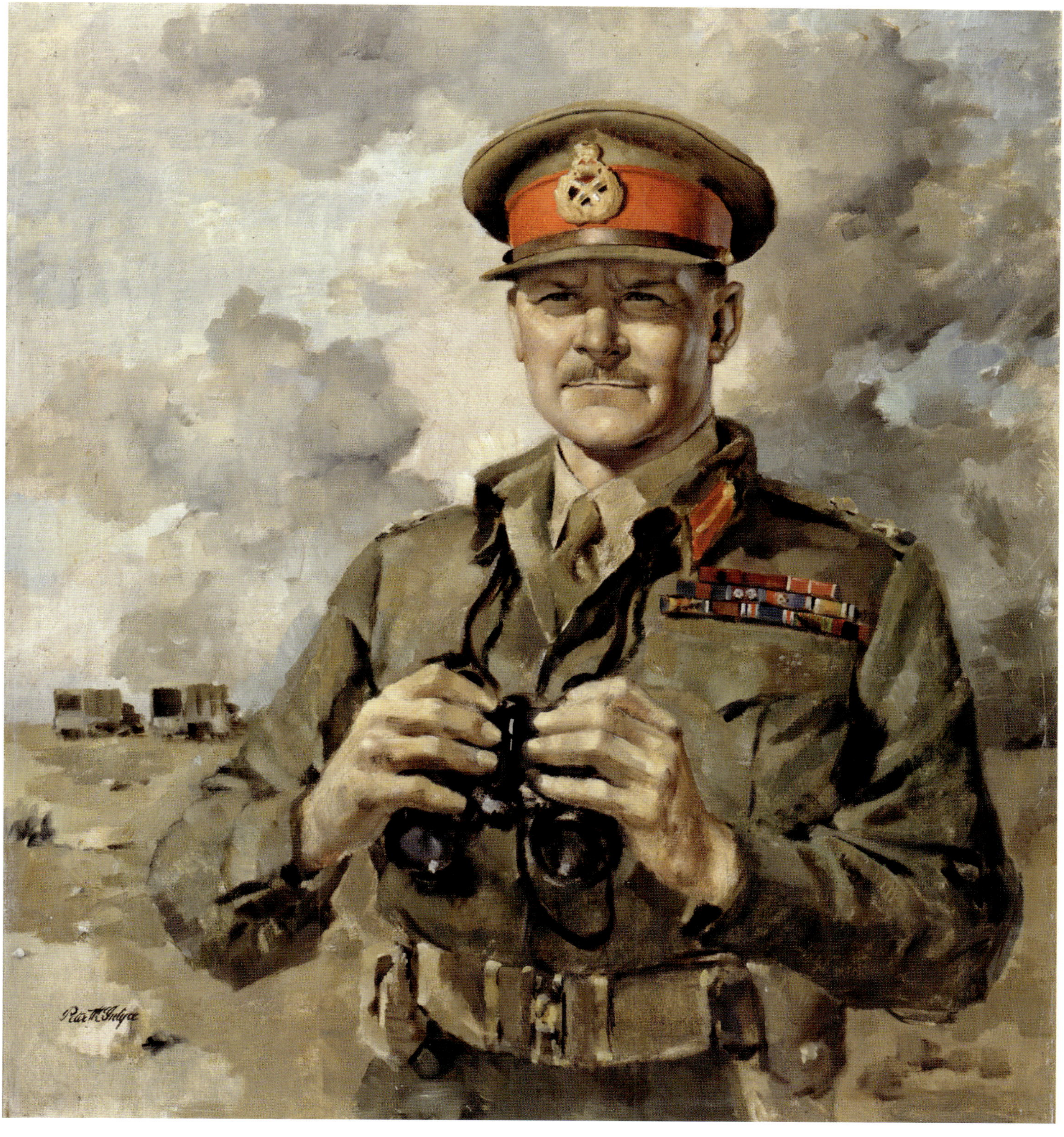

missing, literally all the bits I missed SEEING. I thought then at least I might have something new and interesting to contemplate. 'Paint what's missing,' I read somewhere; paint what you want to see. Paint what isn't there.

With the emergence of the New Image movement in the early 1970s, a small group of us found oblique and underhand ways to smuggle 'abandoned' ideas like pictorial depth and narrative into the existing modernist framework. But it wasn't until a few years later when I was illustrating *The Magpie*, a poem by Denis Glover, that I actually went back and had a fresh look at those 'bad' painters like Peter McIntyre, Austen Deans and co, studying their abstract conventions for 'bush', 'grass', 'fence post', so I could find a way into rendering the landscape of the poem in a way that felt upfront and personal – beyond irony (though the irony that I was even doing this didn't escape me). And, most significantly, beyond modernism. Way beyond.

This was the point where I actually reconnected with my youthful enthusiasms, where I recognised that I did have a personal belief system and that it might be worth investigating.

And this is the misty outline of that list I glimpsed when Jenny rang me up with the idea of a personal history of New Zealand art.

Having said all that, I don't think there's anything particularly unique in this selection, and in fact there's a lot of my list that weaves back and forth over the more established narratives. Some names are obviously going to appear on every list. No one's going to write a credible history of New Zealand art without mentioning Colin McCahon. I'll never forget how genuinely 'awesome' it was seeing his Gate series in Christchurch's Robert McDougall Art Gallery way back in 1962. The paintings seemed fabulously substantial in ways that I'd never seen 'live' before: the rough masking tape marks (masking tape?!), the 'kitchen cupboard' enamel paint surfaces – how was it possible to make art out of such brutal and unsympathetic means?

Not all my 'moments' have been so emphatic of course. But I have concentrated on looking back for those names that made me sit up and take notice when I came across them in the course of my life. Some of these moments can even be summed up in one painting. The Edward I Halliday portrait of Ed Hillary is a good example. It never occurred to me to follow up on the artist; I just loved that one image. Everything I wanted was in there; the vigorous rendering of the light on the face (very 'cinematic'), the work on the rope. I remember it seemed to follow me around town, originally hung halfway up the main staircase in the Auckland

Austen Deans
Camp in the Kowai
1952, oil on canvas

It looks like a snow-capped hill but it's actually only paint. Very clever paint.

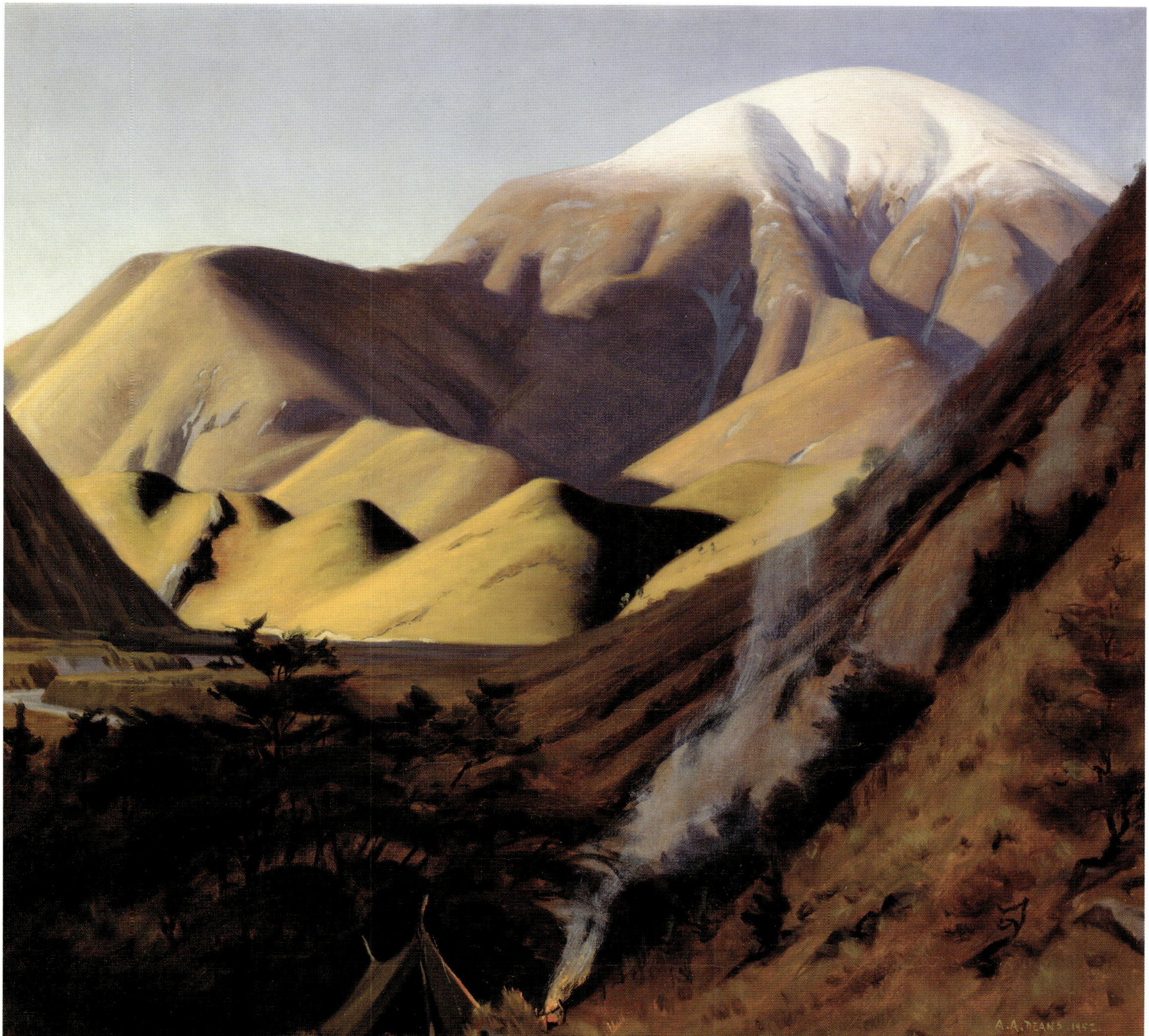

War Memorial Museum and then in some office lobby in town. Rushing past it on some mission, I'd be registering 'face', 'light', 'rope', 'mist' . . . refreshing myself.

As I went back to confirm the names, titles and dates for this book, I had to constantly resist the temptation to reinvent my own past, to add to and refine the sequence of my epiphanies. Sometimes I wondered if I was recovering memories or just inventing them! It was a huge temptation to pull other more marginal artists into the line-up to make me look more original . . . a bit of retrospective colouring-in.

Sometimes the research jogged some real memories. I wouldn't have thought of mentioning the Frank Brangwyn murals in the old National Art Gallery until I came across them in Michael Dunn's *New Zealand Painting.* I remembered how much I would look forward to seeing them as I went up those stairs. (More stairs! – with all the little painted metal kiwis holding up the handrail.) I didn't know who the artist was back then, but assumed he was a New Zealand painter (he wasn't, but that's not the point in this instance), and I know I measured everything else in the gallery against them. Such an odd fluke that something so 'international' was even there, I realised much later on.

If the beginning of this list is only slightly divergent from the sanctioned canon it gets even less so as it moves closer to the present. Nothing much is overlooked now, and ever since modernism's linear narrative was unravelled by the pluralism of postmodernism, the phenomena of fringe movements and unheralded sideroads just doesn't happen. Everything gets a look-in at some point if it looks vaguely like it'll make a contribution to the dialectic. That some ideas fade as quickly as they appear seems to be part of the process.

As we move into the twenty-first century, art broadens out even further. Looking around now at the contemporary scene I'm amazed at how everything has done such a 180 in what is a relatively short space of time. While fashionably déshabillé installations may still win the prestigious art prizes, the sheer number of painters out there working in such a vast variety of modes must be a good thing.

The requisite spirit of 'newness' and originality now seems to come from either an unexpected inversion of the familiar ('the old made new again') or an unlikely combination of genres or disciplines. These mash-ups look as if the artist has just landed on the planet with absolutely no preconceived idea of what is meant to go with what and has proceeded with zero prejudice, roping in whatever is required to complete the picture (as it were).

Frank Brangwyn
Mediterranean Market
1916–17, oil on canvas
1949 x 3887 mm

And this is only part of it!

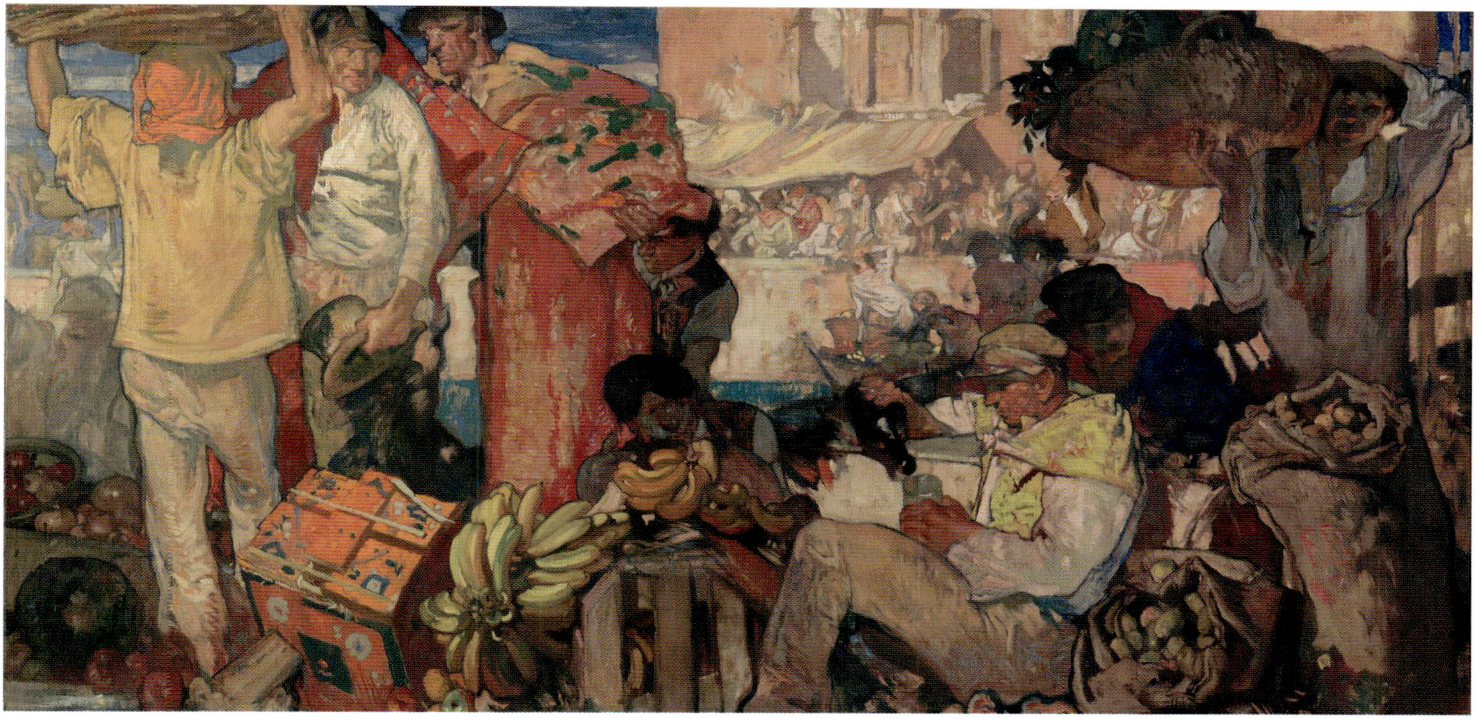

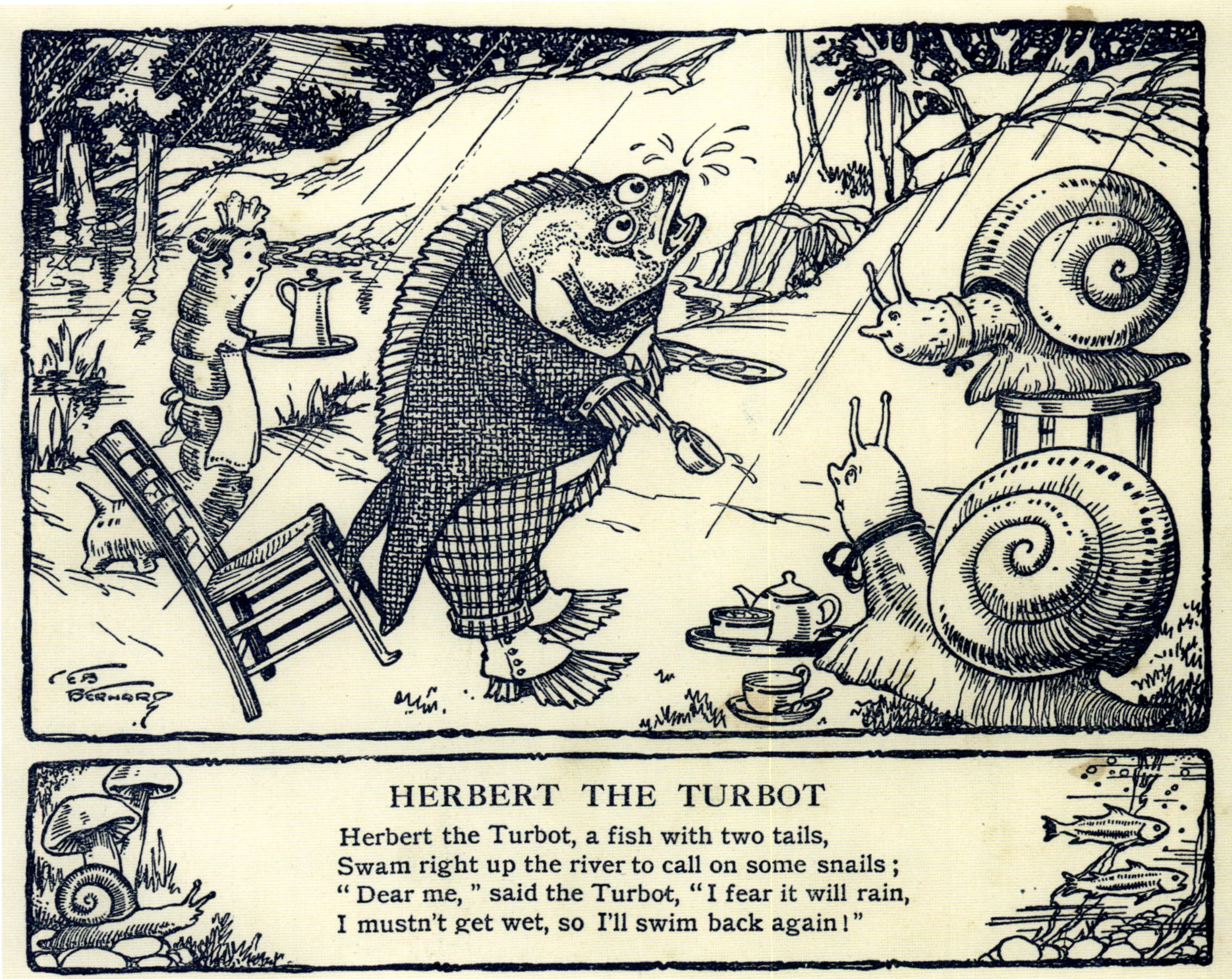

HERBERT THE TURBOT

Herbert the Turbot, a fish with two tails,
Swam right up the river to call on some snails ;
" Dear me, " said the Turbot, " I fear it will rain,
I mustn't get wet, so I'll swim back again ! "

The 'Talking Turbots' illustration from *Tiger Tim's Annual* 1926

Strange how adult children's books were back then.

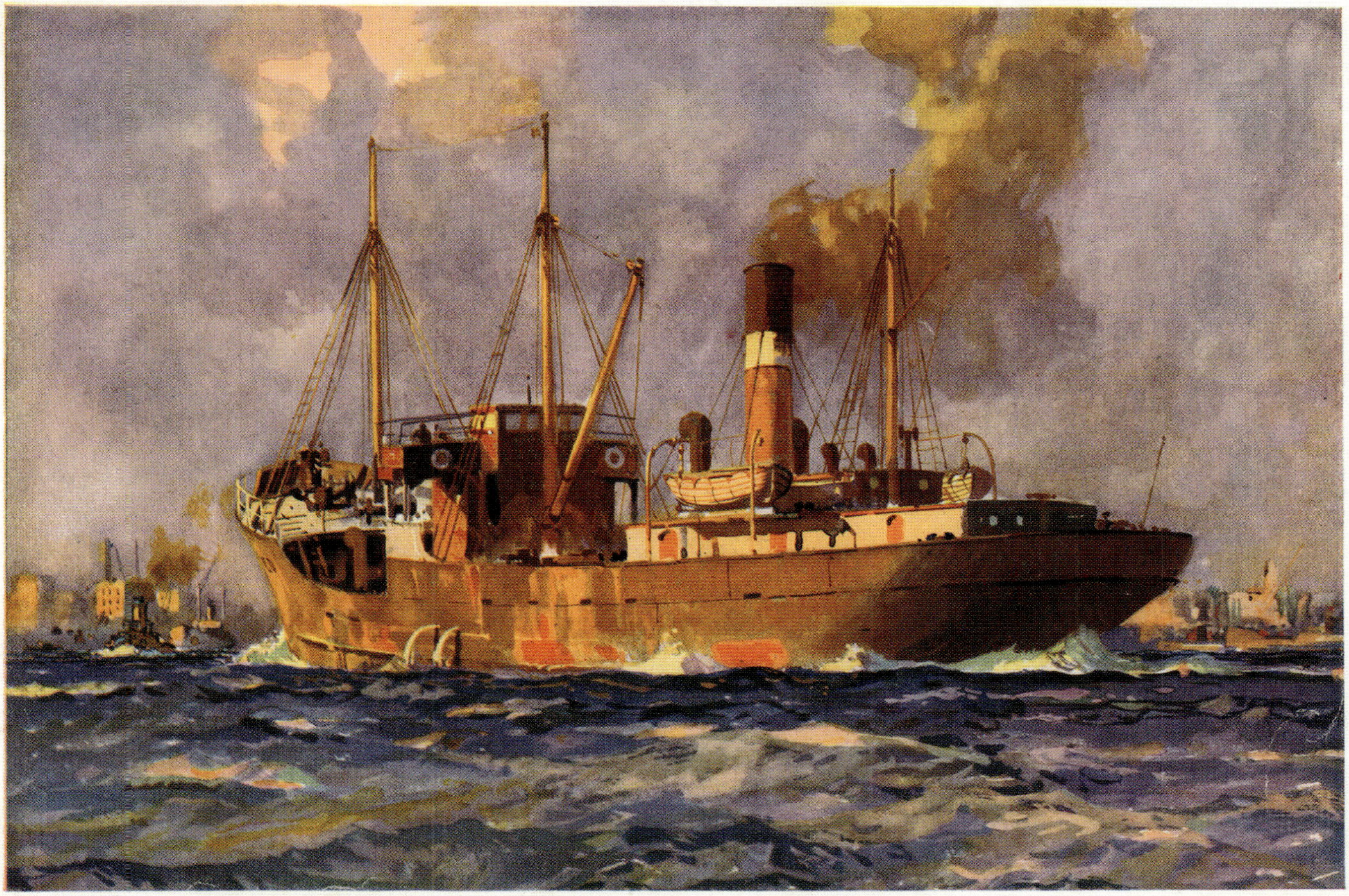

A COASTER ABOUT TO ENTER PORT

Blackie
A coaster about to enter port from *A Book of Ships*, Blackie & Son, Glasgow, 1954

A coastal steamer from one of the most romantic books I have ever owned. Where is that port? I want to be there.

I've heard this cross-cultural and interdisciplinary plundering (and I'm NOT talking about multimedia!) called 'convergence', where art can spontaneously manifest in any creative endeavour if it's driven hard enough. Some people have suggested that it's a sort of cultural dumbing down (and that that's why I'm so fascinated with it!), but I actually think it's the democratisation of intelligence and I'm incredibly optimistic about the future of art.

I find it intriguing that the signals that tell us instinctively when some practice or other tips over into art are so deeply imbedded that we – that is, anyone prepared to spend the time informing the instinct – always know it. I think Denis Dutton was right with his *Art Instinct*; on some level it's essentially an evolutionary transference of information.

If I'm ever asked to put another list together in the future, I'd like to demonstrate the above with less emphasis on painting – but I make no apologies for the present list. Given that the number of images came with a recommended limit (and thank God for that!) and the fact that it was meant to reflect the development of my thinking, this book was always going to be a list of paintings.

I also wondered about the format, whether to actually list the artists chronologically or list them more or less as I came across them in the course of my life. I've gone with the latter because the former tended to make me look almost prescient in the development of my ideas; so we get a bit of time travel in the narrative but I think it better reflects my story.

It's been a fascinating exercise, reflecting on myself like this, and I'm only too aware of the great and the good I had to leave out; but I was never going to write a comprehensive history – hardly a legit history at all, really. It's a tight list, but it's succinct – and it's mine.

Edward I Halliday
Sir Edmund Hillary
1955, oil on canvas
1145 x 8750 mm

Cinematic tricks – the collar describes the incline.

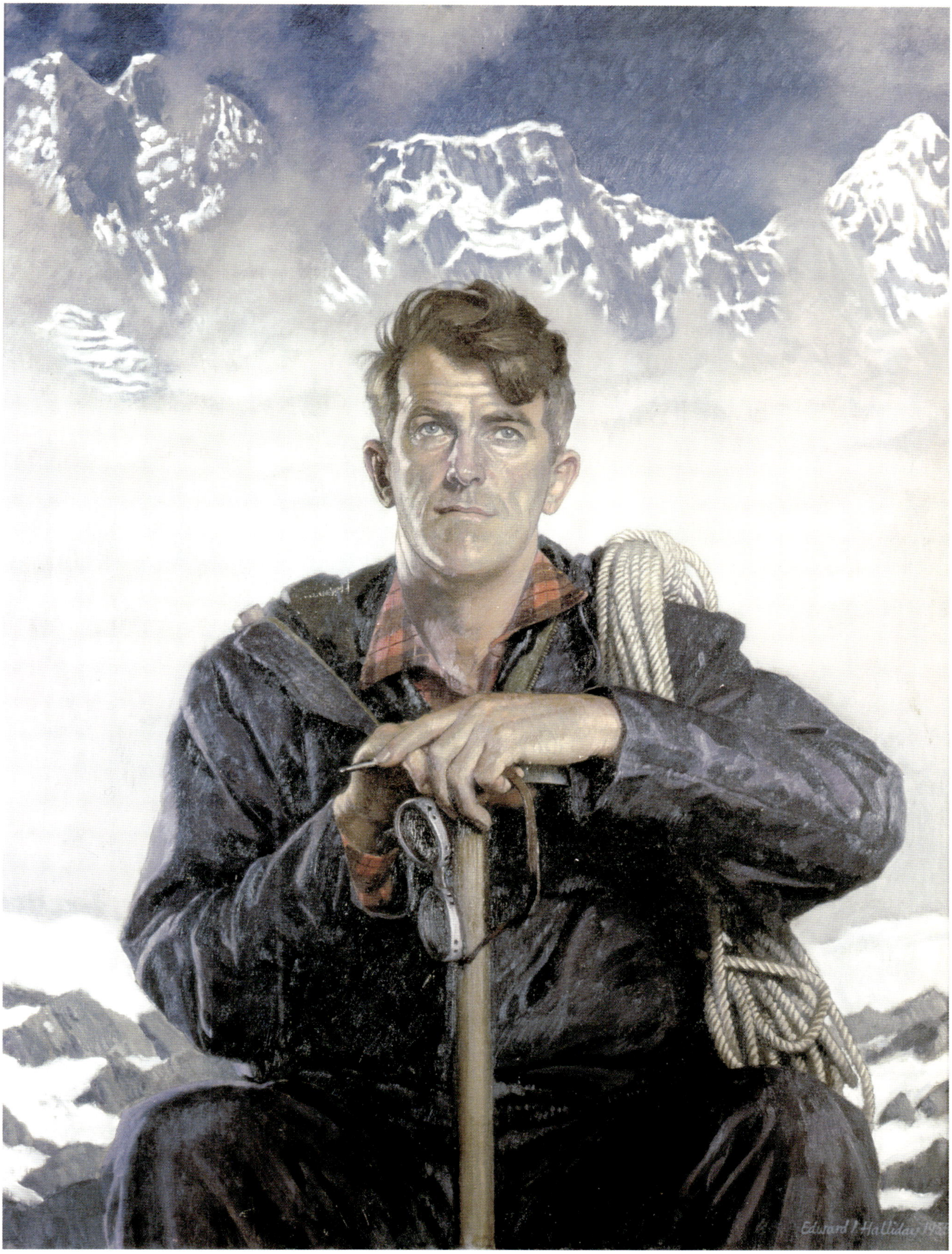
Edward I Halliday

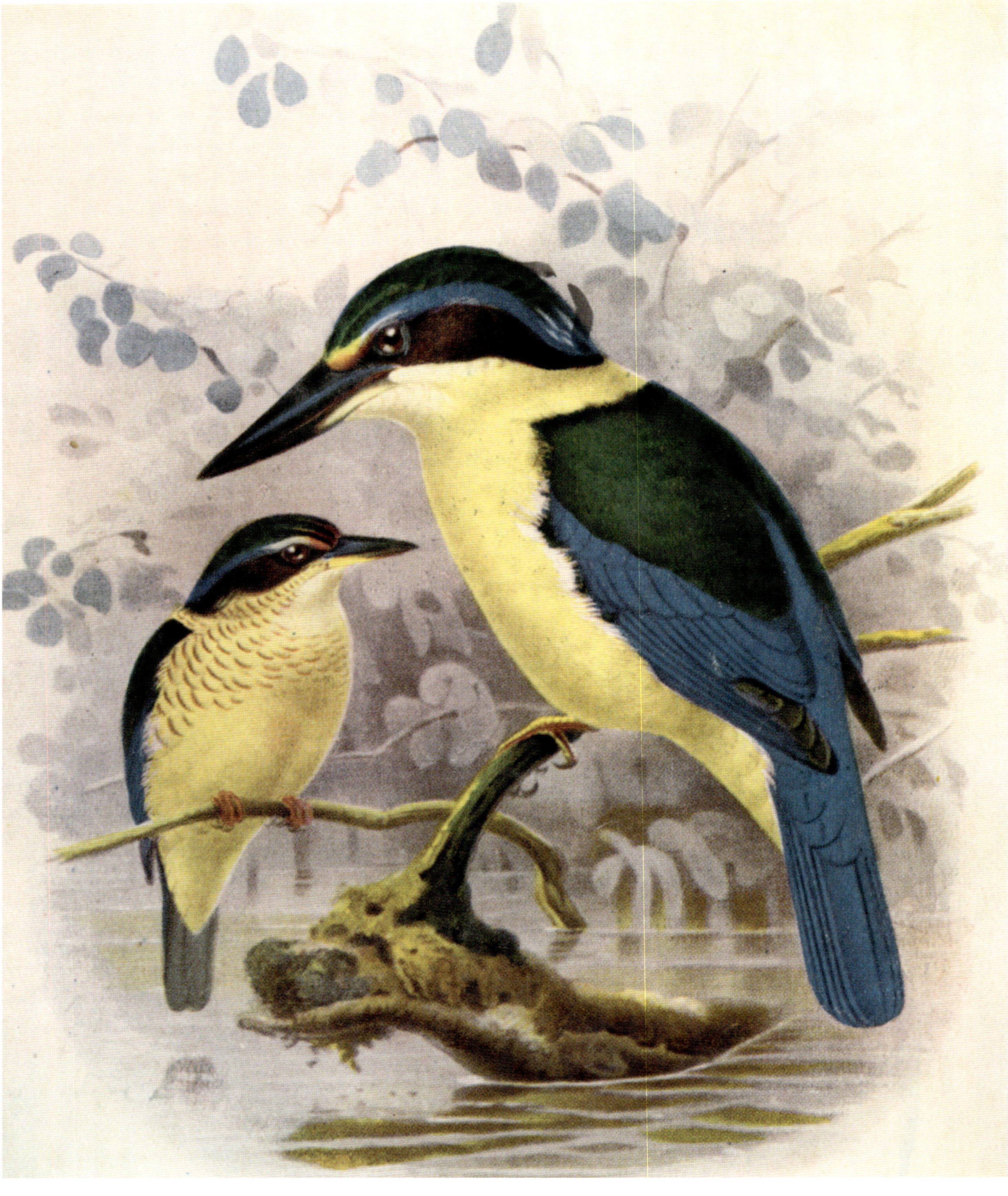

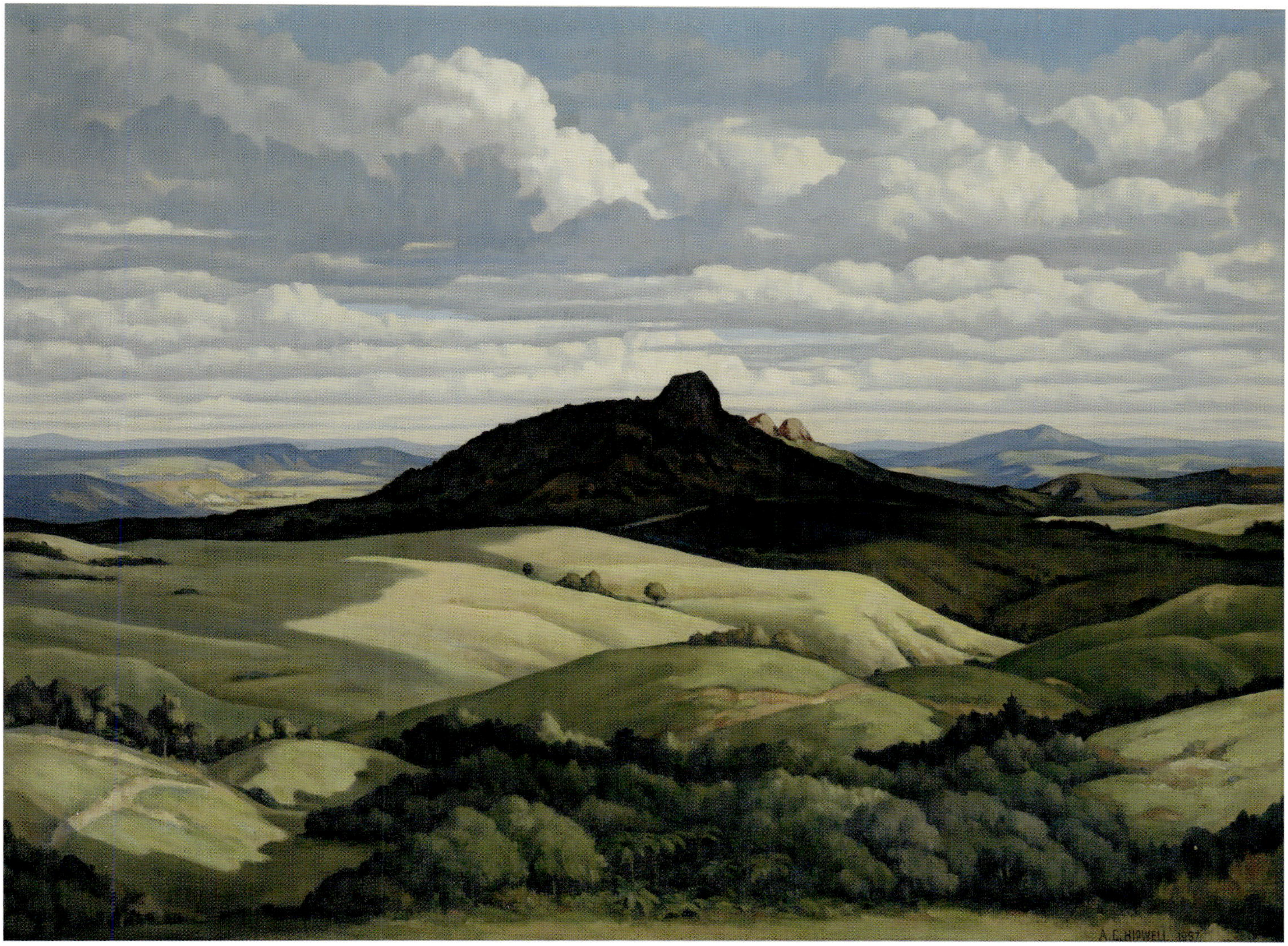

JG Keulemans
Buller's birds — Banded Rail from *New Zealand Flowers and Birds,* New Zealand Tourist and Publicity Dept.

One of my mother's favourite cribbing references. Looks great on a polished rimu plaque.

Arthur Hipwell
Mt Taratara, Northland
1957, oil on board
746 x 1000 mm

How long did he wait for that shadow? The Kelliher Prize winner in 1957.

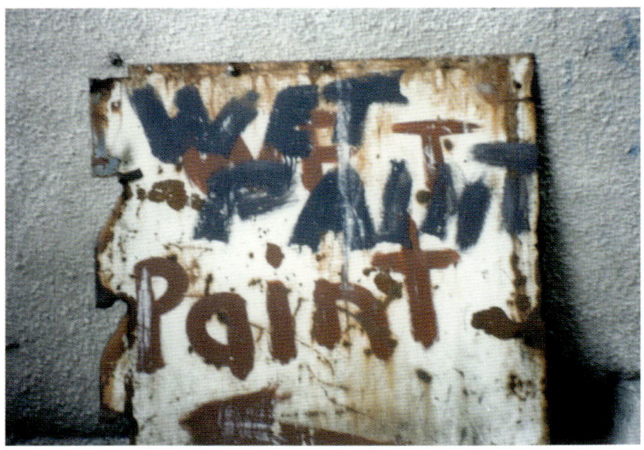
WET
PAINT
Paint

The Artists

Joan Trollope

Joan was a member of the Hawke's Bay Art Society when I was a schoolboy doing School Certificate Art at Hastings Boys' High School. I think her paintings were the first actual in-the-flesh oil paintings I ever saw. I mean I must have seen others, having walked through a whole room full of art society offerings, but Joan's was the first painting I recognised as 'art'.

Couldn't have told you why back then, of course, but it was somehow obviously 'art-intelligent'. Joan knew what she was doing, while everybody else just thought they did. I haven't been able to track down that work, a lushly rendered image of a pink Italianate villa, a fondly remembered holiday moment, worked up with a palette knife, brush and, most wondrous of all, the pointy end of the brush, drawing back into what must have been the paint when it was wet. No one ever told me that you could use both ends of the brush! (I've got a strange feeling I'm making most of this up, but something definitely did happen, and it involved some amount of pink.)

I can only begin to imagine what a strangely lonely life it must have been, to be that good a painter in such an isolated community back there in the late 1950s, and I might be imagining it wrong anyway because, to be fair, I did get taken up by some determinedly older bohemians who had started a sketch club in the basement of the Hawke's Bay Museum, so something was going on. This painting is the only one of hers I've been able to track down; fortunately it's a particularly good one.

Joan Trollope
Tomato Pickers
c.1959, oil on hardboard
580 x 905 mm

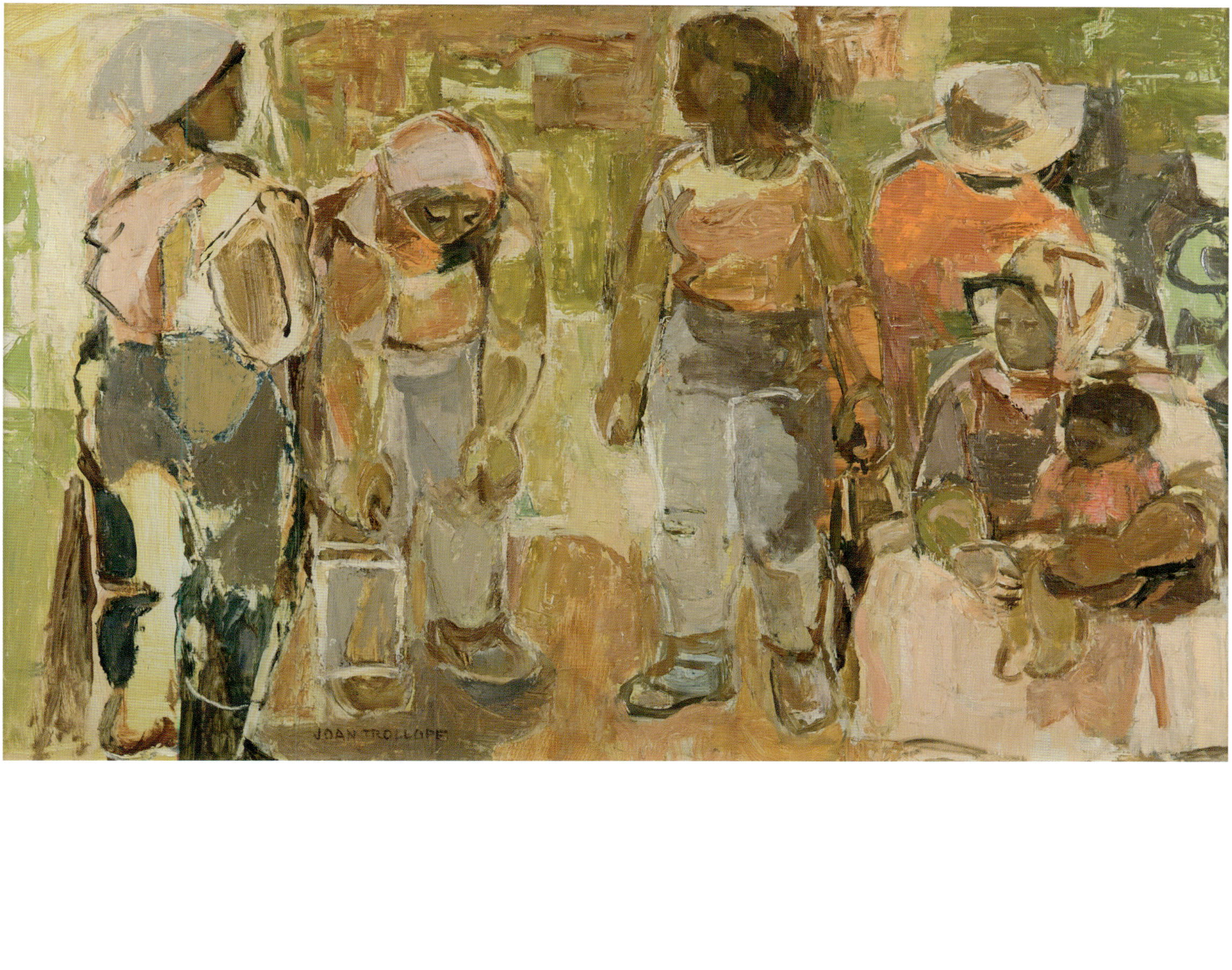
JOAN TROLLOPE

Bryan Dew

I was in my School Certificate year when Bryan was doing his prelim year, one form ahead of me. He had a special little fenced-off enclosure at the back of the art room at Hastings Boys' High.

I could stand there and look over the fence at Bryan drawing and painting away in such a confident and seemingly effortless manner that it made me seriously doubt my ability to occupy the same space the following year. (I never did; three of us took the course and the 'enclosure' was abandoned, though I doubt if it ever officially existed; such was Bryan's confidence in his own superiority he probably engineered the whole thing himself!)

I lost what little touch I had with him when he went off to Auckland and I went down to Christchurch, and I couldn't get my head around these paintings when I came across them up in Auckland four or so years later. That anyone in New Zealand at that time could produce a socially satirical body of work with such consummate professionalism – and an art student at that – beggared belief!

The artists I was currently in the sway of, Ben Shahn, John Bratby, James Ensor, were right there in that plate of sandwiches. All of them soaked up and spat out in an unmistakeably New Zealand way. Could it be possible that we could be represented in such a contemporary fashion? Could our humble rituals be something more than a cultural embarrassment? Bryan certainly made it look as if they could be!

The fact that he decided to give it all away for a more pragmatic design course at the Royal College of Art only serves to suggest a realistic, or cynical, point of view, far too sharp for this world. And maybe that astonishing facility came too easily for him to really believe it.

Bryan Dew
The Key
Oil on canvas
1235 x 780 mm

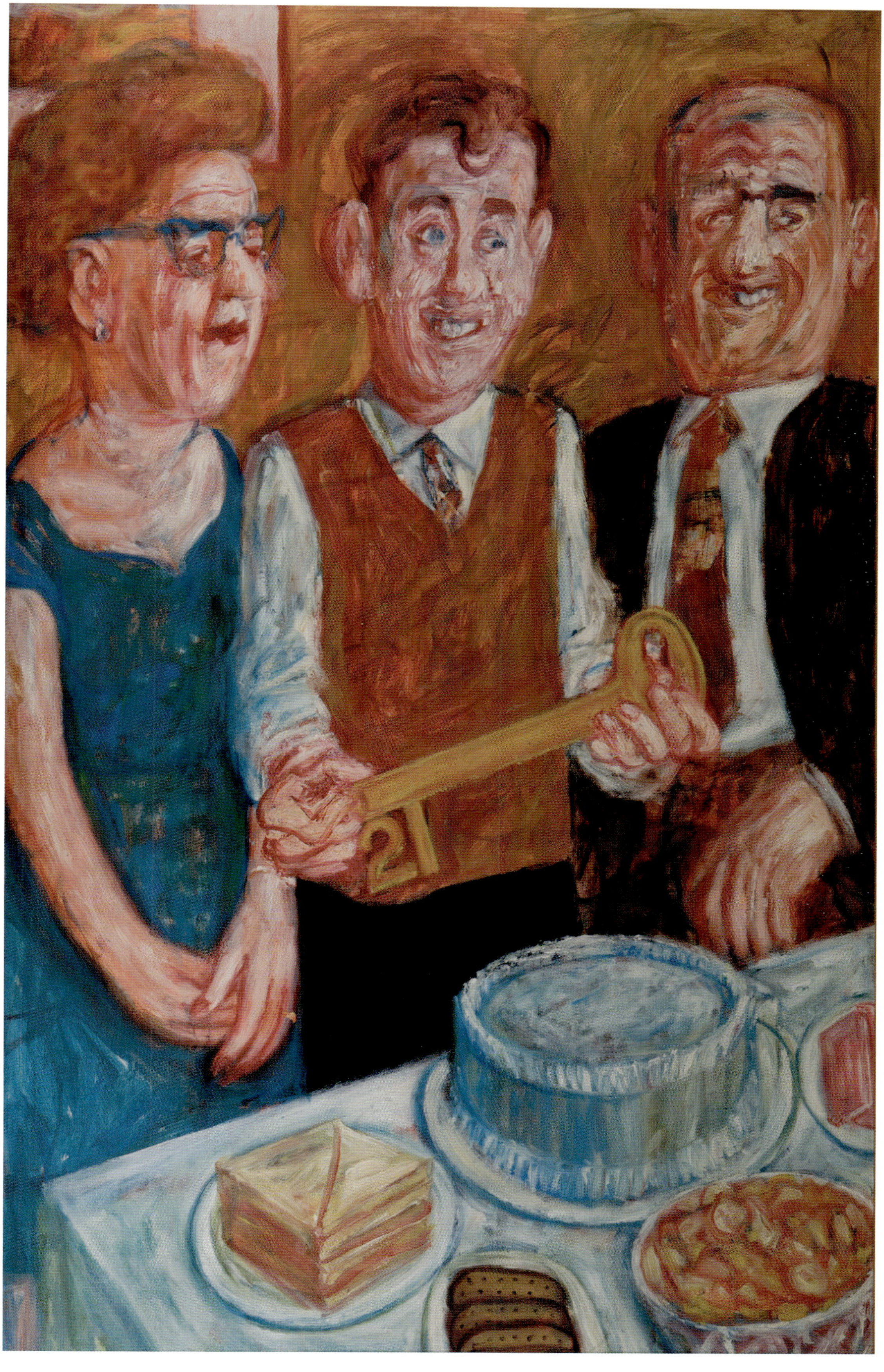

Peter McIntyre

This is a tricky one because I can't say I'm a huge fan of Peter McIntyre, but he just keeps popping up in my life. He seems to be necessary on some level and if he hadn't been around and published all those books, there would definitely be a gap in our history.

I've chosen to include this painting because the Maori boy in the foreground was the 'model' for the Maori boy dragging the guitar at the bottom of my Ngaruawahia Rock Festival poster.

When I get overwhelmed by the technical and physical challenges of my own landscape paintings, when I get too literal about it, Peter's deft shortcuts to illusion are always a reminder that it's all just paint and brushes at the end of the day. Snap yourself out of it and get cracking!

Peter McIntyre
Maori Children, King Country
1964, oil on canvas
600 x 700 mm

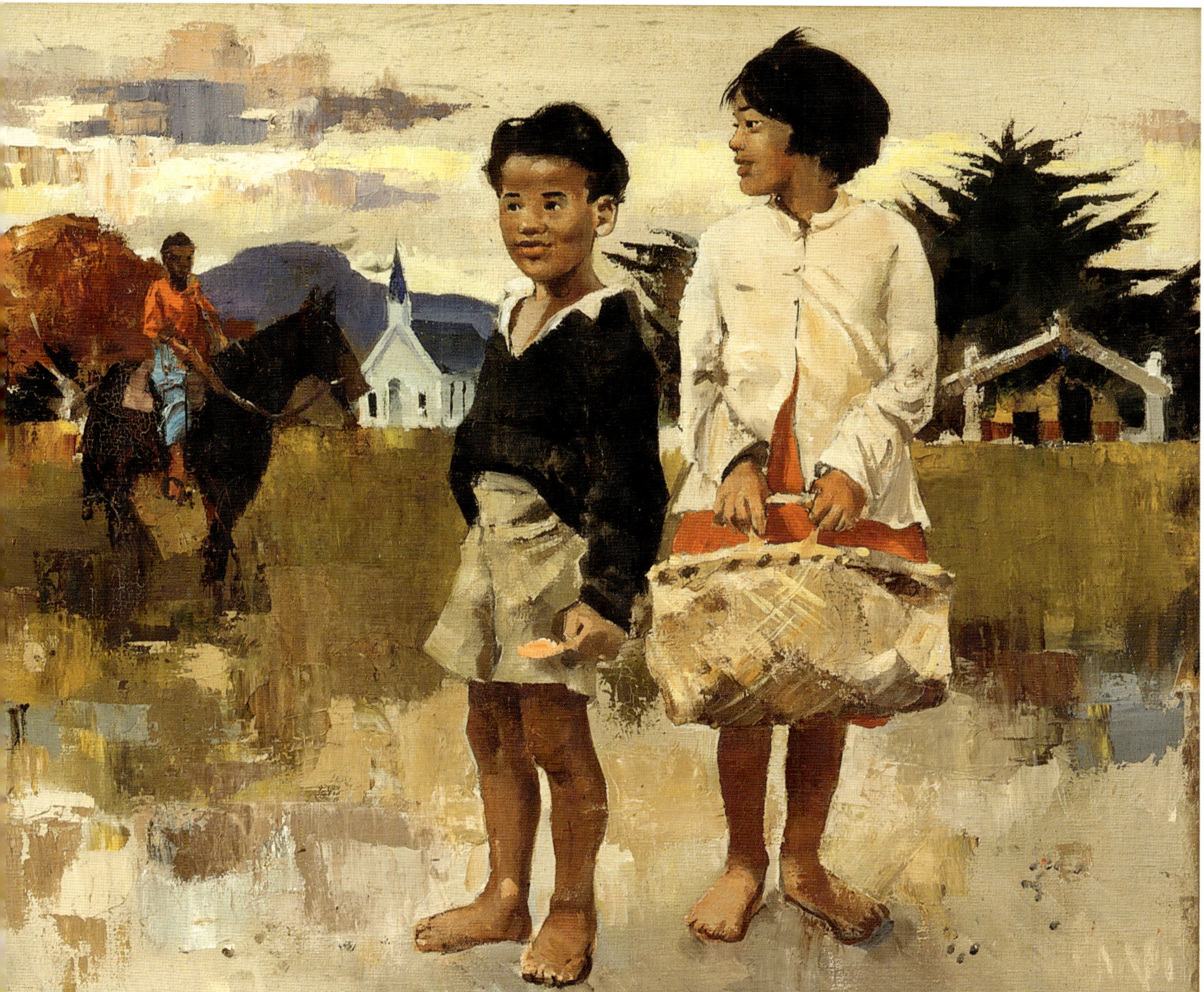

John Coley

John was one of a group of 'grown-up' artists working in Christchurch when I was a student. Every second week or so we had a 'critic's evening' at the school and John or Pat Hanly or whoever was passing through would come to critique our work, usually after a warm-up at one of the inner-city pubs.

John was always hugely entertaining and wouldn't offer specific criticism so much as regale us with fabulous tales about what we were (hopefully) in for further down the track. John's 'recitations' were a welcome relief after Rudi Gopas's gloomy prognostications.

At some point my wife Jude and I were invited to John and Fay's house for dinner and I fell in love with this work. That you could paint something as significant as this, then frame it and hang it over your own couch was a mighty revelation!

John Coley
Cut Back Macrocarpa
1960, oil on canvas

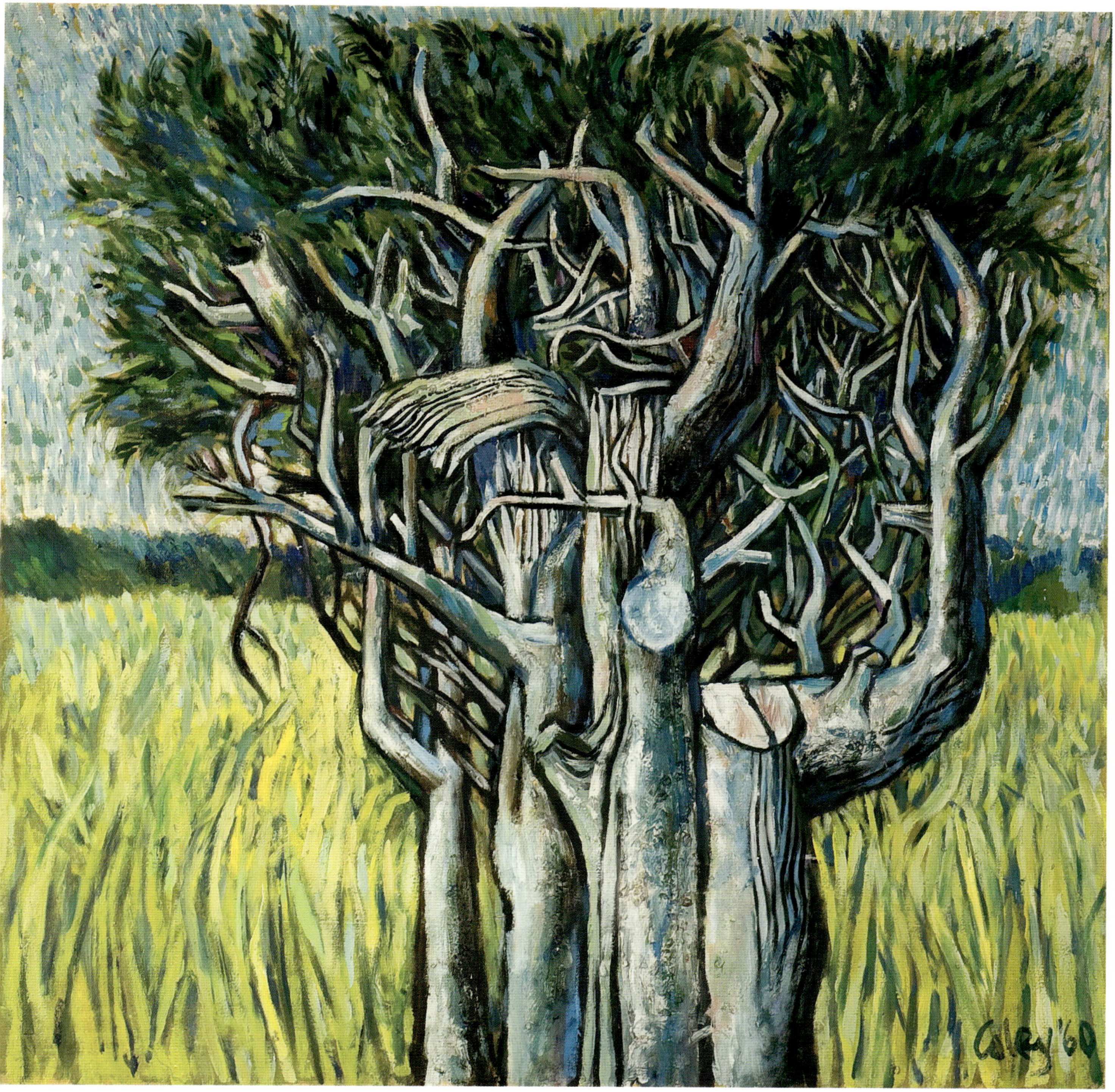
Coley '60

Bill Sutton

This is the first painting I thought of when I was asked to write this book, must've always been a secret ambition of mine to see it published somewhere.

Every time I visit Te Papa (reluctantly, because I'm still waiting to see the national collection housed in an actual art museum) I always drop by to have a quiet moment with Bill's dad. I'm not quite sure what it is that captures me, maybe because it's so modestly consummate, perfectly poised between an obviously deep respect for the sitter and a stunning display of self-confidence from the painter himself.

Bill shows off, but not at his father's expense.

The quiet accumulation of each perfectly placed mark and the soft colour relationships contribute to a powerful gesture that goes way beyond sentiment but brushes past it gently on the way.

Bill Sutton
The Artist's Father
1943, oil on canvas
905 x 694 mm

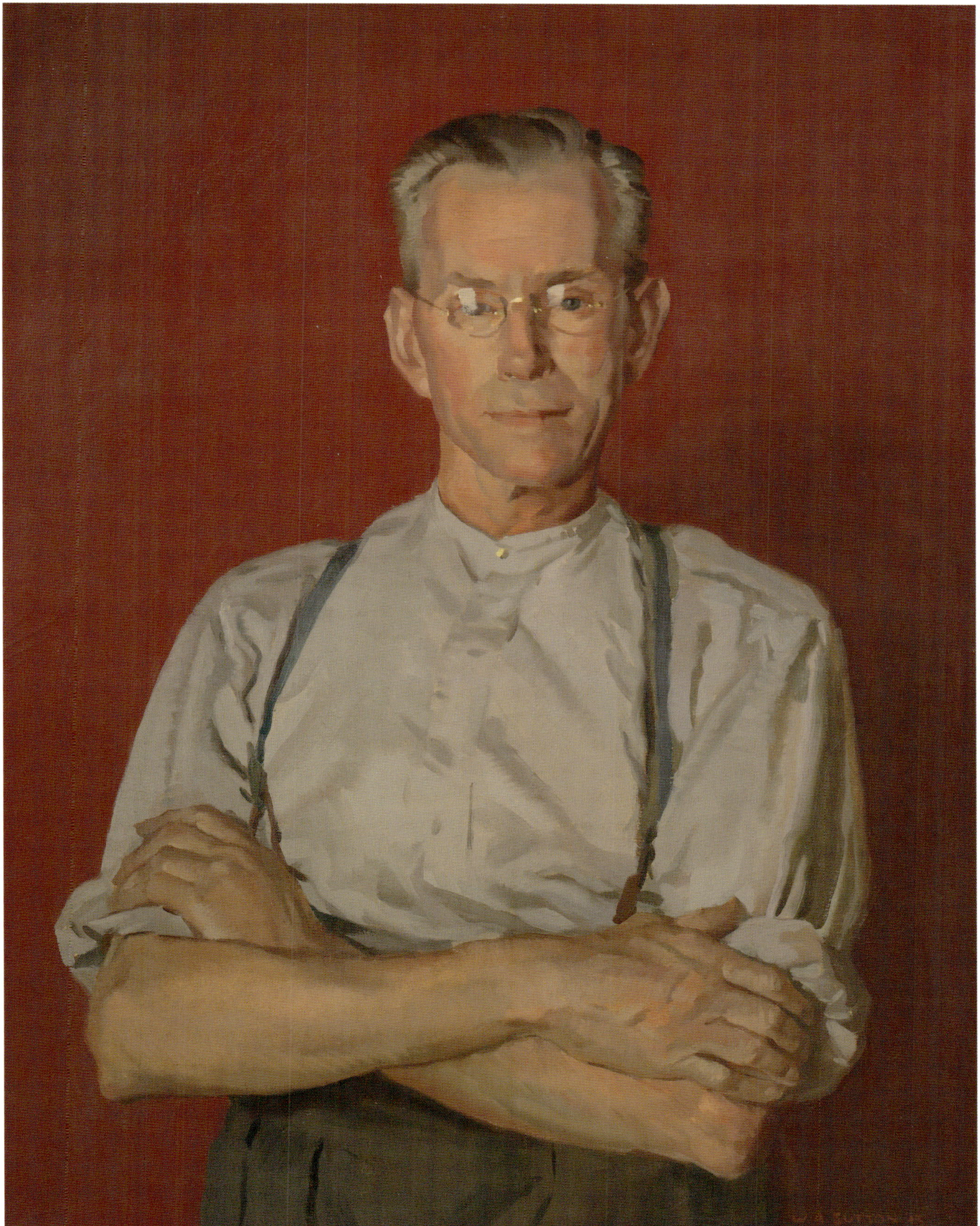

Rudi Gopas

Rudi, our scary bohemian art school hero lecturer. Striding about our modest campus in his dark tweeds, tousled hair over furrowed brow and pipe clenched in gritted teeth . . . startling the horses. An 18-year-old's mythic image of a painter.

I took Rudi's class in abstract composition, whatever that was. He sent us out to find something in nature to work from. I was flailing away at this knot in the side of a tree (I'll never forget it) when Rudi came up and offered me this advice: 'Take za painting, lie it down on za floor, and zen rrrrrub it wis a rag soaked in turps.' Which I obediently did, and the painting gradually (and thankfully) disappeared. Oh, I thought, what strange advice! But it taught me a lot about cutting to the chase.

And we'll have to cut to it here because, despite some desperate plea bargaining, we couldn't secure permission to reproduce the Gopas painting I wanted . . . couldn't have any of them actually! To see the image you'll have to go to: http://christchurchartgallery.org.nz/collection/objects/69-83

The Trawlers is a fabulous painting. I can imagine Rudi painting it, scrubbing away with his vermilions, squinting at it with a baleful eye. It's an irony that we can't see it here because Rudi was one of the reasons I initially felt excited about writing the book! Would've given me the space to go on about how a painting will bend its own internal rules to get to where it wants to go.

In the meantime you can contemplate this earnest student effort. One that Rudi couldn't talk me into wiping off. The severely limited palette is a result of Rudi's terrifying colour theories that took me 15 years to figure out.

Dick Frizzell
Gas Stove
1961, oil on board
700 x 500 mm

One Rudi didn't make me wipe off.

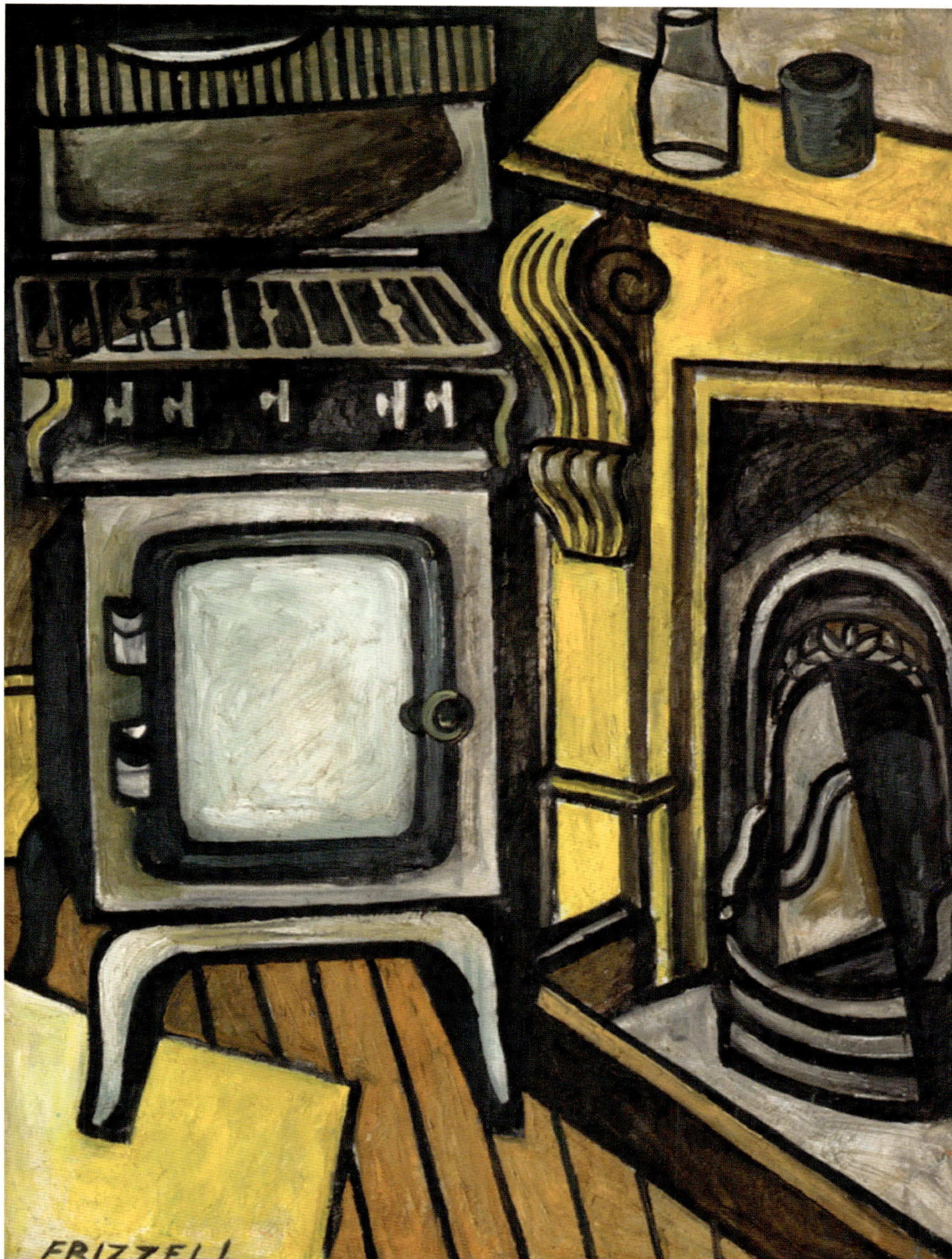
FRIZZELL

Russell Clark

Another 'Famous Artist' lecturer at Ilam while I was there. I got off to a bad start with Russell, walking out of his illustration class because I couldn't do it, couldn't 'illustrate', mostly because Russell forgot to tell us about research and reference (or I was down at the pub for that lesson).

By the end of my third year I'd come round a bit and was actually invited back to his studio, probably my first visit to a real artist's workplace, and I remember how perfectly 'arty' it was: the plaster maquettes along the windowsills, the canvases stacked around the walls and on the easels, the paraphernalia of painting, the dust, mess, and the obviously ordered system within all that.

I knew that Russell was somehow lower down in the general hierarchy than, say, Sutton and Gopas, but I also recognised a like mind. A strong graphic sensibility and – dangerously attractive to me – a fondness for the gussied-up finish. A bit too much of the old palette knife . . .

His best work managed to transcend this inclination for the obvious and the over-decorated, and like with McIntyre, I can't imagine how our history would've looked without the contribution of his professional and disciplined draughtsmanship.

Russell Clark
Cabbage Tree in Flower
c.1954, oil on canvas

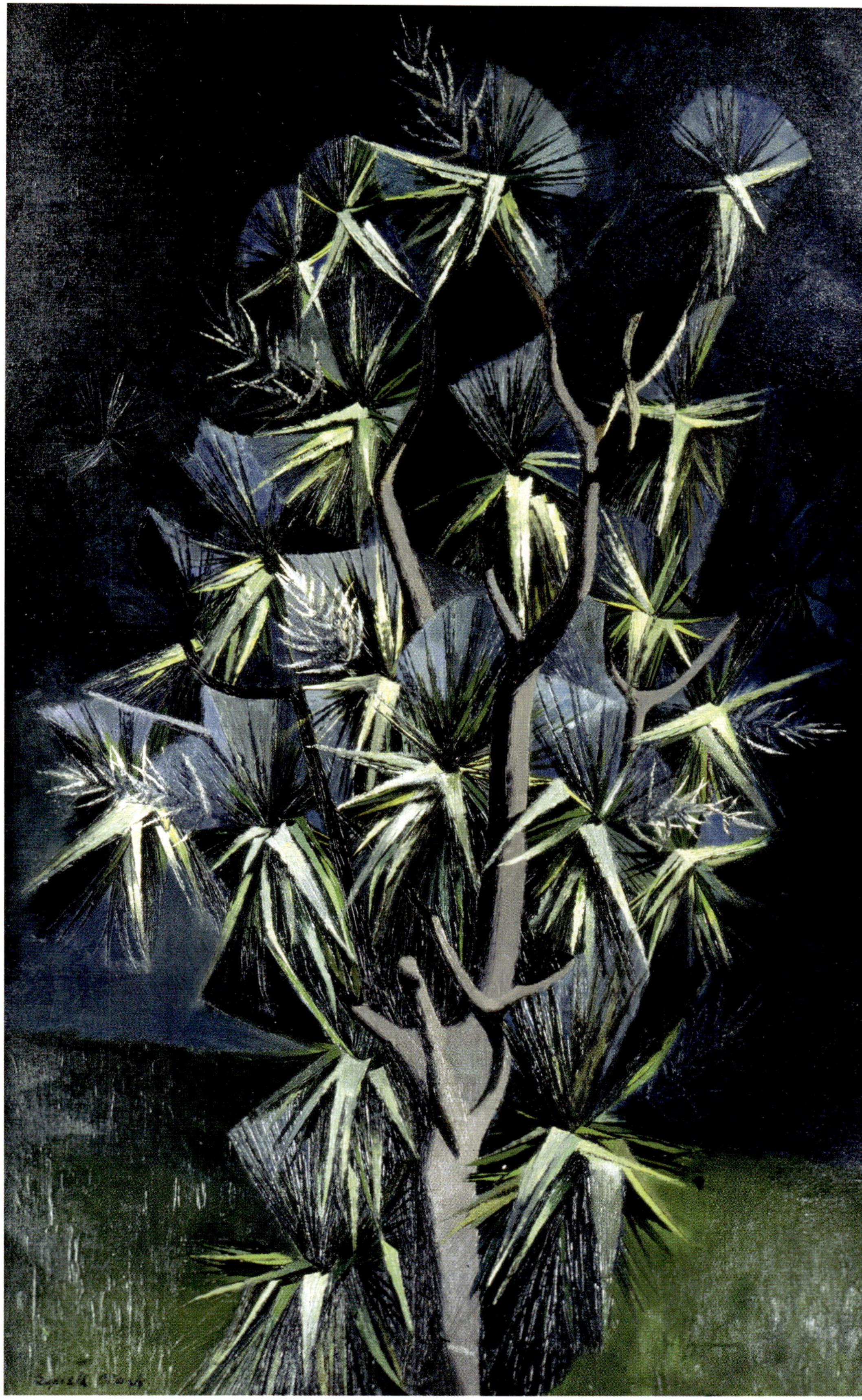

Eric Lee-Johnson

Why do all these chaps have double-barrelled names? Dick Lovell Smith, Dennis Knight Turner . . . I imagine them all painting away with leather patches on the elbows of their painty coats.

And there's something terrifically blokey about the look of the name as well. 'Eric Lee-Johnson' looks like it's composed of sea wrack, twisted stumps and bent sheets of corrugated iron.

Eric never quite grabbed the gravitas he so obviously aspired to with all his tortuous writhing about and gloomy weather patterns but he did record some essential New Zealand history both with his painting and his photography. And some of his earnest desire for atmosphere did rub off of course, because, despite a selective view that favoured the 'forsaken motif', a certain truth did leak through.

Besides, I suspect that he hardly had to be very selective given that there couldn't have been much else to take in at the time but the obviously picturesque. Even a cliché has to start somewhere.

Eric Lee-Johnson
End of the Assembly Line
1945, oil on cardboard
445 x 561 mm

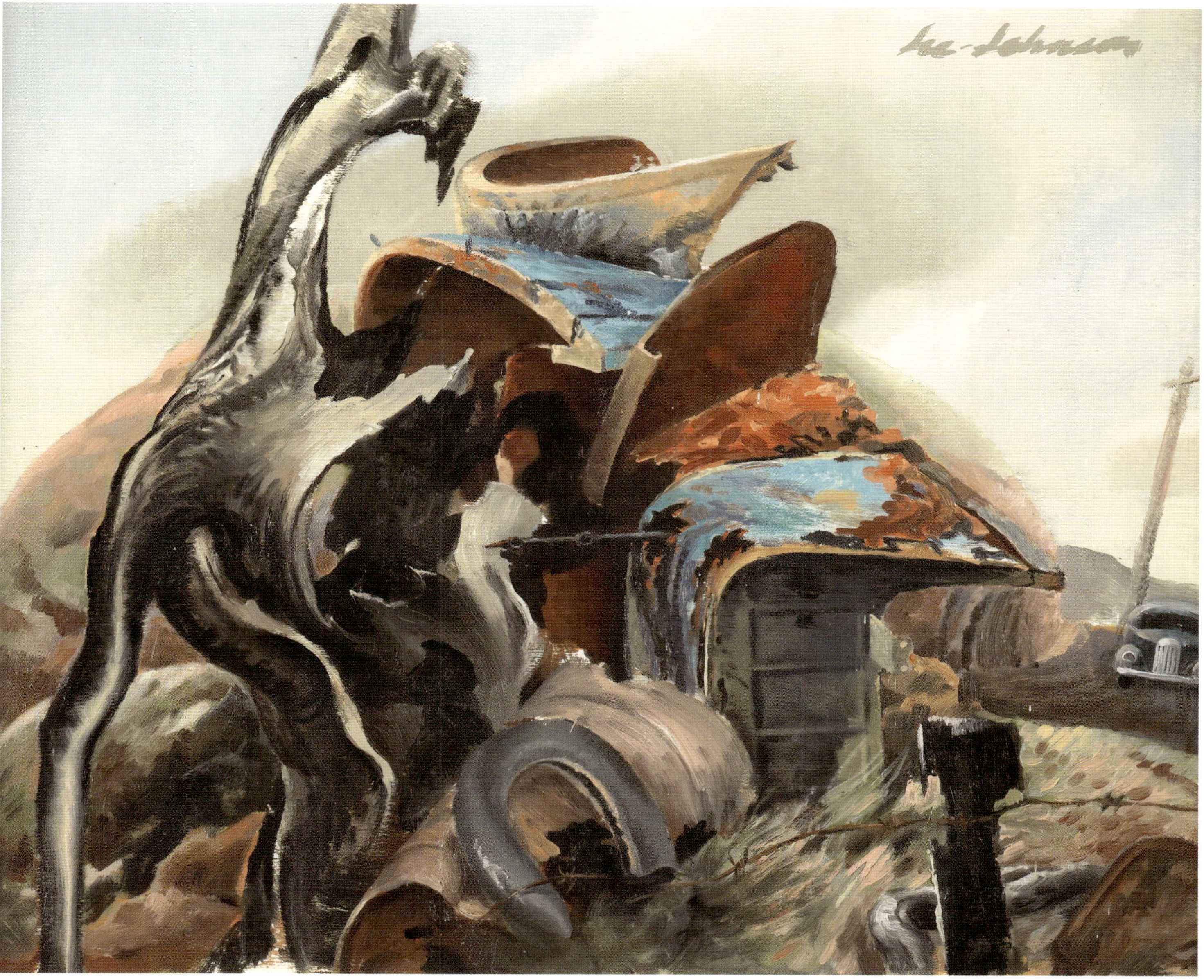
Lee-Johnson

Reverend John Kinder

I've left out a whole raft of colonial artists, your Gullys and Blomfields, because I have no burning interest in them. I'm not sure why exactly: too genteel? Too many antique polished frames or something.

I prefer the odd mannered or naïve renderings of the occasional army lieutenant or pragmatic surveyor, and I guess that's what I like about Kinder's work. While he was still hampered to some extent by 'the English eye', his unusual technique of gradually tickling the forms into existence with his watercolour brush seems to have led him to a more deeply rooted understanding of the reality of what he was looking at.

The Rev was very much an inspiration to me during my very early experiments in trying to find a personal way of reflecting my environment.

Reverend John Kinder
Rotokakahi. 1866.
Outlet of Lake
Watercolour on paper
220 x 330 mm

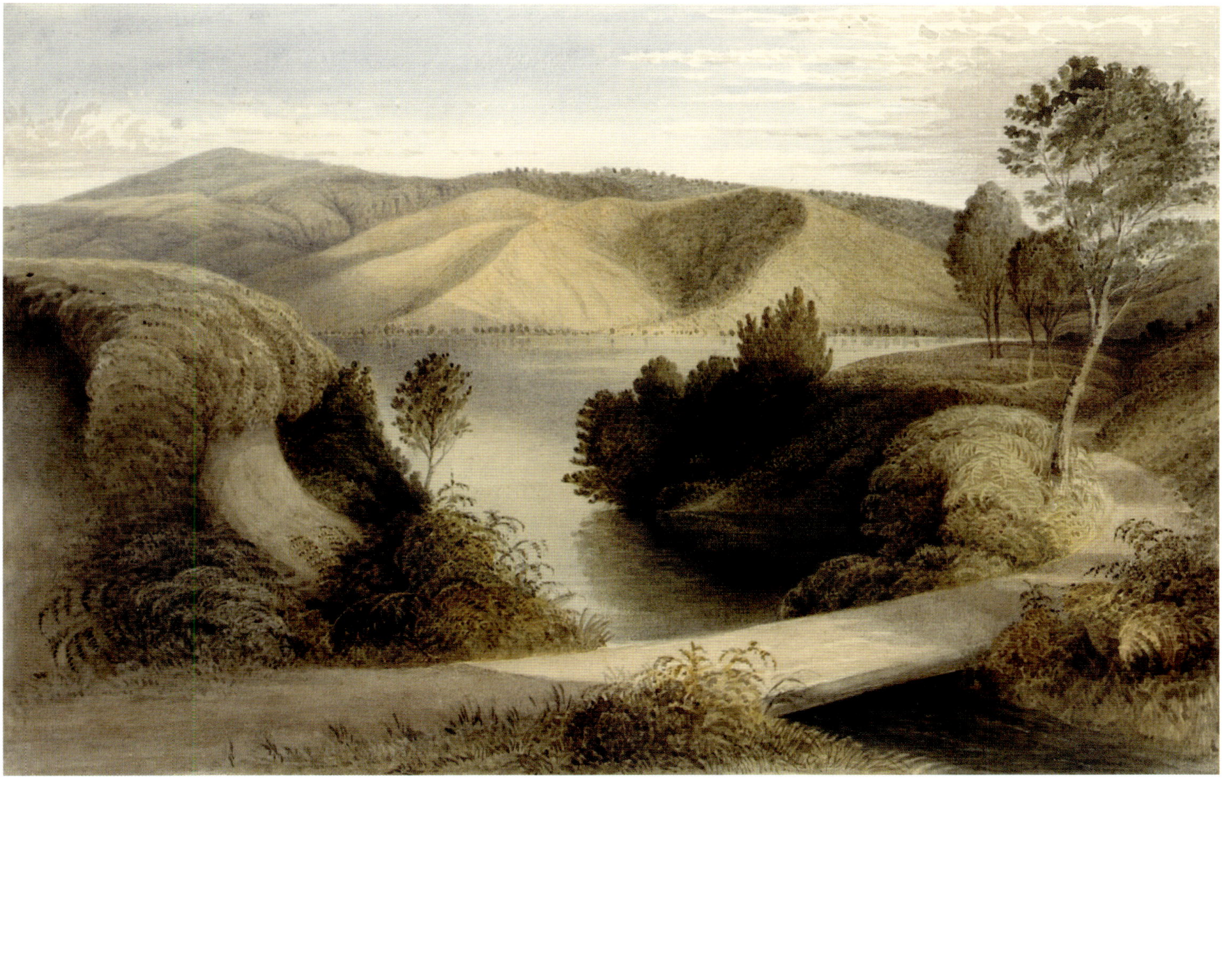

Dennis Knight Turner

I knew Dennis first as the illustrator of the Barry Crump books so it was interesting when I came across his painted work much later in my life, interesting because I (even me!) had to climb over that hump of disdain, very much prevalent then, which made it hard to take an 'illustrator' seriously as an 'artist'. But once I got over it I became a big fan.

I love this guy's stuff: his design, colour, graphic textures, those half-brushed passages, knowing when to go on and when to leave off. I still can't understand why he's not taken more seriously; well, I can actually.

He let himself down a bit with his larger more 'vernacular' compositions, slightly 'over macho-ed' and straining for manly effect, but I can forgive him for all the man-alone stuff because it was de rigueur at the time and it would've taken a bloody huge talent to use it without falling into those sentimental traps. And very few managed that.

Dennis Knight Turner
Untitled (fish and figures)
1952, oil on canvas on hardboard
393 x 445 mm

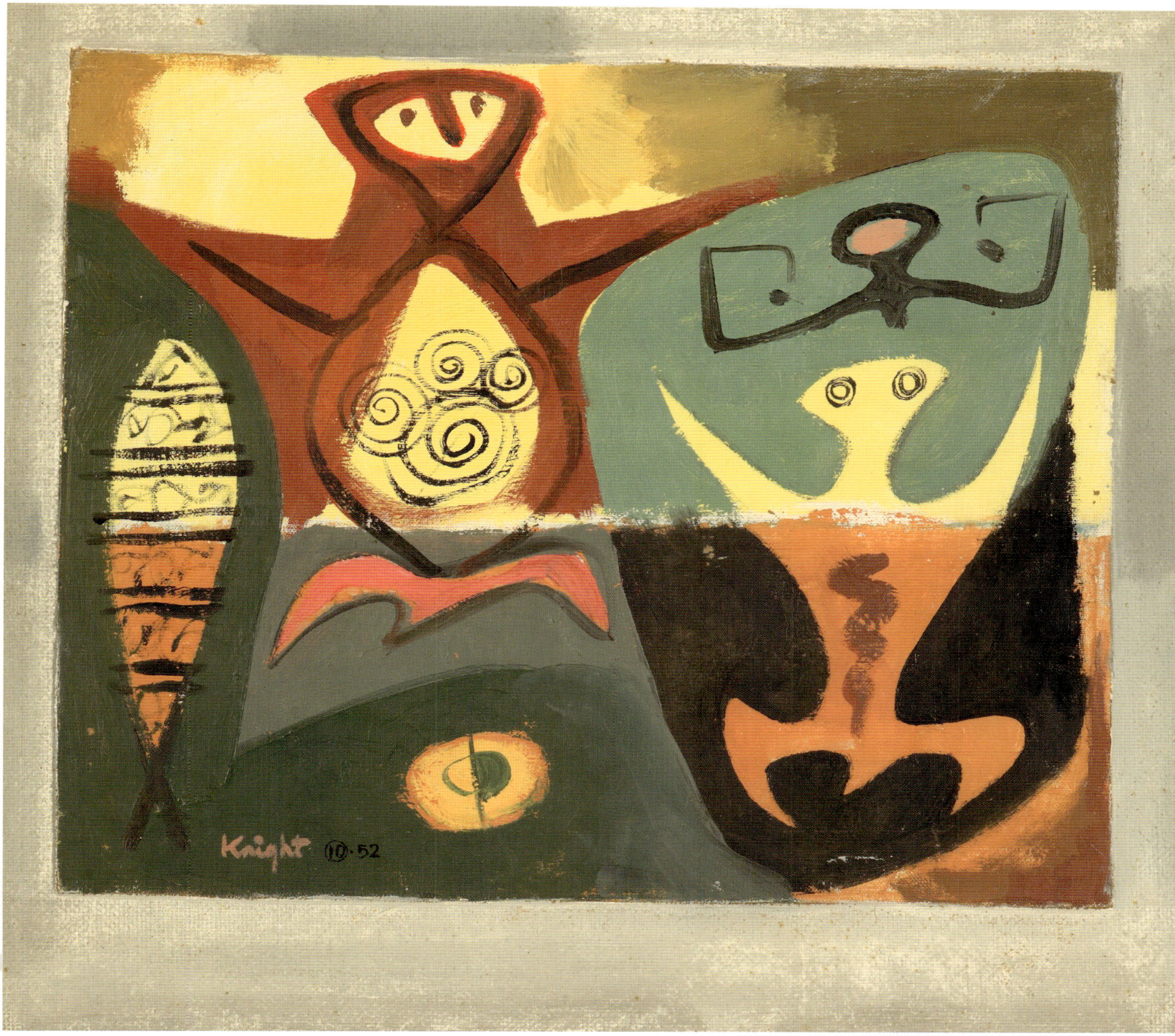
Knight 10·52

Petrus van der Velden

Not a lot I can add to the van der Velden story really. The only point I can make, which is the point I'm making by reproducing this particular painting, is that I find all the sturm and drang of the Otira Gorge works so bloody obvious that I can hardly look at them. Well, I can look at them but all I see is this macho 'citizen of ze vorld' bravura. Though to be fair, I do wonder how you paint roaring water like that without a lot of photographic reference . . . perhaps that's what he did.

With the painting opposite, *The Dutch Funeral*, I can go back and back to marvel at the extremely modern composition, the 'idea' of the painting, the black rectangle of the clustered group in all that white space, the rendering of the fabric textures as crisp as the snow they're trudging through, and so on.

He certainly knew what he was doing; perhaps it all went to his head.

Petrus van der Velden
The Dutch Funeral
1875, oil on canvas

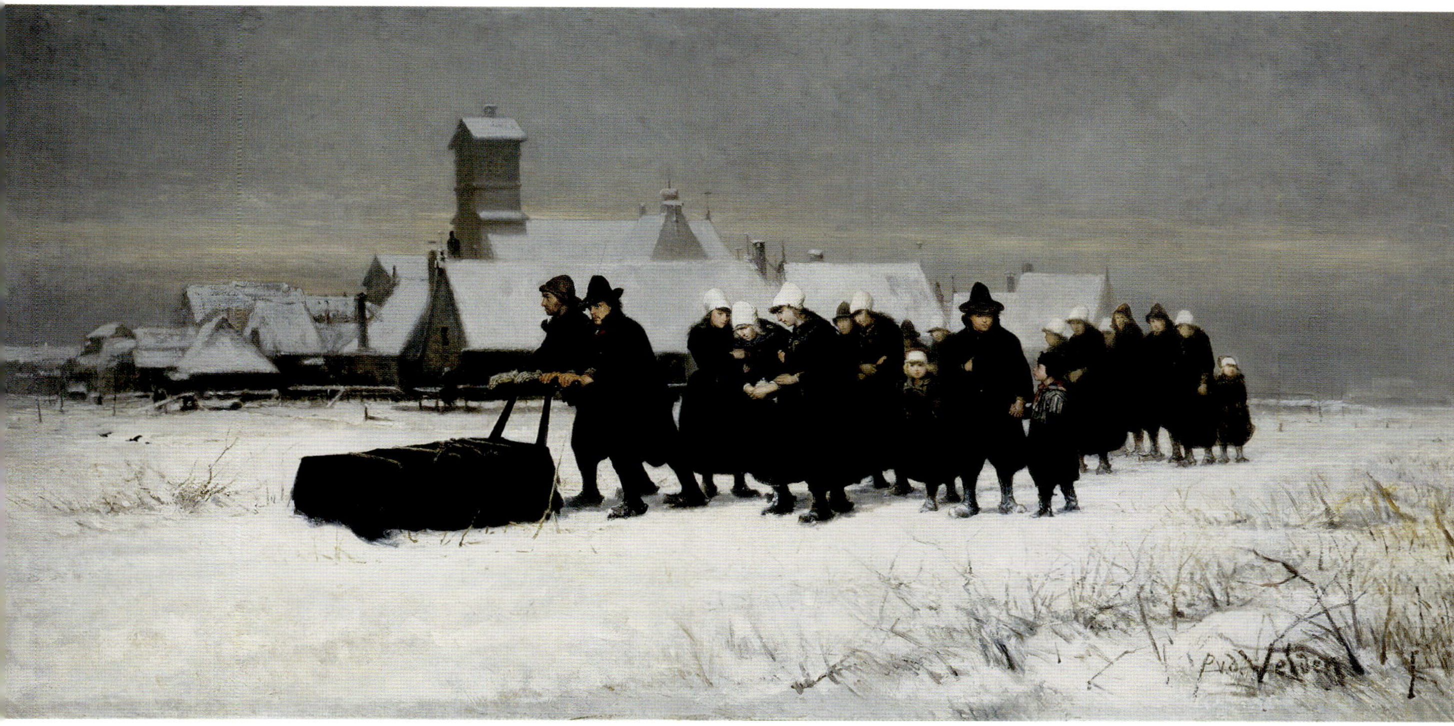

Archibald Nicoll

I know this is a bit of an old chestnut, been in just about every New Zealand art book published in recent years, but I wasn't going to leave it off my list. It's hard to say exactly why it's a favourite; I just think Archie got it 100 per cent right on the day.

The heft of the composition is created by the boldest lines all falling dangerously away to the right only to be pulled back just in time by the curve of the track and the line of the fence, and emphasised nicely by the three left-sloping fence posts upper middle. Then the whole thing is nicely tied up by the perfectly registered tones of light and dark in the snow – love those snow shadows! – and the foliage. Fine form transcending academic discipline.

Archibald Nicoll
Peninsula, Winter
c.1932, oil on canvas
614 x 792 mm

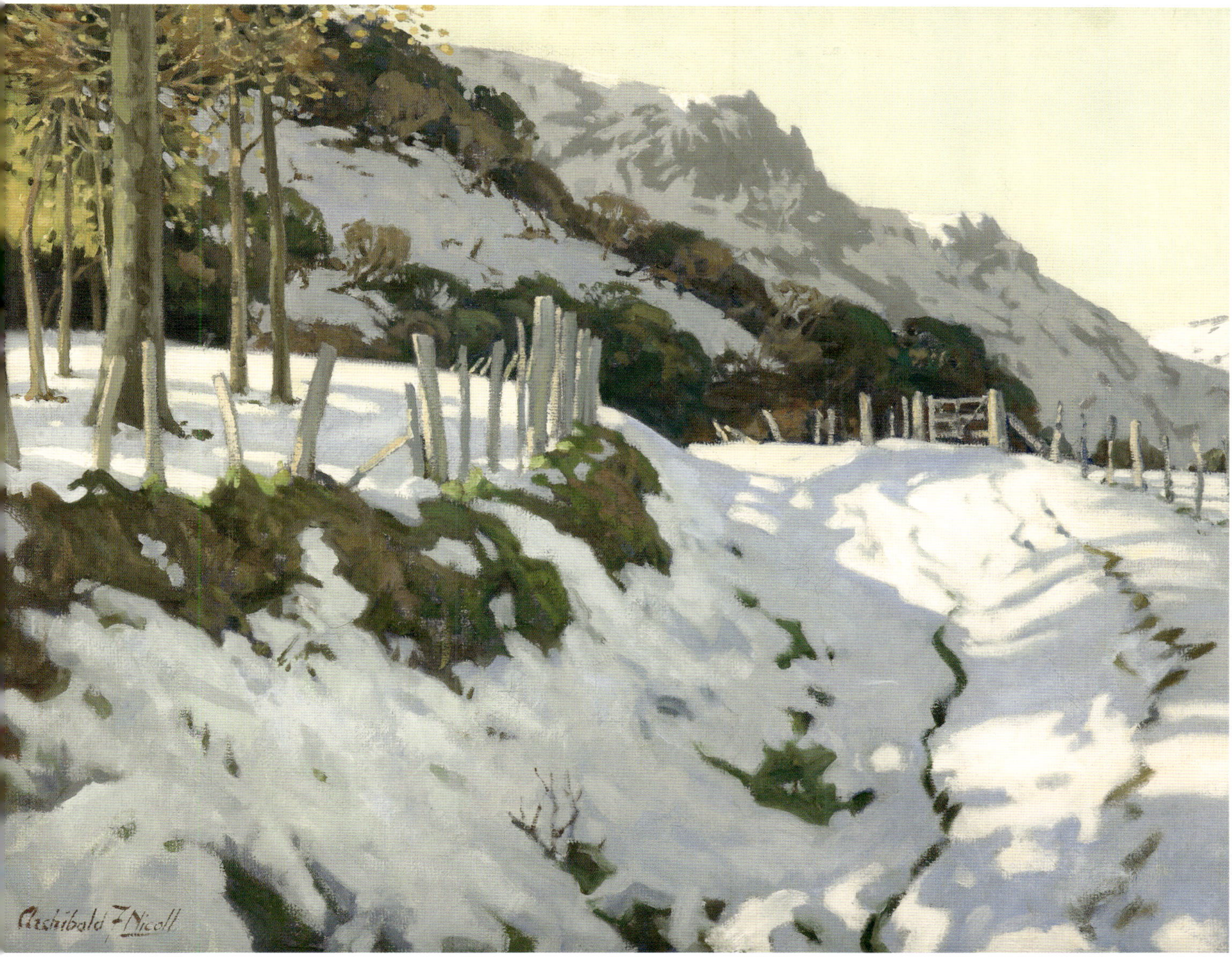
Archibald F Nicoll

Charles Goldie

It must be strange living with a Goldie, your dark little treasure in its big black frame sitting there on the wall, rendered virtually invisible by familiarity. I wonder if the owners even think about them much. I obviously do or I wouldn't be labouring with this torturous exposition. I do want to acknowledge the Goldie story, but struggle with it a bit.

I enjoy his works technically and certainly prefer their crisp brushwork to Lindauer's vaporous and strangely boneless apparitions, but if you relax your gaze for a second they slide into a dull fog of wrinkled tattoos and wispy grey hair. And then I get pulled back in by a beautifully articulated piece of woven flax or fabric, and the fact of the image being a masterful act of portraiture asserts itself again. The truth caught, by the skin of its teeth, in a web of lies.

Charles Goldie
Hamiora
1901, oil on canvas
456 x 560 mm

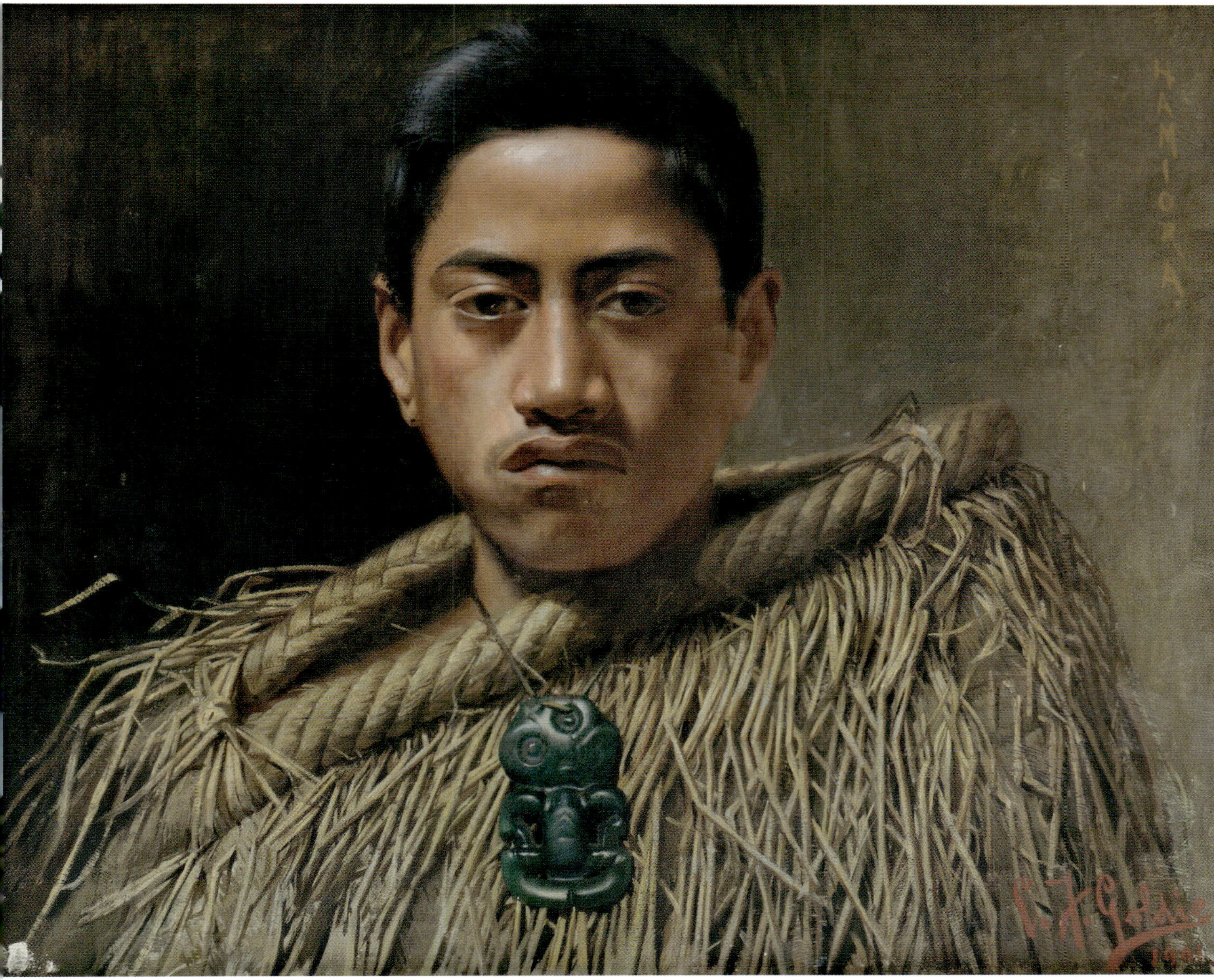
HAMIORA

Doris Lusk

Sounds a bit misogynistic to say it, but Doris obviously bashed her way to the front of the queue by virtually beating the boys at their own game. I wonder how it went down at the time?

Hers are tough, uncompromising paintings, boldly taking in huge chunks of geography and taming them with extraordinary leaps of scale, tone and colour stitched together with dynamic patterning that cleverly uses mass and tertiary detail in constant tension across the surface of the composition. Even her dry scrubby brushwork seems to be the perfect vehicle for describing these raw environments.

With time, and practice, one suspects, she evolved a more sedate technique which never really captured the energy that her early works radiate so confidently. It would've been an exhausting act to maintain, I'd imagine.

Doris Lusk
Landscape Overlooking Kaitawa, Waikaremoana
1948, oil on board

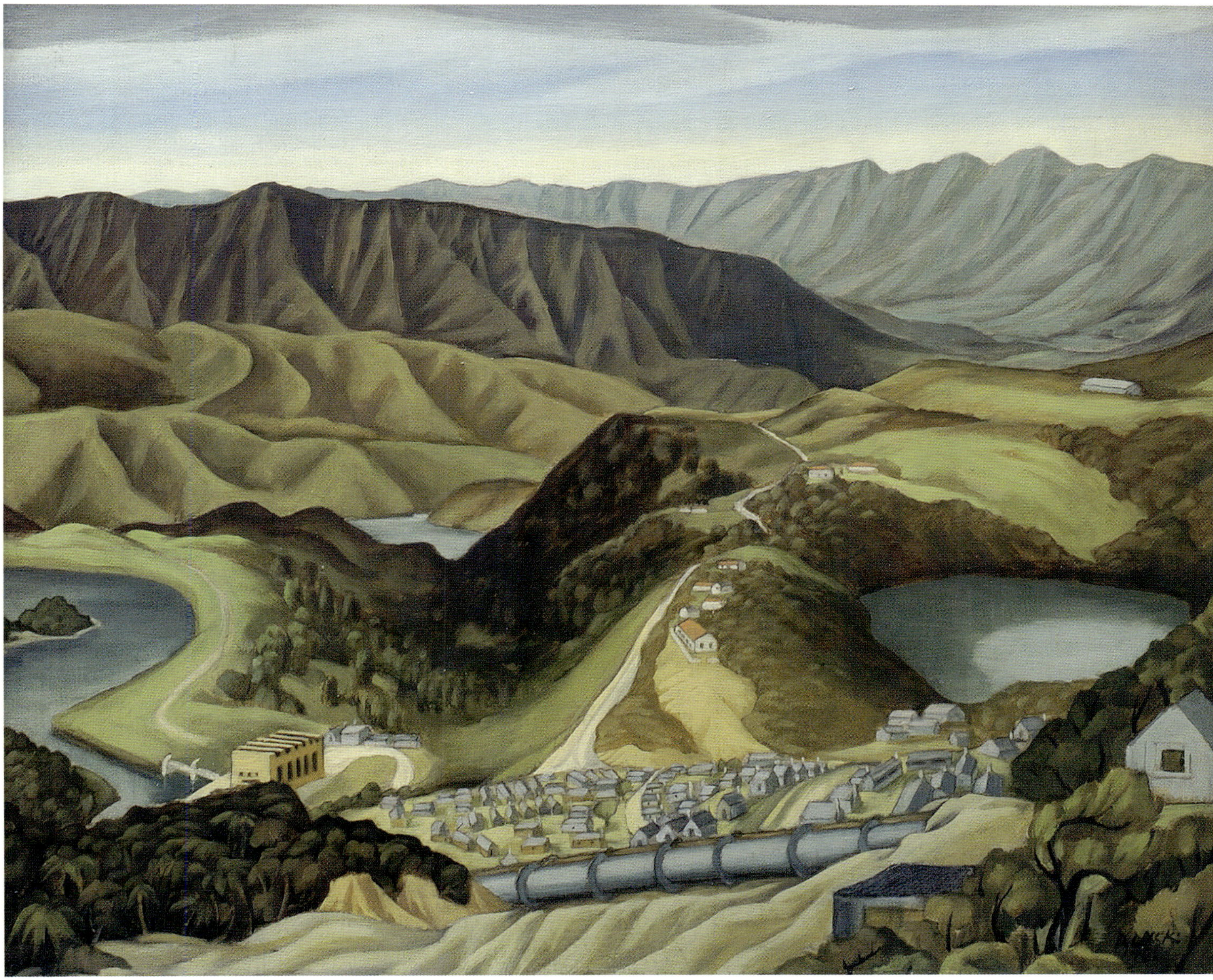

Christopher Perkins

One of my true New Zealand painter heroes. Every time I scumble a loaded brush down a bush-clad slope it feels like a handwritten letter from me to him.

Christopher's sense of proportion, his point of view, even his chunky brush work, were all so perfect for the task he set out for himself – to represent New Zealand. He wasn't alone in all this of course, as the time he was painting was without doubt the beginning of a new New Zealand cultural self-consciousness. But Christopher gave this a peculiarly solid heft, a British sort of gravitas grounded in a new, muscular way of exposing the landscape's underlying anatomy. And he managed to do all this transplanting without the work ever falling back into soft echoes of Sussex Downs.

Christopher Perkins
Volcanic Country Near Rotorua
c.1930, oil on canvas
609 x 685 mm

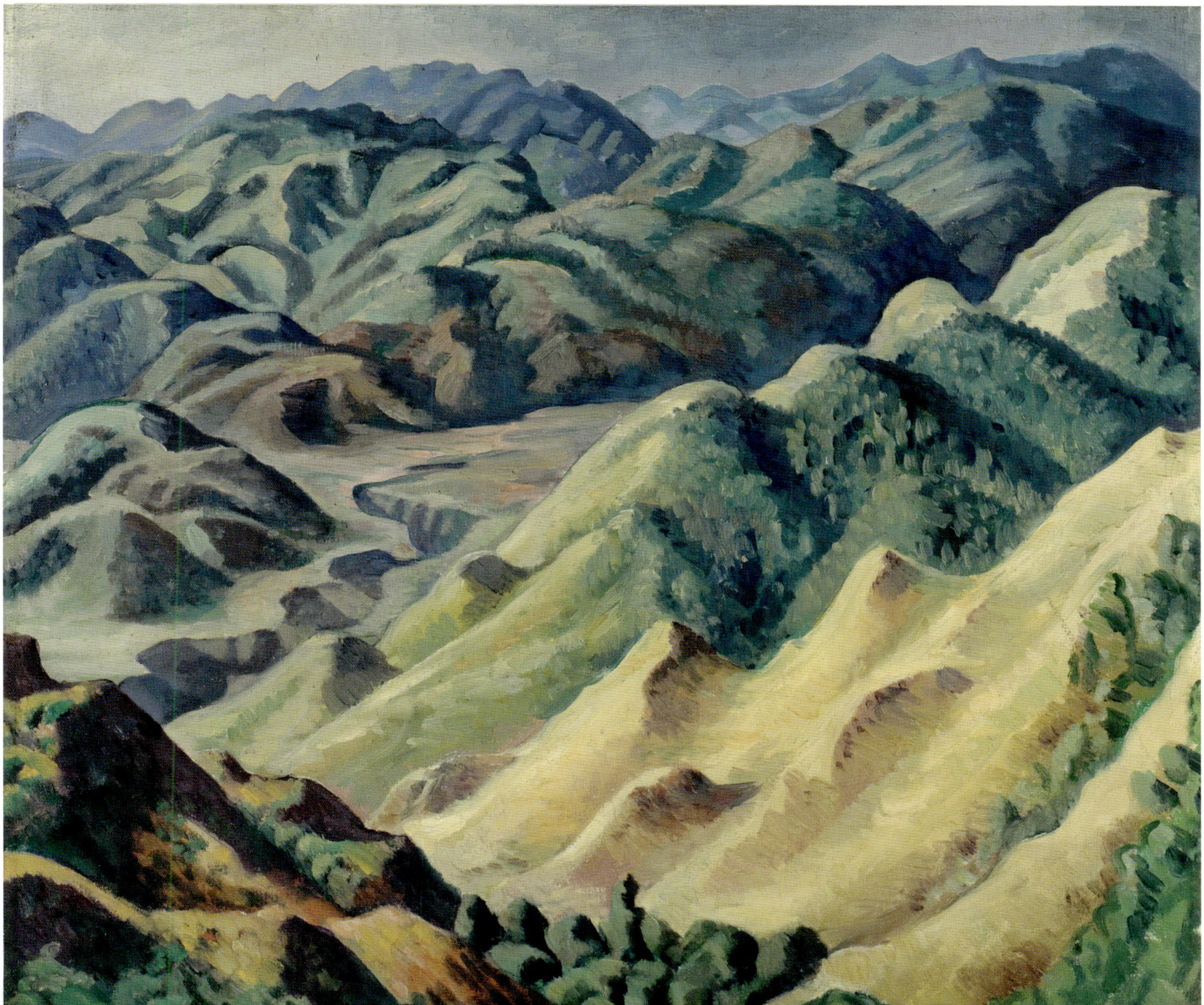

Margot Philips

Unique among her contemporaries, Margot is one of those rare individuals, the 'informed innocent'. Informed by some significant informers to be sure, Colin McCahon among them, and we have to be thankful for the inspiration he gave her, but no amount of summer schools or huddled art groups had any real impact on her very personal vision.

At one glance her works look like conventional landscape images, but at another it becomes apparent that they're almost entirely made up! And not made up as in making a new landscape out of different sources but REALLY made up, dreamed up even. But their fidelity to something is so convincing you'd almost believe that when Margot looked out her window this is what she saw. I mean, it's not mediated or manipulated for pattern or philosophical effect but is painted from some pure poetic impulse.

How true all this is, I'm not sure, but it certainly provides a clear way into appreciating her work.

Margot Philips
The Nearby Hill
1975, oil on
canvas board
745 x 835 mm

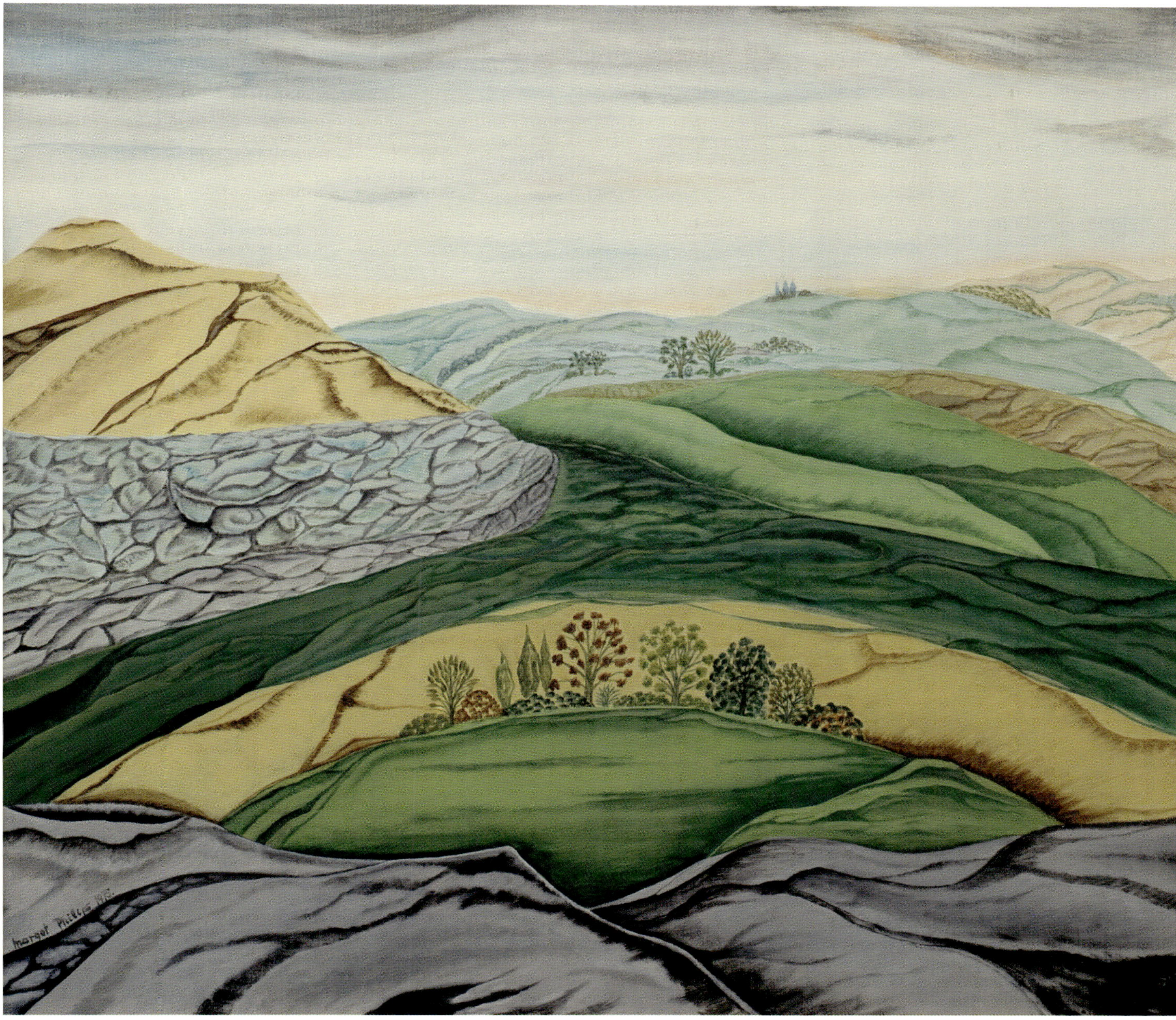

Cedric Savage

There seem to be a lot of trees in this book; a universal theme, I suppose . . . conveniently filling the picture plane. I'm a big fan of British painters like Paul Nash and Eric Ravilious and you can see Cedric has made a similar study. How to chop the raggedy edges of reality into a manageable pattern.

What I find fascinating about this painting is that the patterning is so deceptively simple: a modestly 'abstracted' landscape in the style of the time – a straightforward tree study – but if you examine it closely you can see that an impressive amount of information has been smuggled into the composition.

From the large co-ordinated mass of foreground trees, the tertiary details reduce in scale right down to the river winding into the background at bottom left. And then there's the gentle suggestion of the 'aftermath' itself . . . the post-storm glow in the clouds.

This is a very . . . I don't know . . . 'civilised' painting. Simultaneously modest and staunch. Even something as ordinary as the close earth tones in the eroded bank in the foreground is strangely reassuring on some level.

Cedric Savage
Aftermath
Oil on canvas
965 x 1130 mm

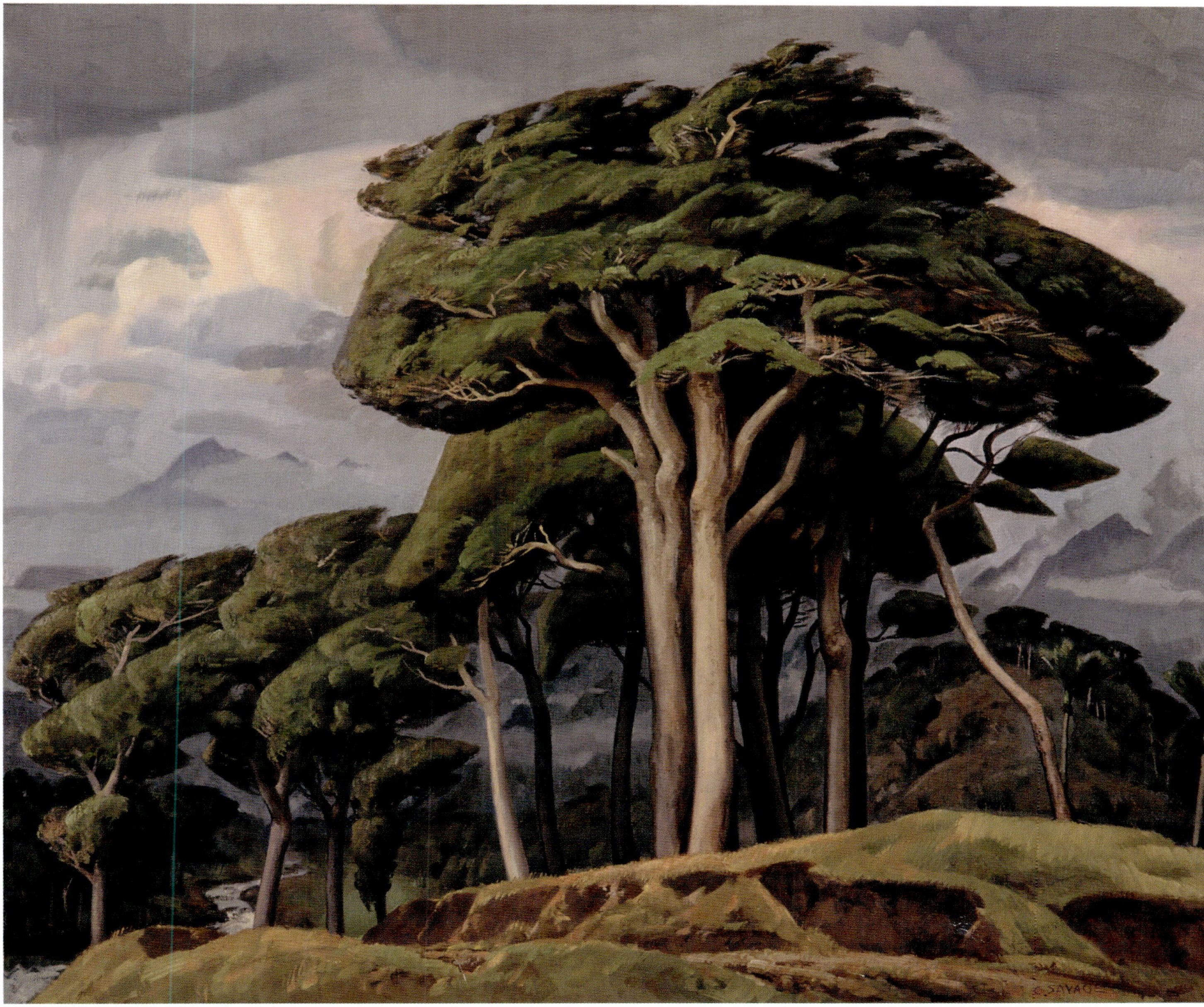

Patrick Hayman

A quiet poetic genius who drifted away from us and left a sketchy legacy. But enough of one to give me a charge whenever I come across it.

I'm not quite sure what it is about his work that I find so engaging; maybe it's that 'knowing' graphic modernism, a sort of Kiwi Milton Avery. Or the sophisticated sense of style that seemed to come so naturally to him. His paintings look almost as if they 'just came out that way' and that he would have been subsequently surprised to find out just how hip he was when he discovered the work of like-minded contemporaries in his travels.

I could be entirely wrong in all this of course but if a painting sets you off on a journey of any sort then it's doing its job.

Patrick Hayman
Blue Harbour and Camouflaged Ship
1942, oil on board
590 x 590 mm

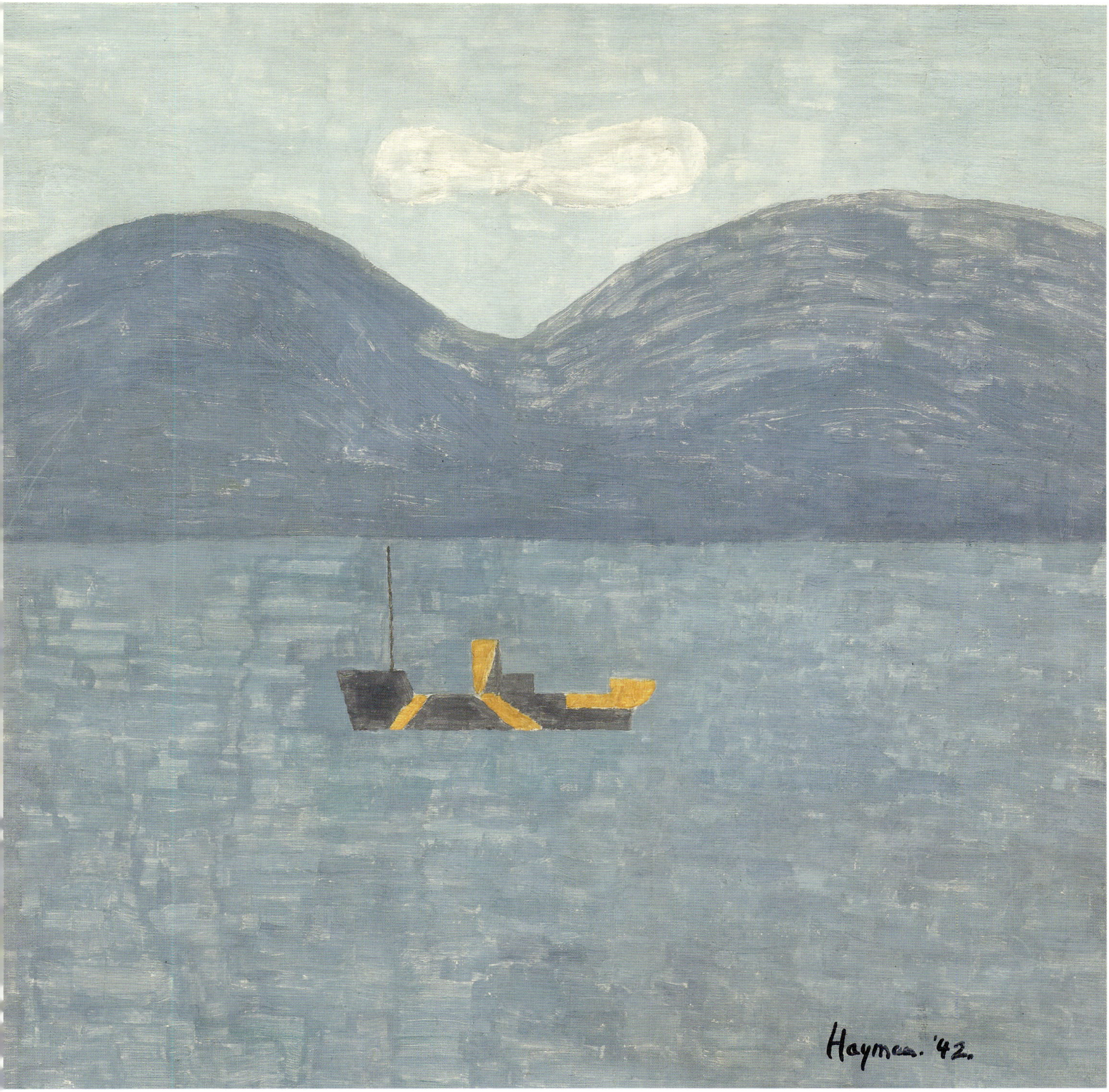
Hayman. '42.

Frances Hodgkins

Pretty much one of our greatest claims to fame, and deserving every bit of it, Frances is very much the complete artist. Her oeuvre conveniently demonstrates every aspect of how people expect a 'real' artist to evolve. The obvious skills displayed in her early watercolour work give the untrained eye the licence to 'approve' of even her most wayward experiments later on down the track. And believe me, they do get wayward.

In an effort to break free from the conventional modes of construction at the time, Frances occasionally wobbled off into complete structural chaos. You stand there in vain waiting for the resolution, which is usually and magnificently there.

But even at her worst she was still better than most. This work goes beyond gorgeous. I love it.

Frances Hodgkins
Berries and Laurel
c.1930, oil on canvas
640 x 763 mm

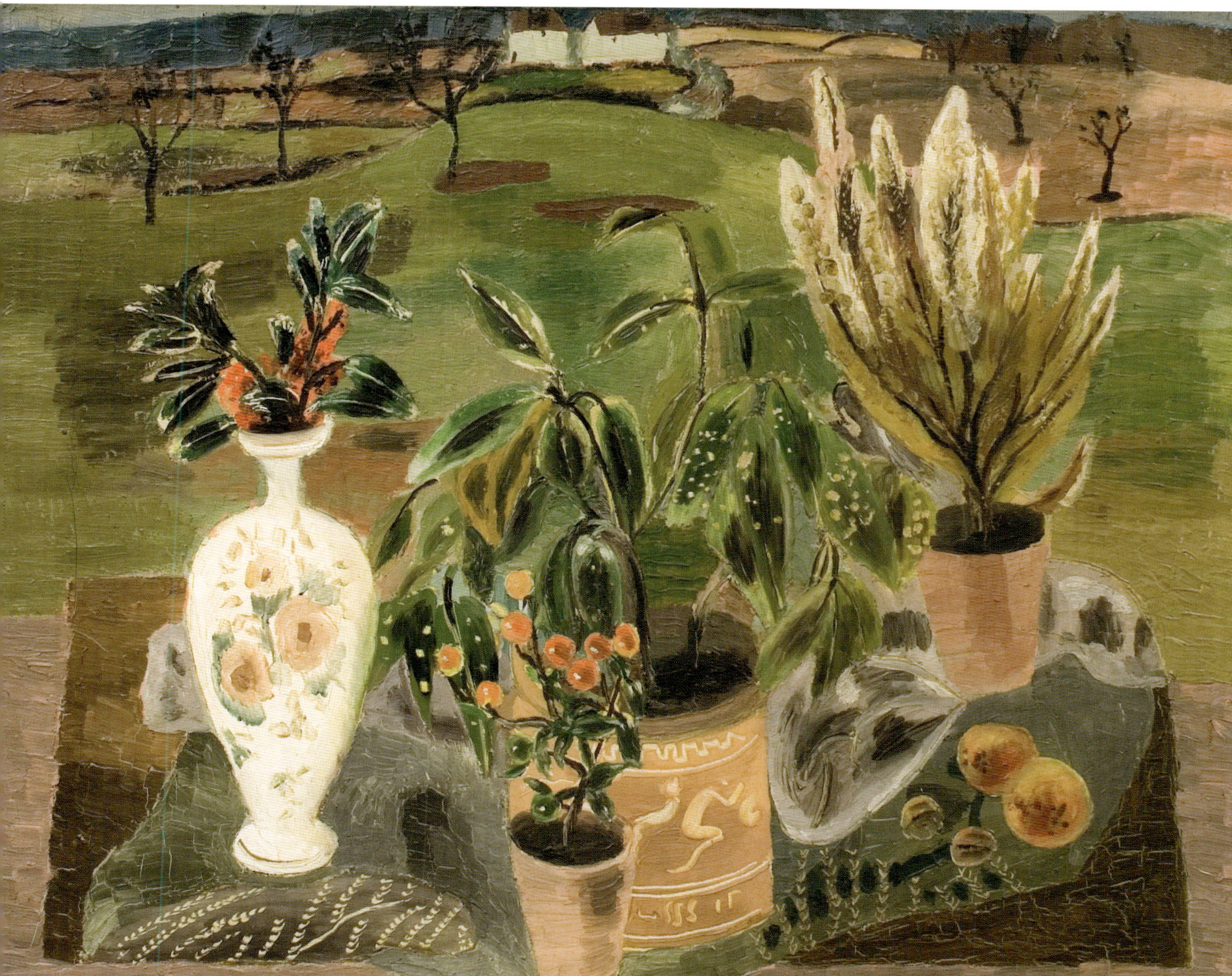

Raymond McIntyre

I really should've used Raymond's self-portrait with a hat here; it would have made writing about him a lot easier. The portrait says it all, the fantastically urbane young man with a sleepy sneer. The style of the man, the style of the painting, the insouciant economy of the execution.

But I'm going with this sublime piece of work, *Felice.* The obvious influence of Japanese painting, the Whistlerian brevity and precision show us a young man painting with incredible skill and fashionable know-how.

I wonder if he was familiar with Matisse's work of the period? (He must have been, I doubt he missed much.) The influence is all there, the cursive line, the flattened colour (what there is of it; his cool, northern sense of colour was never going to stray too far from the grey end of the spectrum).

It's actually a bit of a long bow to keep calling him a New Zealand painter, but we do that, don't we . . . rope them in for the continuity, and to keep the bar high.

Raymond McIntyre
Felice
c.1913, oil on panel
290 x 203 mm

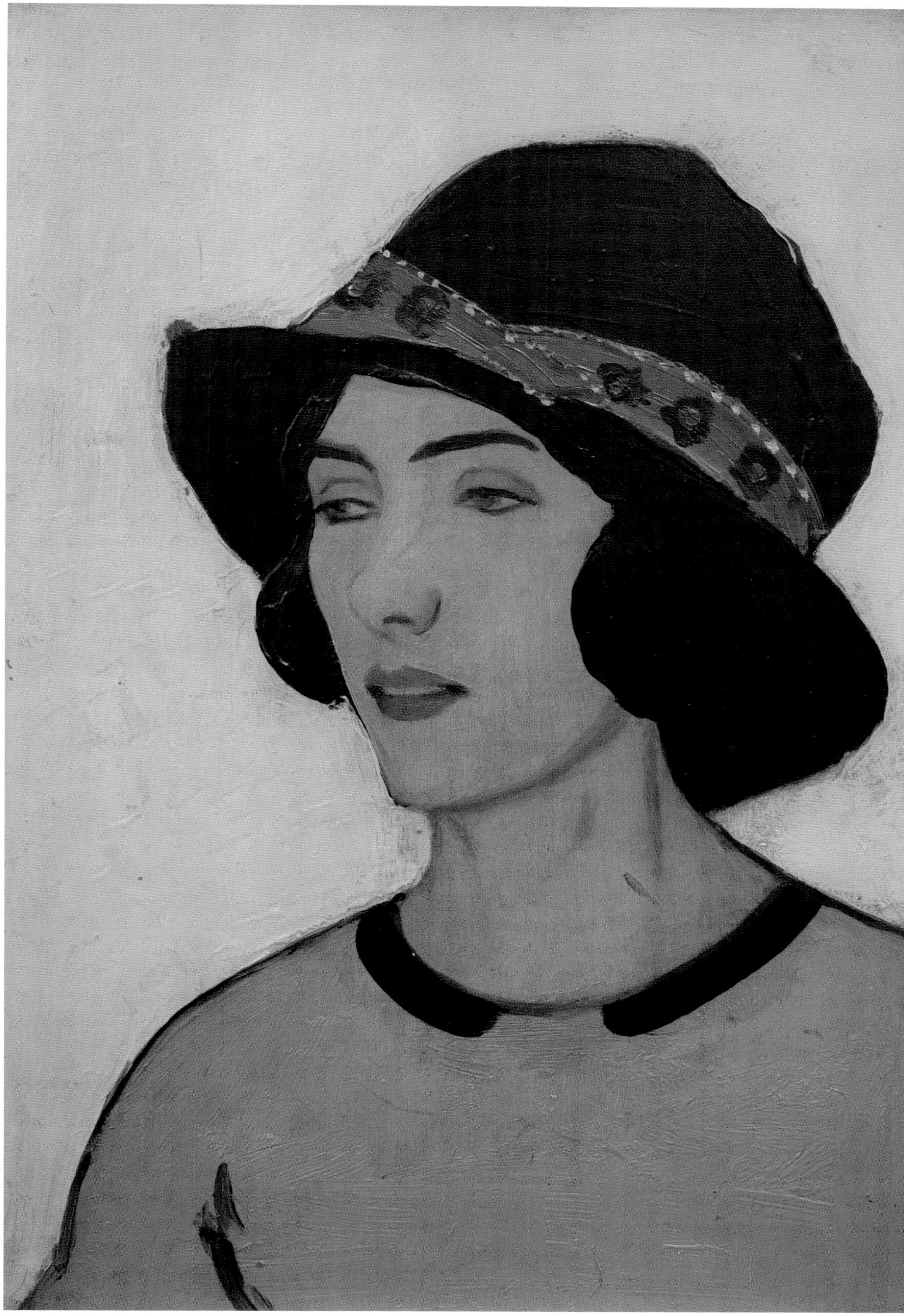

John Holmwood

I bet John was a nice man; his works always express a sunny optimism rare in painting from this period.

Even when the subject was appropriately gloomy something always gives the game away. A lonely farmhouse deep in the godforsaken burnt-stump-and-wet-bush backblocks would have, say, a plume of smoke from the chimney that was so cheerfully rendered it'd make you want to drop by for a cup of tea!

This strangely lyrical work *Horses and Children* is typical of what I mean: the children and the horses frolicking in an almost bucolic happy place . . . where's the introspective angst in all that? It shouldn't be allowed.

Fortunately, and why the works always have a respectable grip on the credible, John gets there with his lively way with paint and a point of view that sees beyond the standard text.

John Holmwood
Horses and Children
1953, oil on board
735 x 805 mm

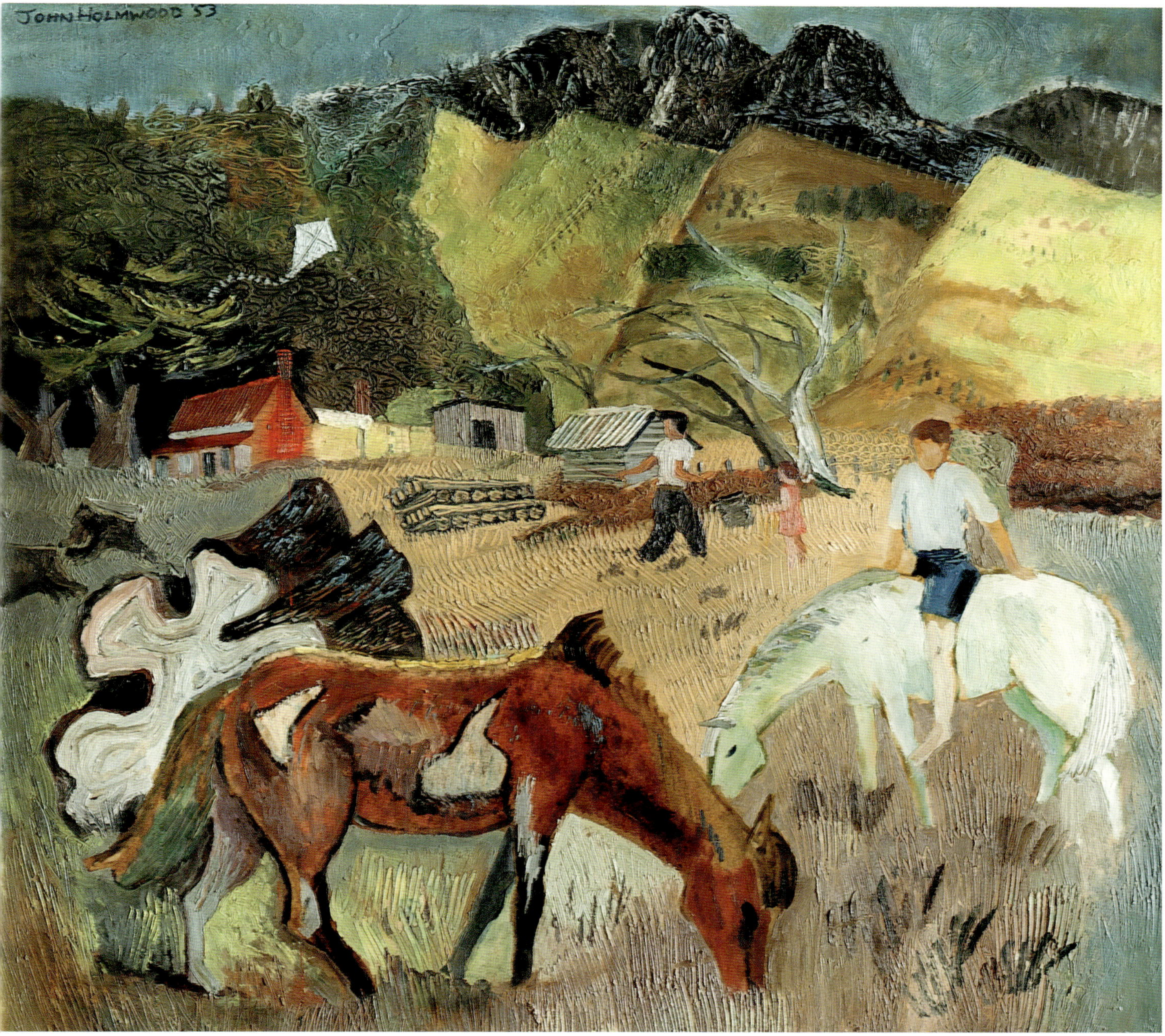
JOHN HOLMWOOD '53

Rita Angus

We're getting into very familiar territory here, and again there's not a lot I can add except to be a bit of a spoiler.

I'm finding I have to tread a little carefully with Rita who is so adored that any criticism sounds churlish and, well, somewhat redundant really. But I do find an awful lot of her work to be a bit silly. Those over-fussed composite landscapes and her 'goddess' stuff seems like a complete intellectual failure to me. Possibly she should have got out more. But when she did get it right, she really got it right and her *Cass* painting deserves its number-one ranking.

I've included this painting, *Head of a Maori Boy*, because of the marvellous conflation of generosity and restraint, not too much and not too little in just about every measure. It's an image that really gives you faith in the formal language of painting.

Rita Angus
Head of a Maori Boy
c.1938, oil on canvas
423 x 311 mm

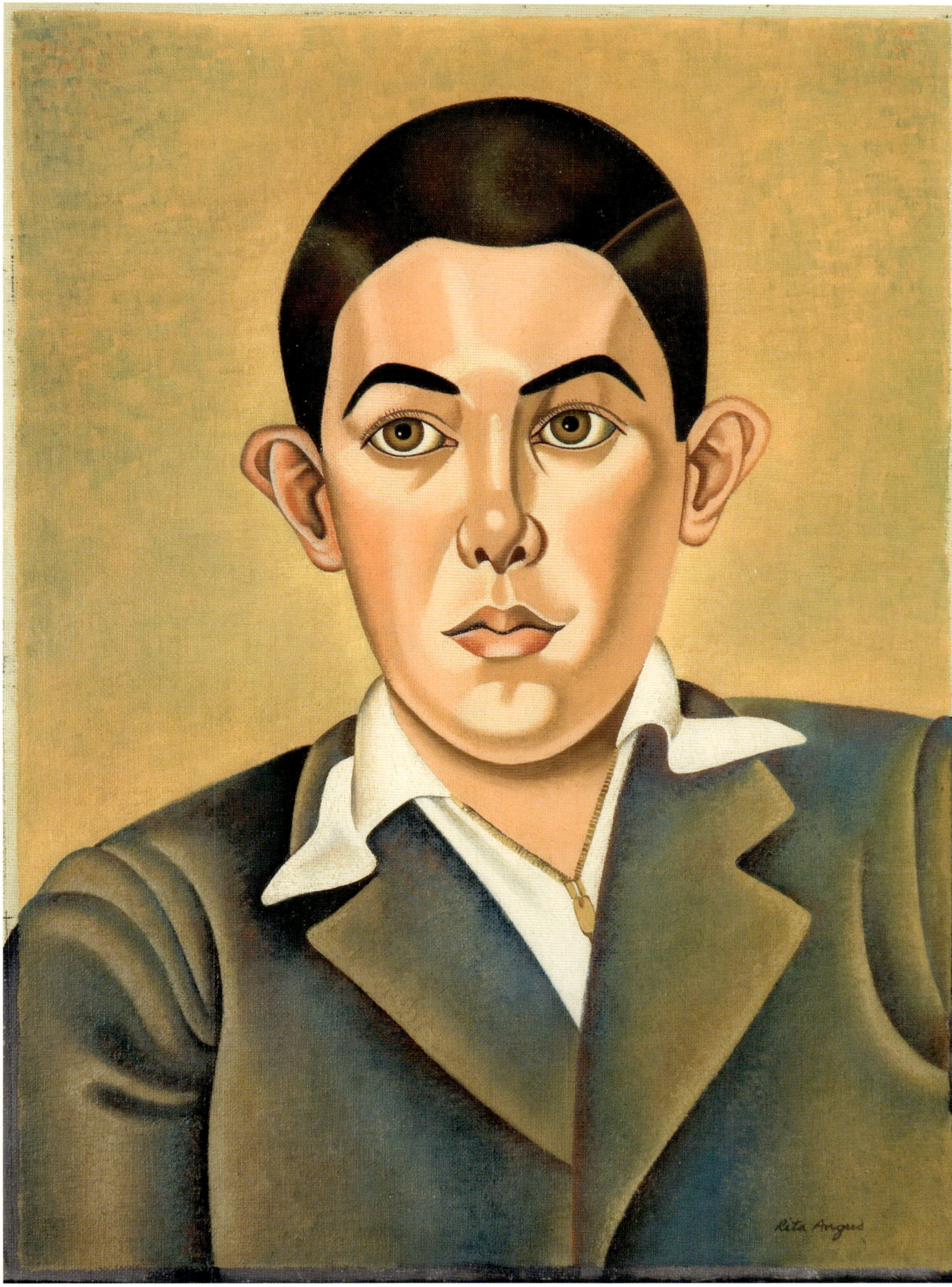
Rita Angus

Douglas MacDiarmid

Don't know much about Douglas, just love this painting. I had a photocopy of *Portrait of Constance, wife of Maurice Sochachewsky* – from *New Zealand Art* – the old black and white mag, pinned to the wall of my studio for years. My neighbours at the time, artists John and June Ritchie, had a great pile of these ancient treasures in their downstairs studio.

The thing that captured me about the image is the bold way the face fills the frame off-centre, squeezing the narrative background details over to the right-hand margin of the painting. A very unusual compositional device. And the other remarkable aspect is that the portrait is so obviously from a photograph, a highly eccentric one with the strong overhead light source casting very dramatic shadows about the place – under the nose, for example. And look at the way the hair tumbles down the stairs – accident or design?

You'd almost have to wonder what Douglas was thinking, but the whole thing very much exceeds the sum of its peculiar parts.

Douglas MacDiarmid
Portrait of Constance, wife of Maurice Sochachewsky
1948, oil on softboard
308 x 247 mm

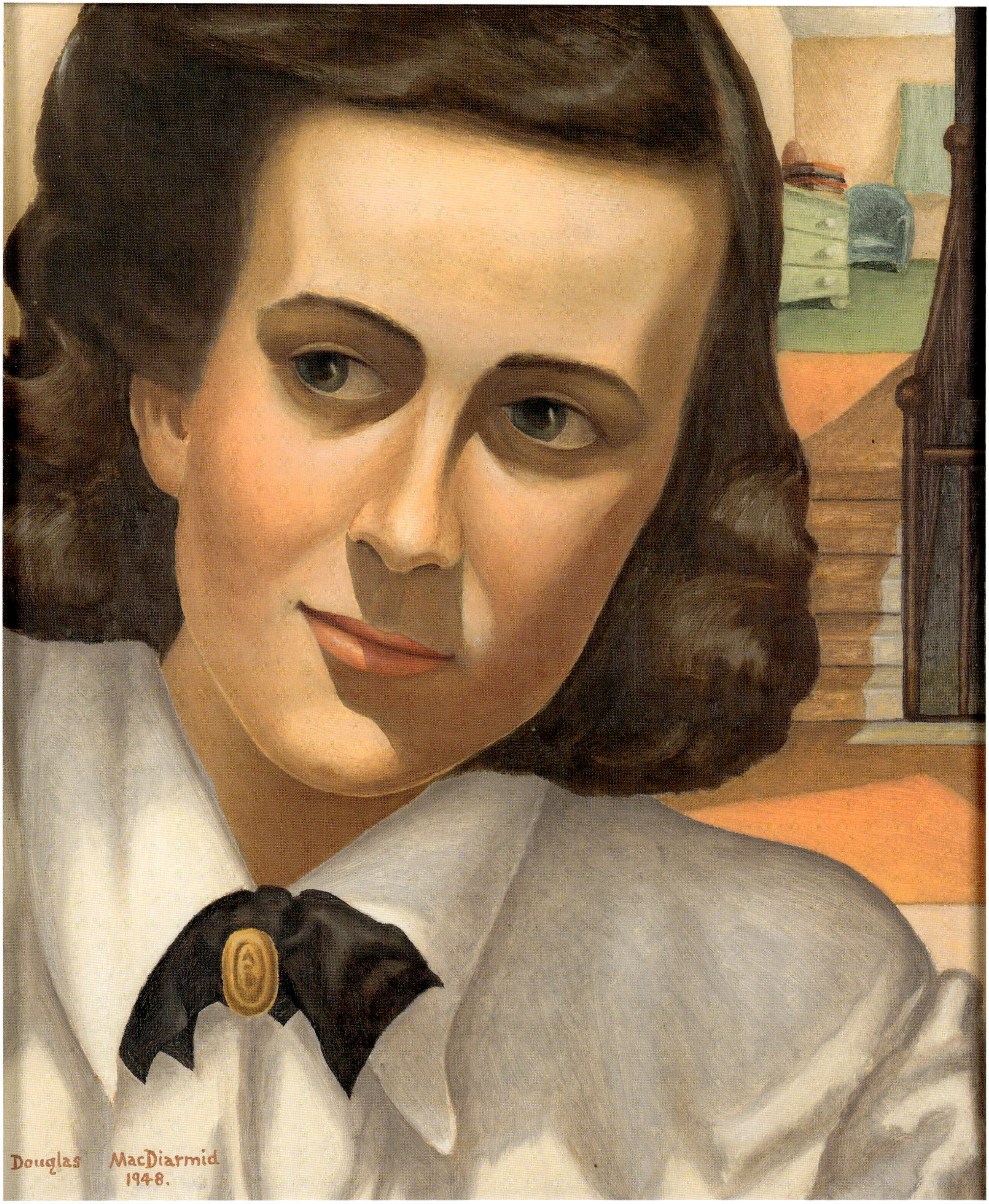
Douglas MacDiarmid
1948.

Nugent Welch

I don't know anything about Nugent apart from what I've just read in Christopher Johnstone's book, *Landscape Paintings of New Zealand*. I just love this painting – it's completely perfect. I should hang a copy of it on my wall.

Look at it – it's hollow! But what hollowness. The elements round the edge of that space are so cunningly interlocked that they fill the emptiness with their radiating dynamic. And given that only about 20 per cent of those elements are static, the cliffs and the island, the rest being clouds, it's quite a feat of design.

He sounds like a fascinating chap, too, tramping off to his cave on the coast . . . waiting for the moment.

A fascinating find.

Nugent Welch
The Coming Storm
c.1930, oil on canvas
700 x 900 mm

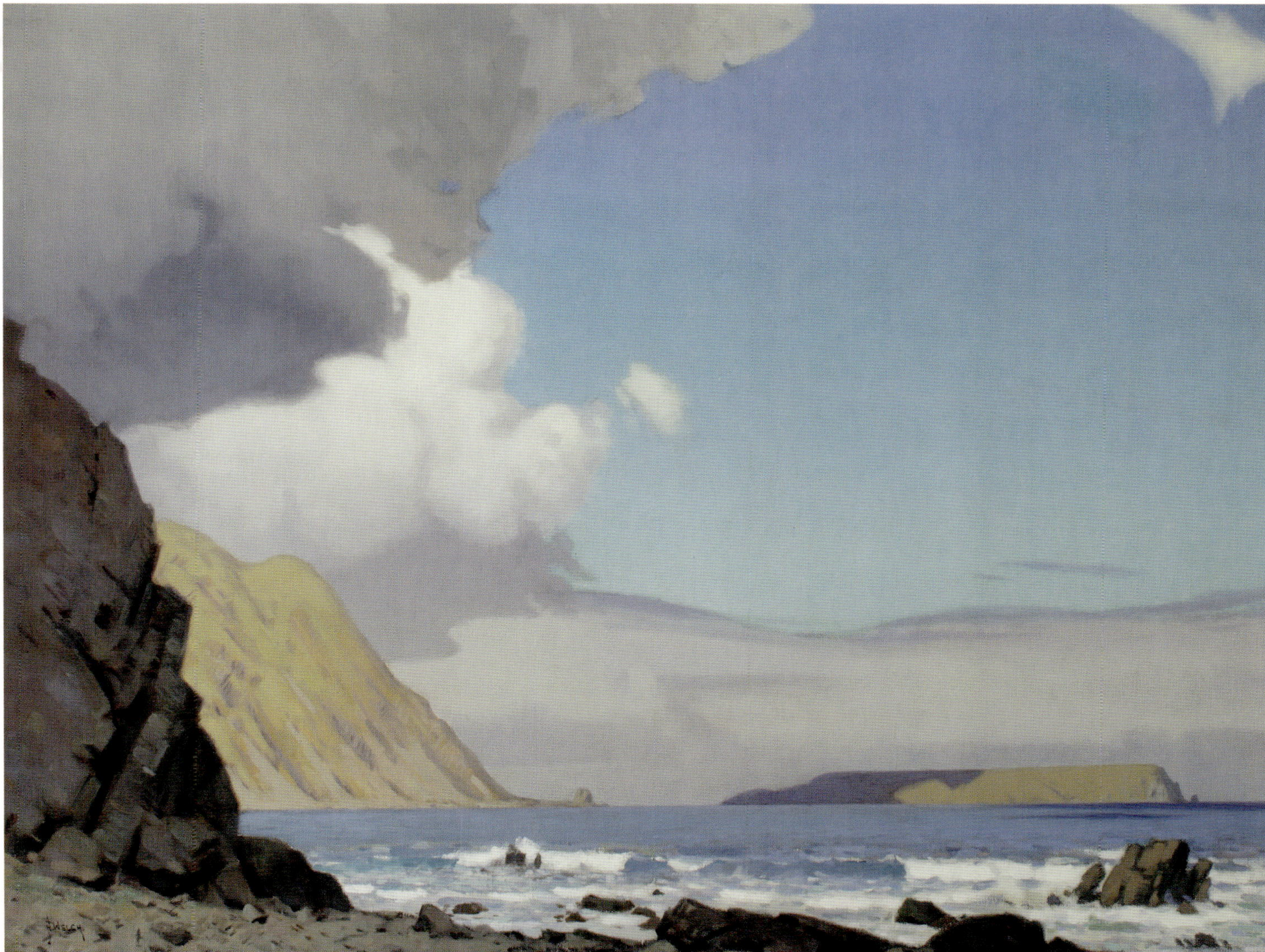

John Weeks

John is another modernist pioneer who has delivered so much to me through his paintings that it's never occurred to me to dig any deeper into his life. Writing this, I'm feeling a little ashamed that I haven't.

He obviously had a fascinating career, painting trips to Morocco and all that, but for the life of me I can't imagine him as a young man. He never really added anything to the movements that excited and inspired him, such as early twentieth-century cubism, but his thorough understanding of how these formal revolutions worked and his ability to pass this information on was an important link in New Zealand's artistic evolution. We were never going to be at the centre of things but we still had to display a coherent understanding of what was happening 'over there' to be connected to an important, global conversation.

John Weeks
Women in Landscape
c.1940, tempera
on paper
435 x 570 mm

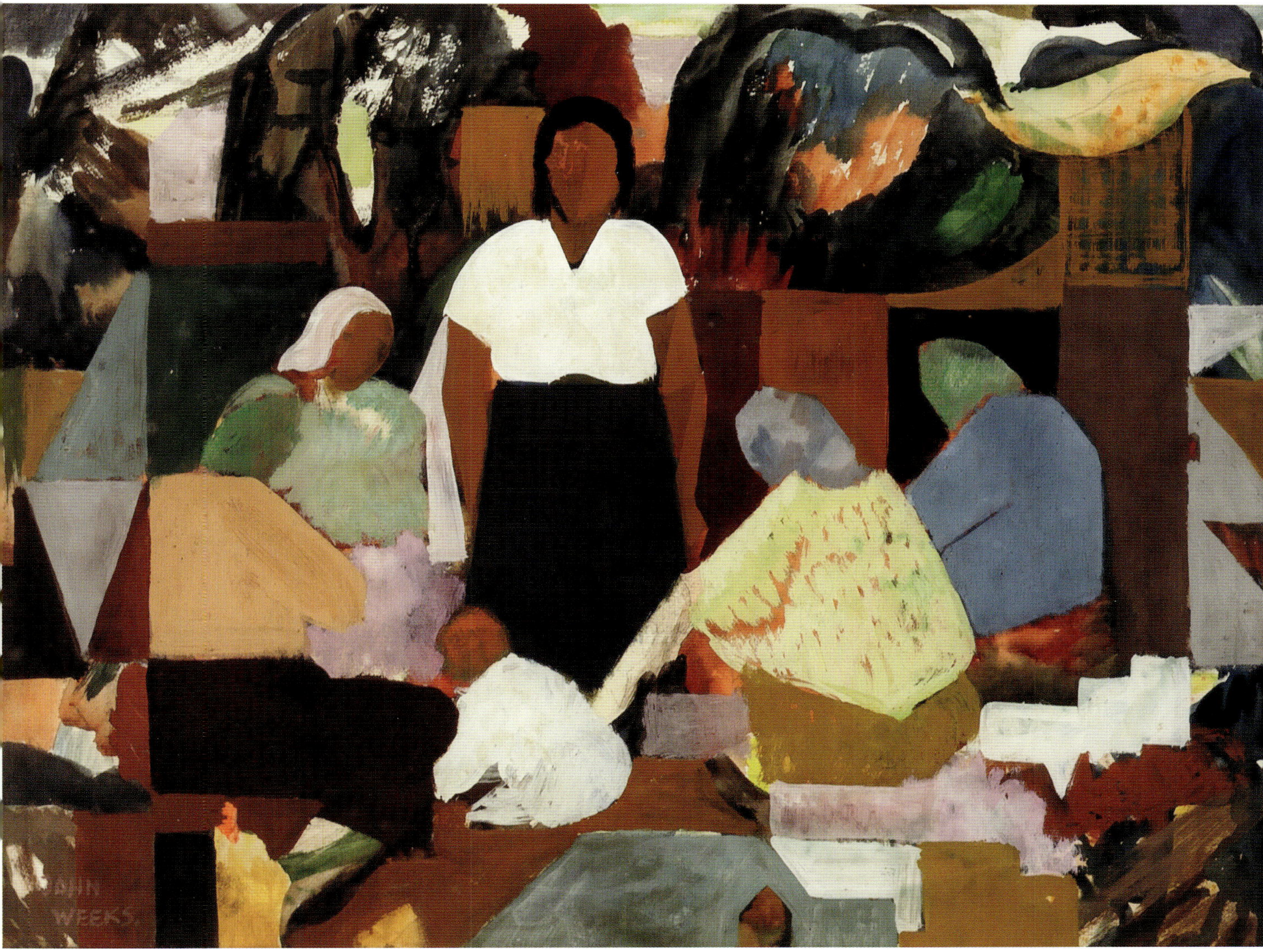
JOHN
WEEKS.

Pat Hanly

Like John Coley, Pat was a great inspiration to us younger students back in the early 1960s. Such was his presence that even before I was familiar with his work I wanted to 'be like Pat'.

In an era where there was little or no art scene to slot into (is there one now?), Pat somehow made the idea of being an artist seem possible. And when I ultimately got to see his Figures in Light series I was stunned. They were so damn MODERN, the flat, bold colour, the open compositions, the little touches of tertiary detail in the larger unmodulated spaces of the design. Picture perfect. Like owning a Binney, every modern Kiwi house had to have one. Lancewoods in the garden, a Barry Brickell casserole on the shelf . . .

And they were here, and about here, summer on the beach! Could it get any better than that?!

Pat Hanly
Figures in Light 14
1964, oil on canvas
on hardboard
1250 x 1198 mm

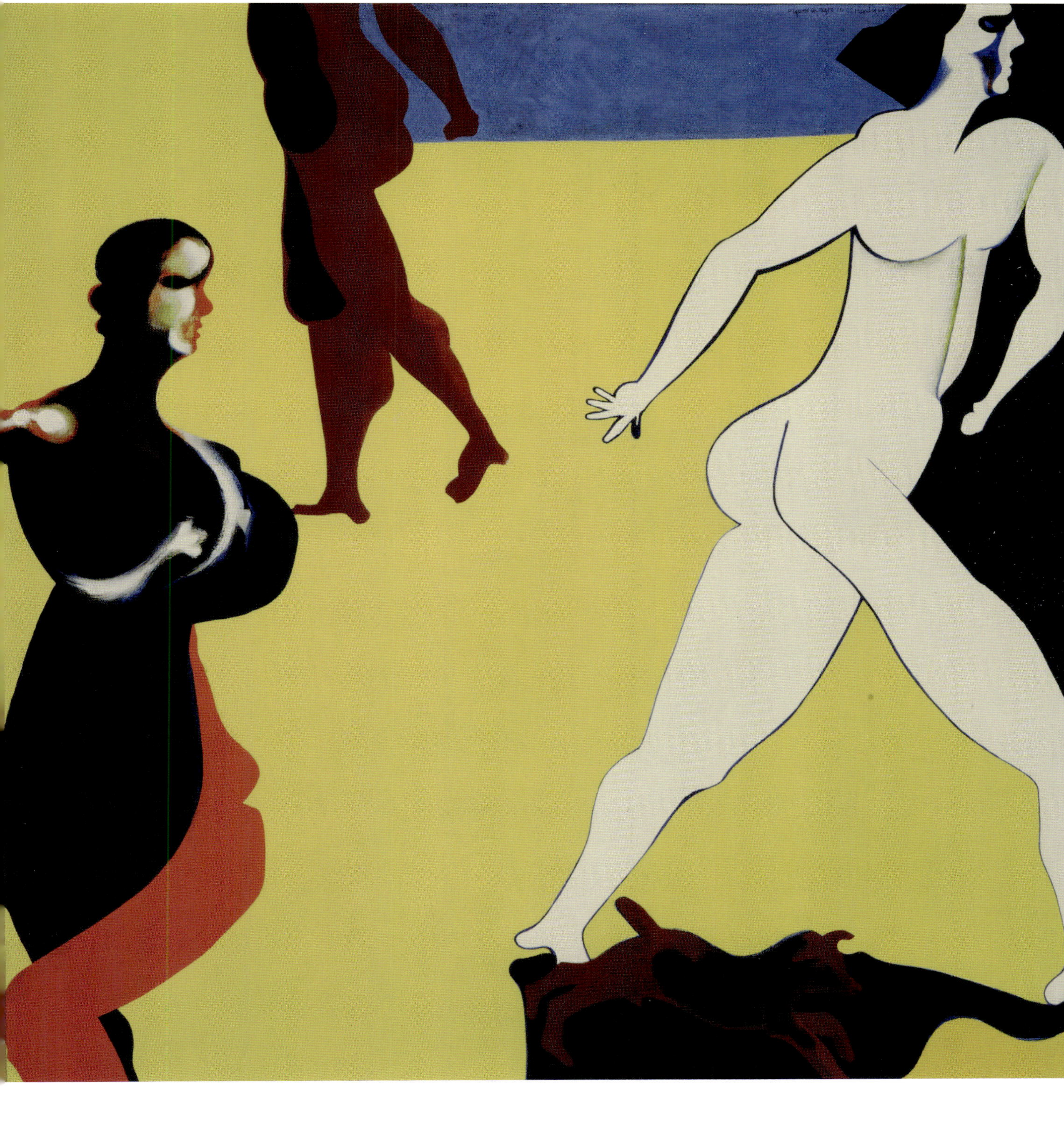

Toss Woollaston

I struggle a bit with Woollaston sometimes, finding it hard to see just what it is with his work that struck such a chord with his earliest admirers. For all the intensity of his well-broadcast belief systems, the actual work often strikes me as remarkably woolly. But that could just be me, and when he does toughen up and dig in you can see why he was always going to be part of the canon.

In *Mount Arthur, Nelson*, all his fidgeting and probing brushwork coalesces into a powerful description of time and space, mood and mass, a manufactured reality as real as the thing that inspired it.

Artists seemed to need to BELIEVE much more in those days . . . to maintain the faith . . . such was the intellectual isolation, and sometimes the proselytising and the product don't quite match up, which doesn't matter because the work's the thing.

Toss Woollaston
Mount Arthur, Nelson
1945, oil on card
606 x 608 mm

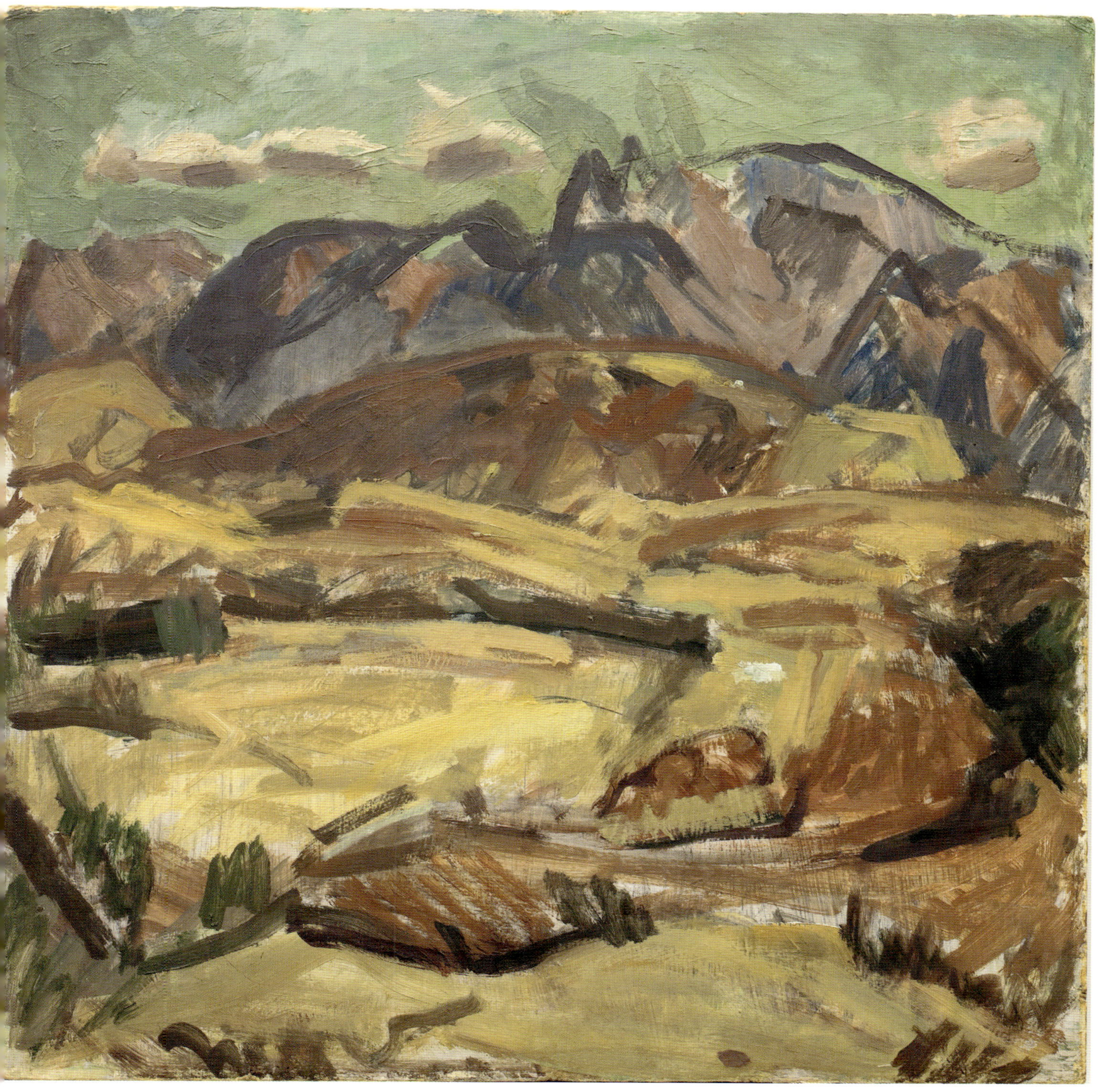

Colin McCahon

Well, I could have filled the whole book up with McCahons and been happy with that. Which one do you choose?!

A Candle in a Dark Room does it for me, the elevation of the crude and the comic to a statement of the best that can be.

I was tempted to show no image at all, just write about them, write about Colin's uncanny sense of proportion, how little he needed to make his point. How the positive spaces and the negative spaces somehow seem to pulse and swell into each other. How the same line can describe a line, or describe a mass, or space, by rolling over onto itself, breaking down then tightening up. How his closed spaces are perfectly poised in their relationship to his open spaces. You have to know EVERYTHING about painting to paint like this.

The truth in a McCahon blows through the work unimpeded by a millimetre of wrongness, like the wind blowing through the back screen door.

Colin McCahon
A Candle in a Dark Room
1947, oil on board
380 x 310 mm

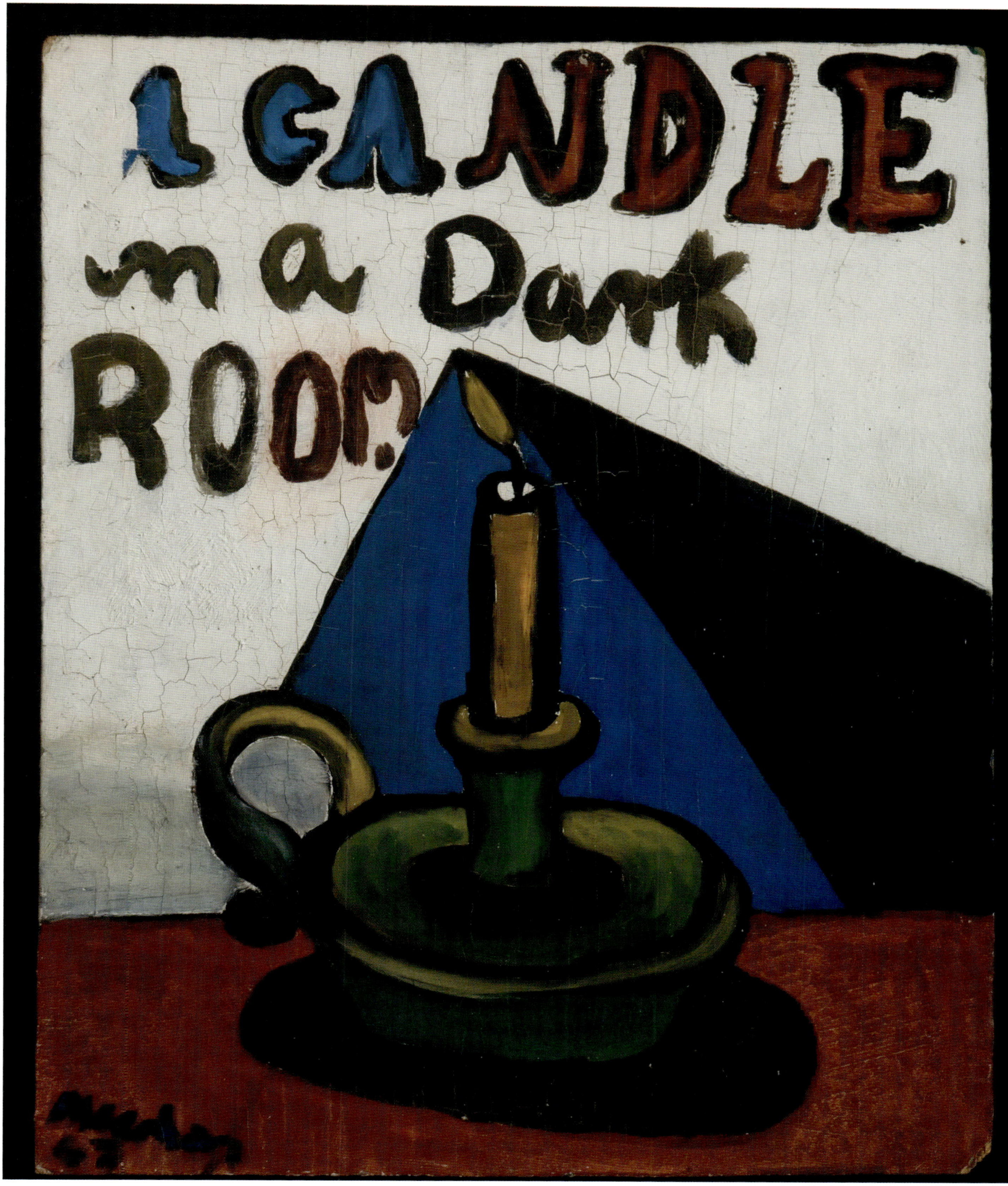
A CANDLE
in a Dark
ROOM

Ralph Hotere

I bought a Hotere once, a modestly scaled vertical of glossy black Ducco divided by a thin green cross . . . fell in love with it and got Rodney Kirk-Smith to put a reserve sticker on it.

Went home and told Jude . . . went back the next day and had Rodney remove the sticker. What was I thinking? The clutch in the Cortina was going and the hot water cylinder wasn't so hot.

So, no Hotere, but I could still enjoy them. And I did: his black Union Jacks, the fantastic mural at the Auckland airport. Large, sparse and elegant; I still can't imagine the control required to scribe those crisp, concentric circles over those beautifully modulated fields of turpsy splatter.

Not sure when I thought the wheels began to wobble and the works started to fall into an odd space somewhere between a hubristic shrug and indignant anger.

God knows it's hard enough keeping it going year after year given that the whole business is governed by attrition – shape up or ship out and all that – though Ralph never lost that elegant touch, he just seemed to let the 'issues' overwhelm the aesthetic.

Anger can be a great thing for getting you out of bed in the morning but you have to park it carefully at the studio door or it can have a pernicious effect on the structural integrity of the work. Illustrating the emotion isn't enough, you have to hope the feeling is so integral to your core beliefs that it'll find its own way to the canvas. I'm still sorry I don't own that green cross though!

Ralph Hotere
Ruia Ruia
1977, acrylic on board
942 x 740 x 15 mm

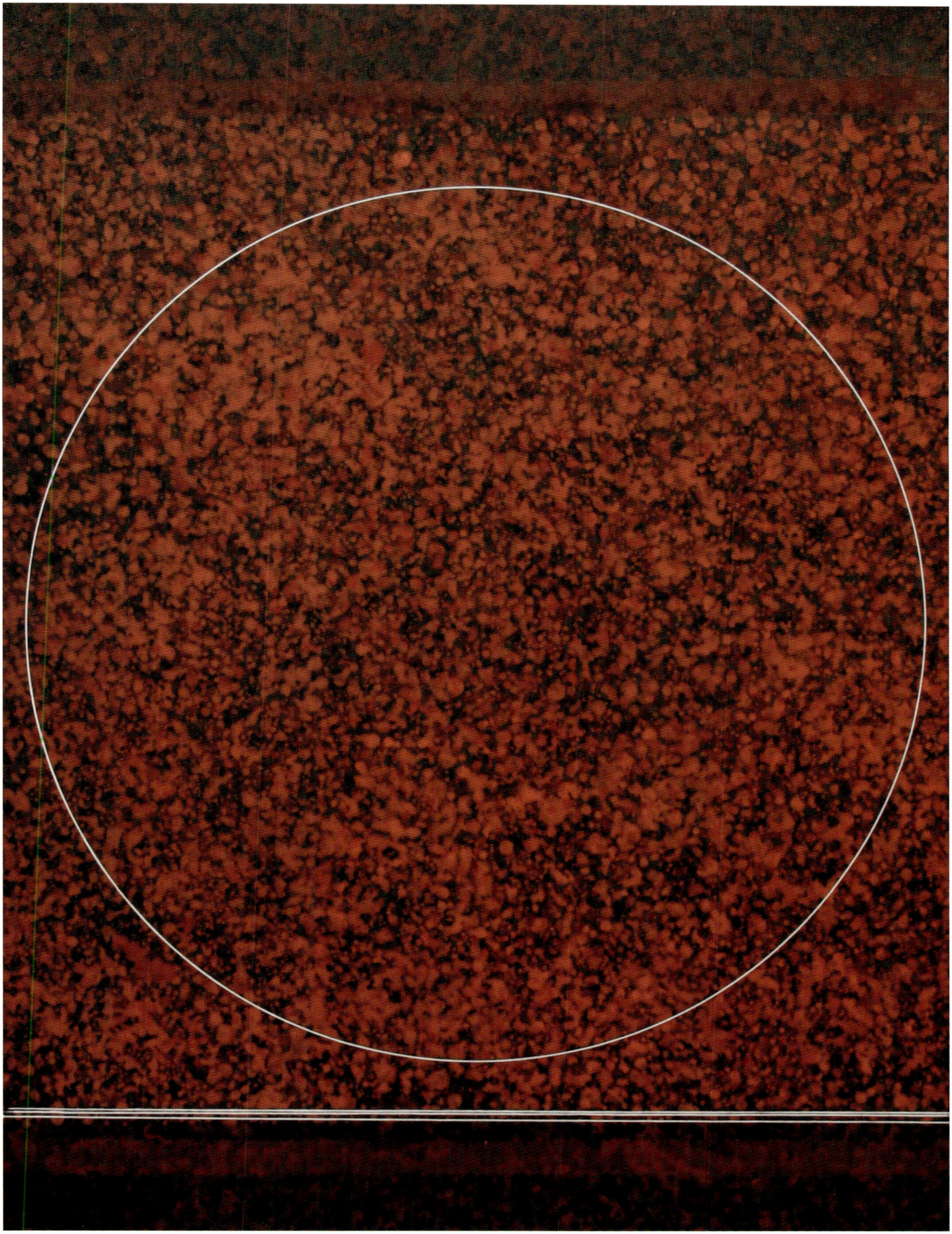

Gordon Walters

I couldn't drag Gordon into my radar in any positive way during the entire writing of this book. He became a sort of benchmark of omission, having decided that I wasn't going to include anyone I couldn't write enthusiastically about. But then I more or less wrapped up the writing and began to relax a bit, and Gordon wouldn't go away. I even started to feel a bit guilty about his absence, as if I was wearing it like a badge of honour. And I was impressed by his works when I first saw them, no doubt about that, so what was going on?

After all it's not Gordon's fault that his kowhaiwhai adaptations have struck such a universal chord, influencing almost instantly every level of local graphic culture. It's hard to look at them without thinking of a government department letterhead or a bad flag. Actually, it's an astonishing story; can you imagine contemporary New Zealand design without Gordon's invention? That positive/negative bobble on the end of a stick has become truly ubiquitous.

So I seriously wondered about the wisdom of reproducing one here, as he did produce a profound body of work that addressed similar spatial and tonal concerns without a stripe in sight. But if we're talking about images that endlessly resonate we'll have to stay with the obvious.

Gordon Walters
Kapiti
1984, serigraph
on arches paper
505 x 382 mm

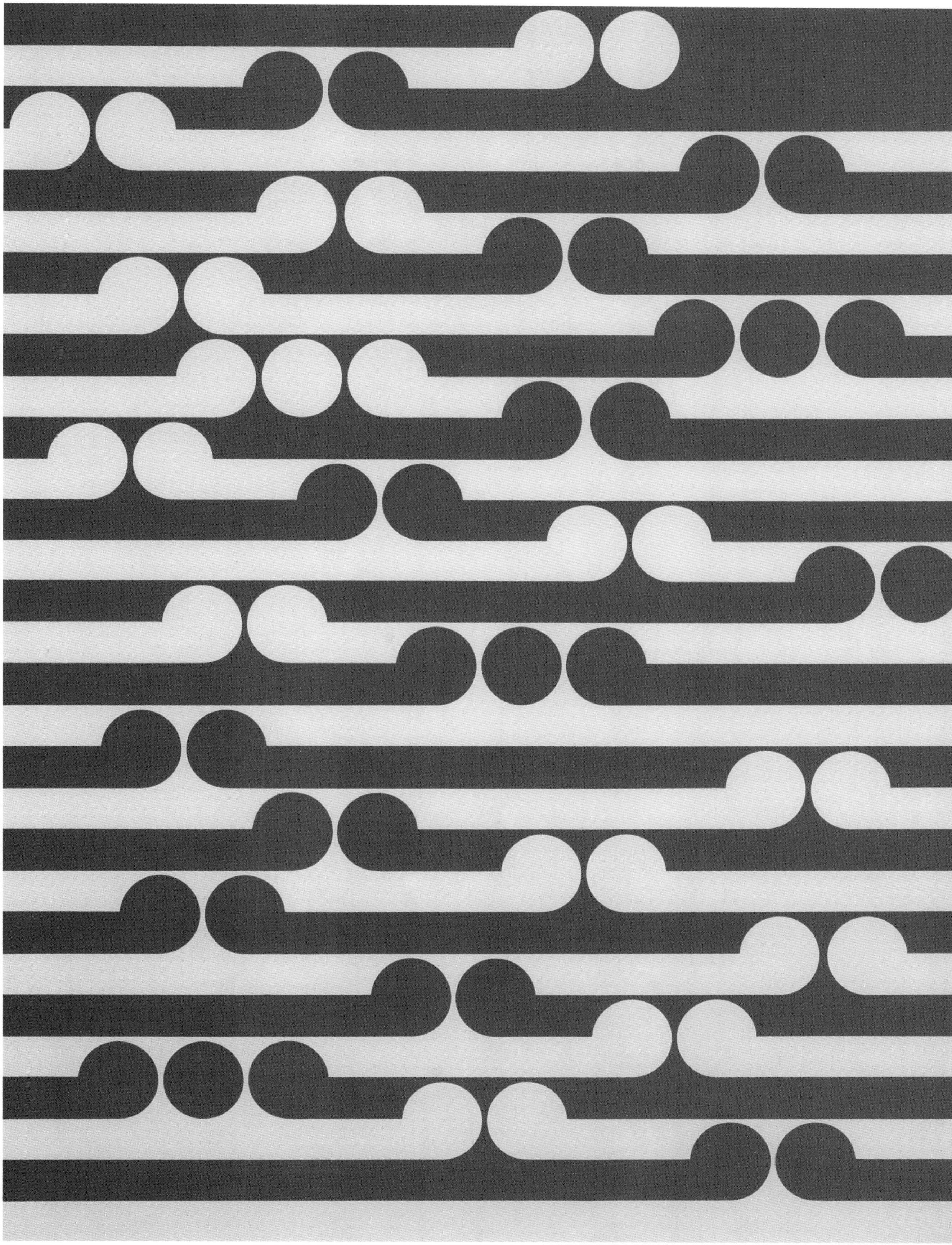

Milan Mrkusich

I know Milan's done a lot of work since 1950 and I don't underestimate the significant contribution he's made in all those years, but I love his early works and how they serve to provide us with a powerfully credible link to a very influential moment in time.

With New Zealand's geographical isolation I think it would have been much harder for us to subsequently move on in our understanding of early twentieth-century modernism without artists like Milan who had a profound understanding of these international movements.

Considering the incredibly small talent pool we had at the time it's a bloody miracle that we have artefacts as sophisticated as this to look back on.

Milan Mrkusich
Untitled (Abstract Composition)
1950, mixed media on canvas stretched on solid board
440 x 345 mm

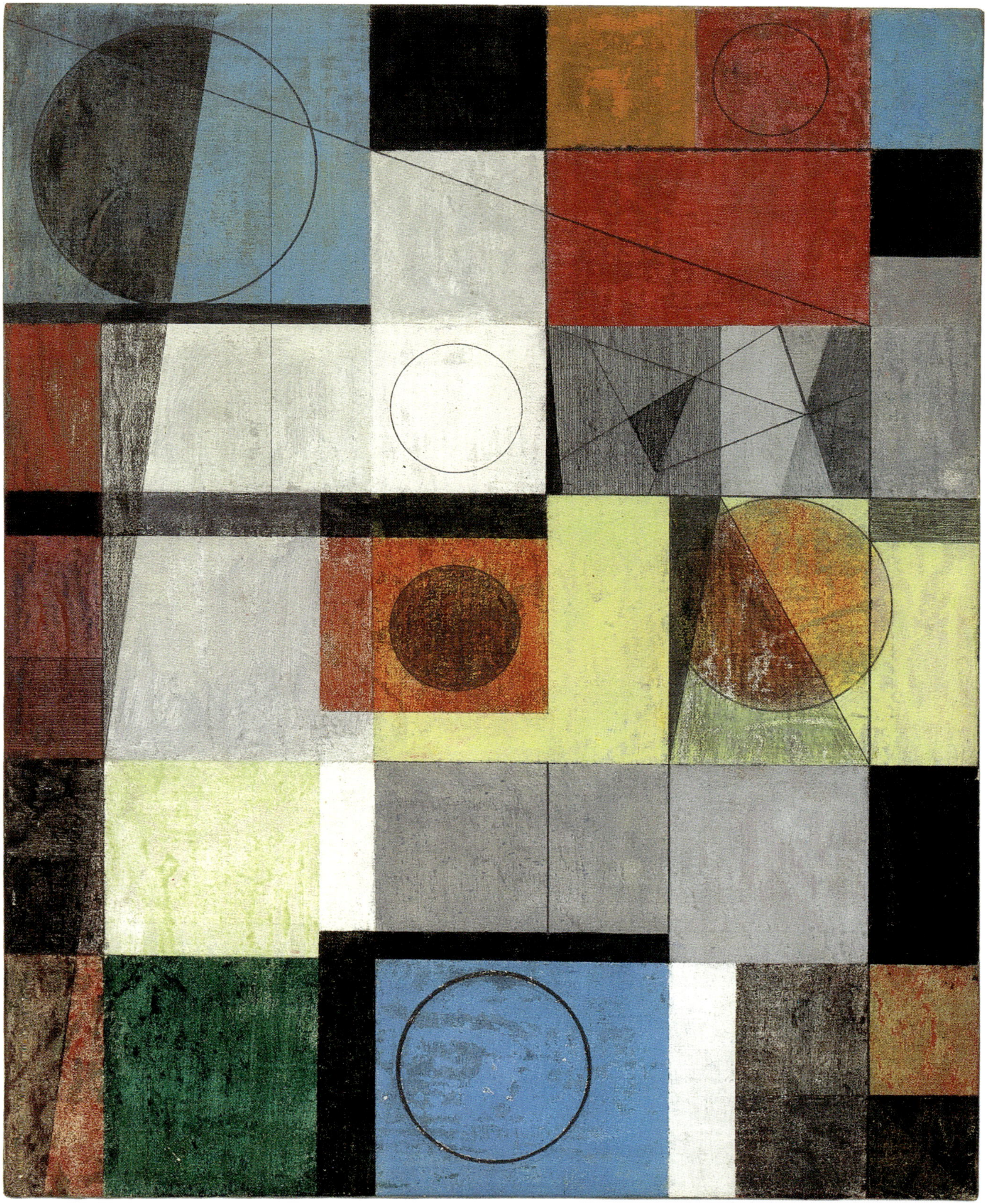

Robert Ellis

Bob came out from England in 1957 to lecture at the Elam art school. We heard rumours about this groovy new guy all the way down south at Ilam. My first glimpse of Bob's work was in the late 1960s in a *Woman's Weekly* of all things. (I guess the *WW* had to struggle to be all things back then given the almost complete lack of any other 'glossy' publication.) They must have had a particularly hip editorial staff because Bob's photo spread was very 'progressive' with Bob hunkered down in Vulcan Lane, his very modern-looking red and orange paintings propped up behind him in a row receding back up the lane. Somehow, it was all very Mary Quant and I remember thinking, I want some of that!

Then, eventually, I ended up working with Bob at Elam, spending time in his studio watching him progress work on his Rakaumangamanga series, where we'd talk technique a lot because Bob has a very sophisticated and curiously 'British modern' control of paint that I've always had a lot of respect for. I don't think his influence on a whole generation of New Zealand painters can be overstated.

Robert Ellis
Motorway/City
1969, oil on board
1219 x 1054 mm

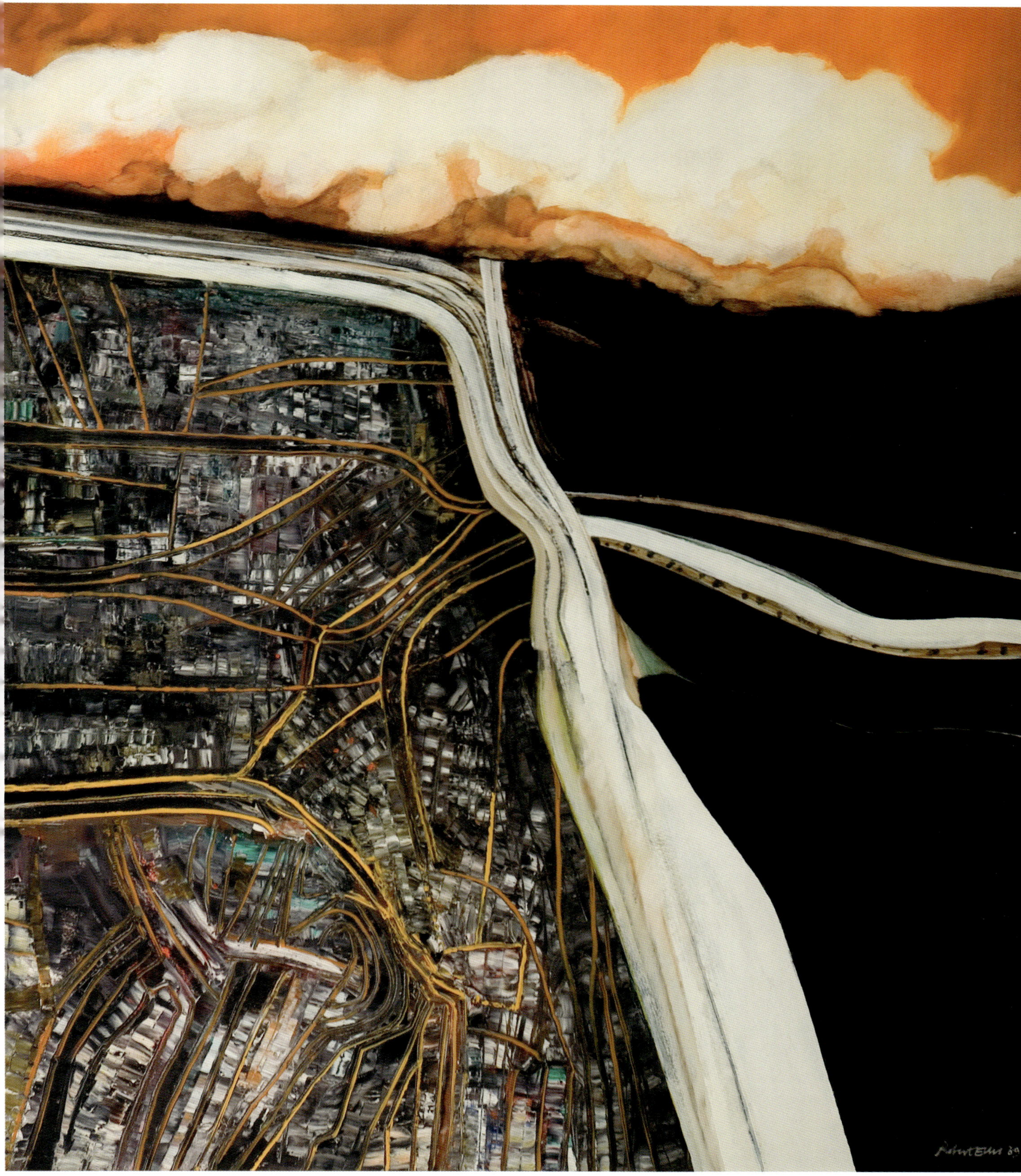

Helen Stewart

A very curious painter, Helen. Where did this strangely dry and scrubby technique come from? And the patchwork abstracting of the elements in the composition – look at those sheep in their diamond pen. Nineteen seventy is not so long ago, yet the work feels like it's from a much earlier time – seems like a companion piece to Patrick Hayman's *Blue Harbour and Camouflaged Ship*. Was Helen looking at Milton Avery too? Avery had a soft sort of patterning eye on the landscape that sat well with a lot of New Zealand painters. The American Marsden Hartley seems to be in there somewhere too. Nothing comes from nothing, we all build our work on a scaffolding of influences from the history of art.

The success of the work depends entirely on how deeply we enter into the engagement, how we take this knowingness into our own time. Usually, if we've done the homework, we can recognise the obvious antecedents in the work of others. But Helen's inspiration escapes me a bit. Not that you have to know all this to appreciate the work, and sometimes an artist will stumble across some source so obscure that the work looks like it came entirely from within the painter.

Someone said Fomison was influenced by Norwegian primitives and on the evidence of the paintings it could very well be true, though I've never found any of these Nordic naïves in my own research. Knowing how much Tony professed to despise modernism as some sort of historical red herring, I suspect he may have dissembled the story himself. All of which doesn't explain Helen, but it gave me plenty to write about. Lovely paintings, luminous, intelligent and very nicely put together.

Helen Stewart
Stable and Woolshed
c.1970, oil on board
753 x 925 mm

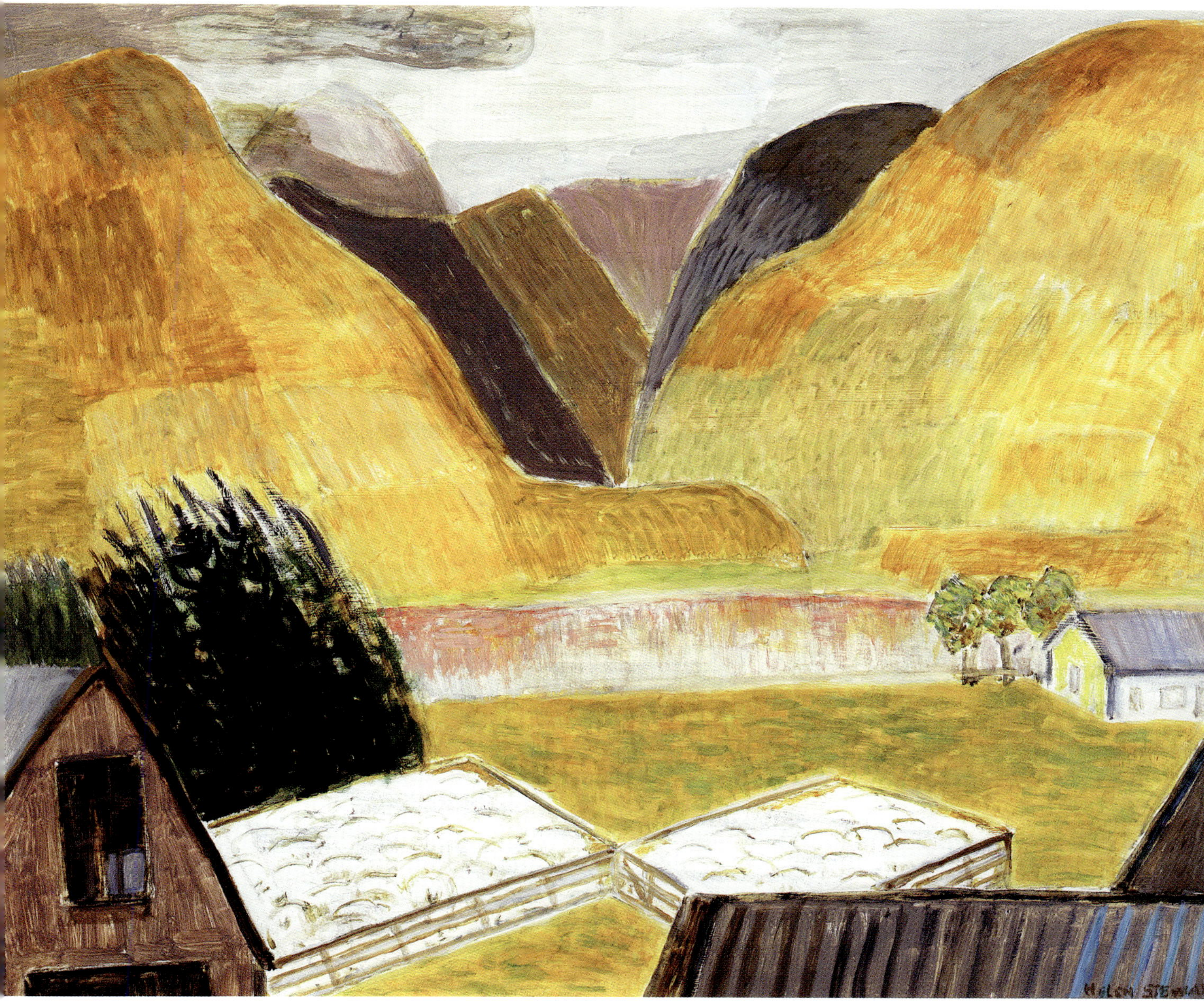
HELEN STEWAR

Don Binney

Don's career took off in the first surge of the search for a national art identity in the 1950s. Whatever the degree of traffic control behind this interesting time, and that's still being debated, Don rose to the occasion like one of his hawks looming up over the wild West Coast.

And the fabulous thing about these 'instant' icons was that they were unassailably genuine.

His passion for the subject, the bird in nature, wasn't an art-political construct but a genuine reflection of his profoundly felt ecological concerns. The technique of combed and palette-knifed paint which he evolved and his magical way of rhyming the forms in the bird with the forms in the landscape lifted these images way up and beyond reportage and polemic.

Later on the backlash kicked in and people started saying, 'Oh God, not those birds again.' So Don experimented with leaving them out and concentrating on the landscape, and everyone said, 'Where's the bird?' Can you imagine?! But Don battled through it and has settled into a comfortable Binney groove that he so thoroughly deserves. A lifetime is longer than you think.

I ran into him at a print workshop in Auckland the other day, heaving himself heavily from the cracked driver's seat of his ancient Corolla, and I said, 'Hell, Don, you still driving that old thing?' And he replied with his manic '60s grin, 'Yes, Dick, driving this car is like nailing a Cuban flag to your letter box!'

Go Don.

Don Binney
Pigeon
1964, oil on board
1030 x 750 mm

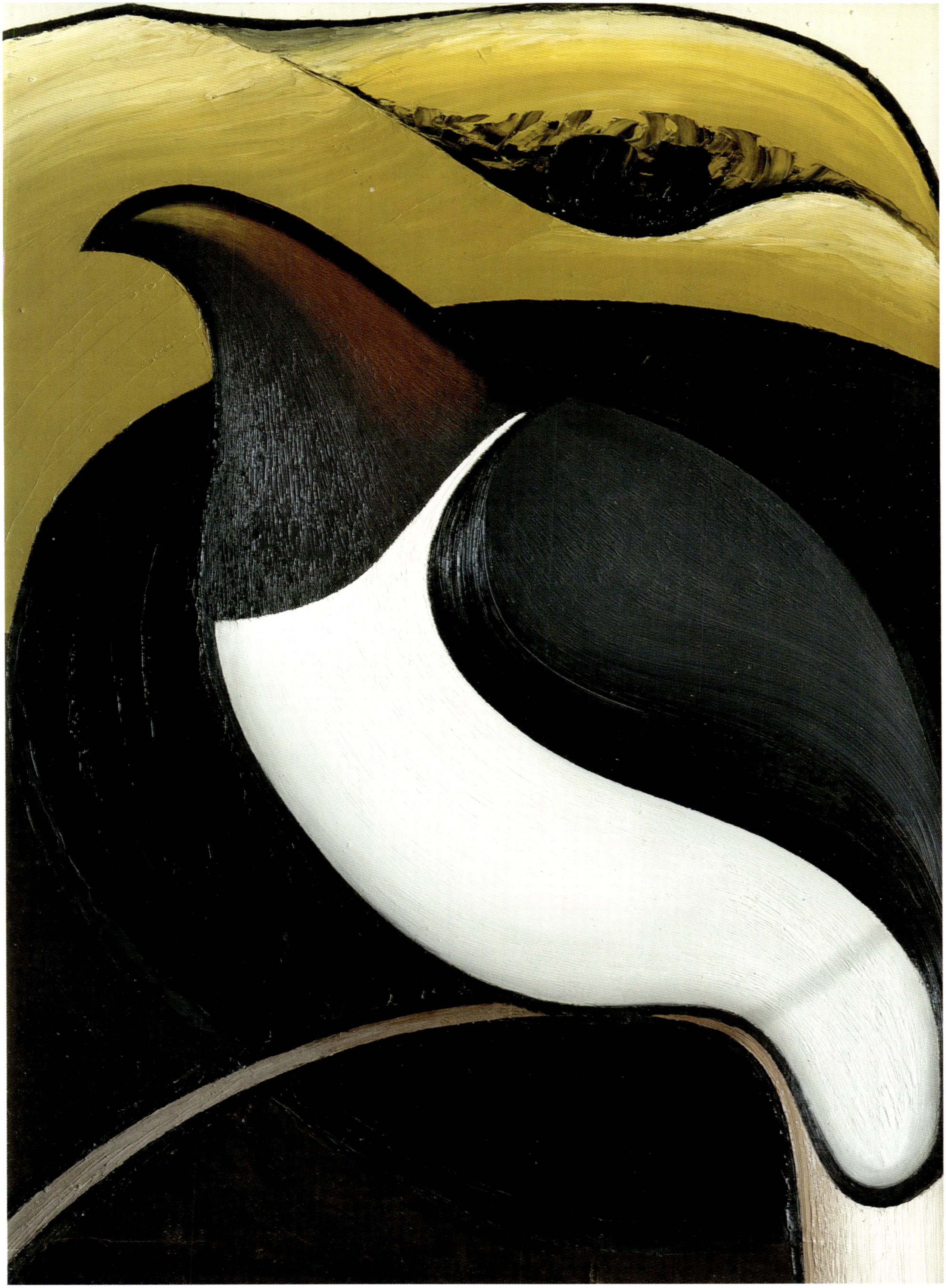

Michael Illingworth

Illingworth is tricky; I nearly didn't include him, but in the end he refused to go away. I never really trusted his anti-bourgeois shock tactics: penises and vaginas were always going to get the police running up the stairs and throwing a blanket over your work back in the '60s and '70s. And his subsequent art hermit holiness didn't impress me much either.

But the work did it . . . convinced me. The adage 'Don't believe what an artist says, only what they do' is particularly salient in Illingworth's case.

Despite the somewhat desperate straining for some sort of spiritual space, in the best of the work he actually gets there! They really do draw you into a mythic netherworld of the imagination. The patient and zen-like application of glazes and soft scumbles combined with extremely odd colour relationships and awkward blends actually carry the gravitas that Illingworth was so serious about projecting.

Michael Illingworth
Adam Figure with Gun
1966, oil on canvas
910 x 760 mm

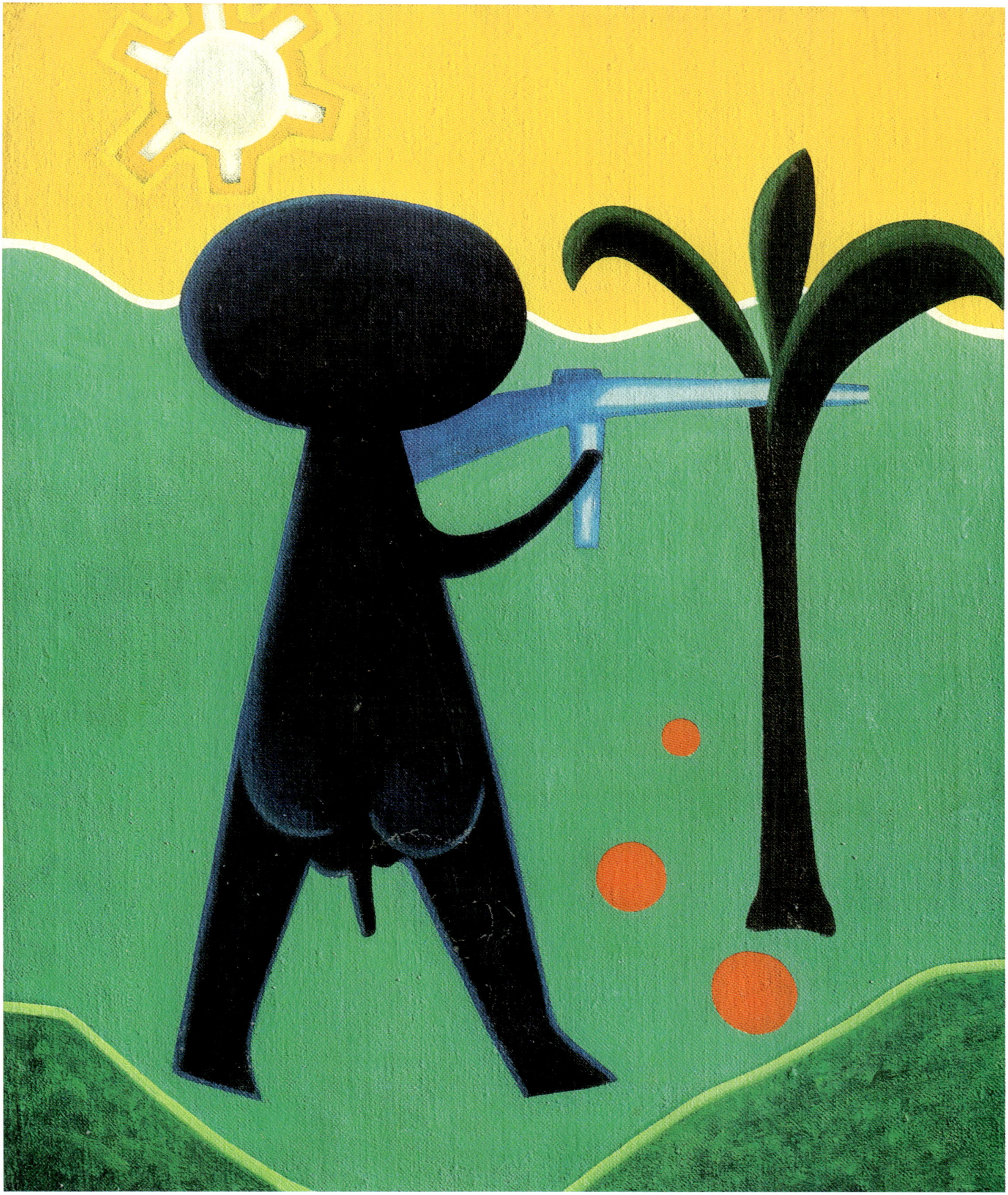

Allen Maddox

Allen muscled his way into the New Zealand art story through a strange combination of raw talent and myth fulfilment. Right when the narrative needed a crazy artist we got three of them: Clairmont, Fomison and Maddox.

Allen didn't have to try very hard to win the role of outraged existentialist as it came entirely naturally to him. Though I think it was less a pose than frustration born out of an ability to see things perhaps a bit too clearly.

He was incredibly art literate and had no choice but to paint, but also found painting, and everything that went with it, such a ridiculous act on some level. It's hardly any surprise that he gravitated to the negating sign of the 'X'.

It was all about annihilation in the end, a losing battle that left some great paintings in its wake. Allen was a nice guy pursued by a really big black dog.

Allen Maddox
Untitled
1977, oil on linen on canvas
1650 x 1500 mm

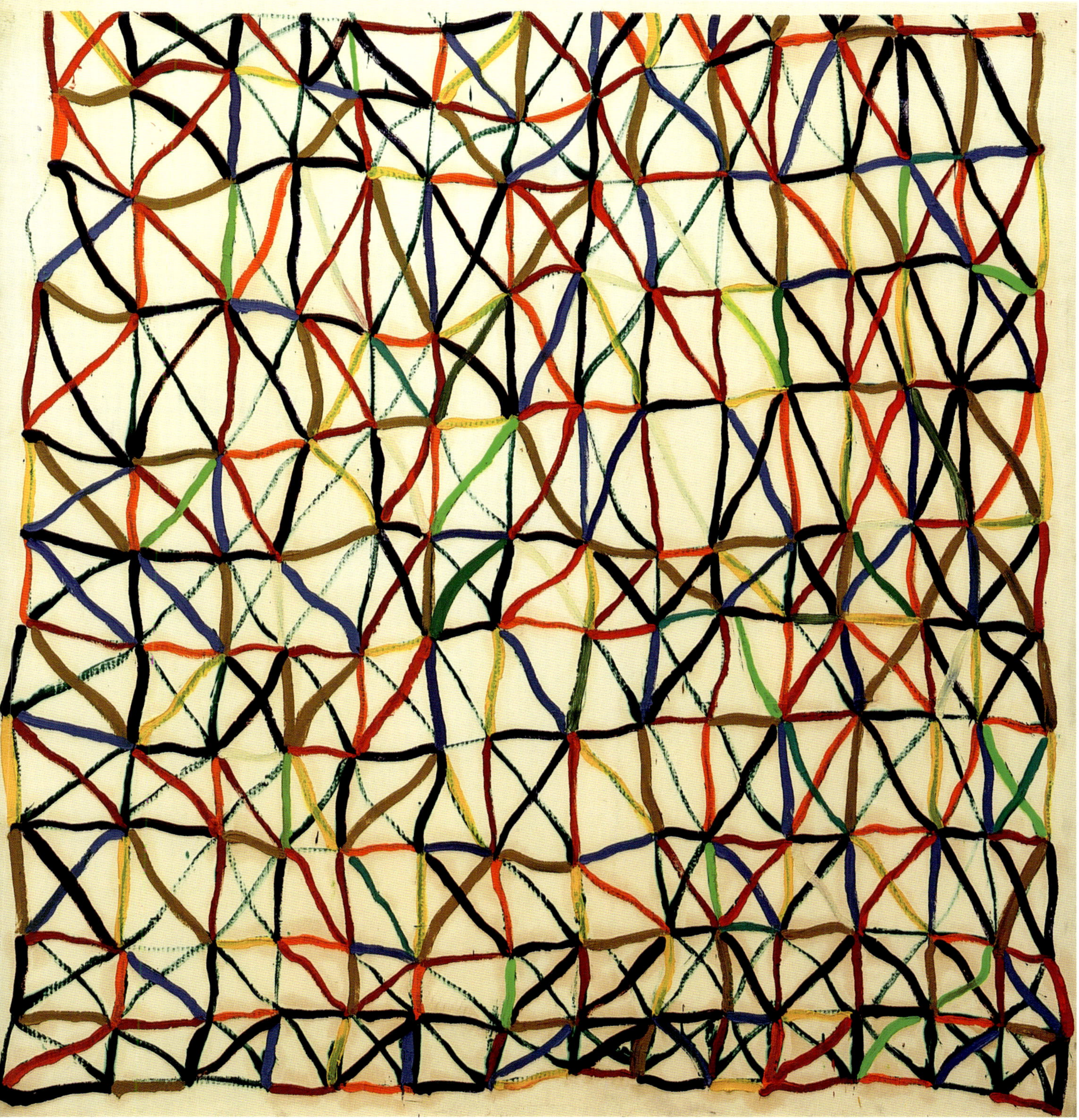

Philip Clairmont

I don't think Phil saw quite as deeply as Allen Maddox but he was obviously dogged by similar demons, and was possibly a wee bit too much in love with the myths that drove Allen to distraction.

I also don't think it's a coincidence that a lot of Phil's language – the teardrop shape, the floating eye – bear a remarkable similarity to the universal identifying signs in Outsider art. I don't think Phil cultivated that language deliberately; he was that odd hybrid that comes along occasionally, the educated outsider, the 'worldly' naïf. A lot of contradictions.

But man, when he got it on none of that mattered, he could animate the most inanimate matter. Even the air, the negative spaces, heave and sigh with mysterious energy. Nothing stands still, but nothing flies apart.

Philip Clairmont
The Scarred Couch, the Auckland Experience
1978, oil and acrylic on hessian
1590 x 2760 mm

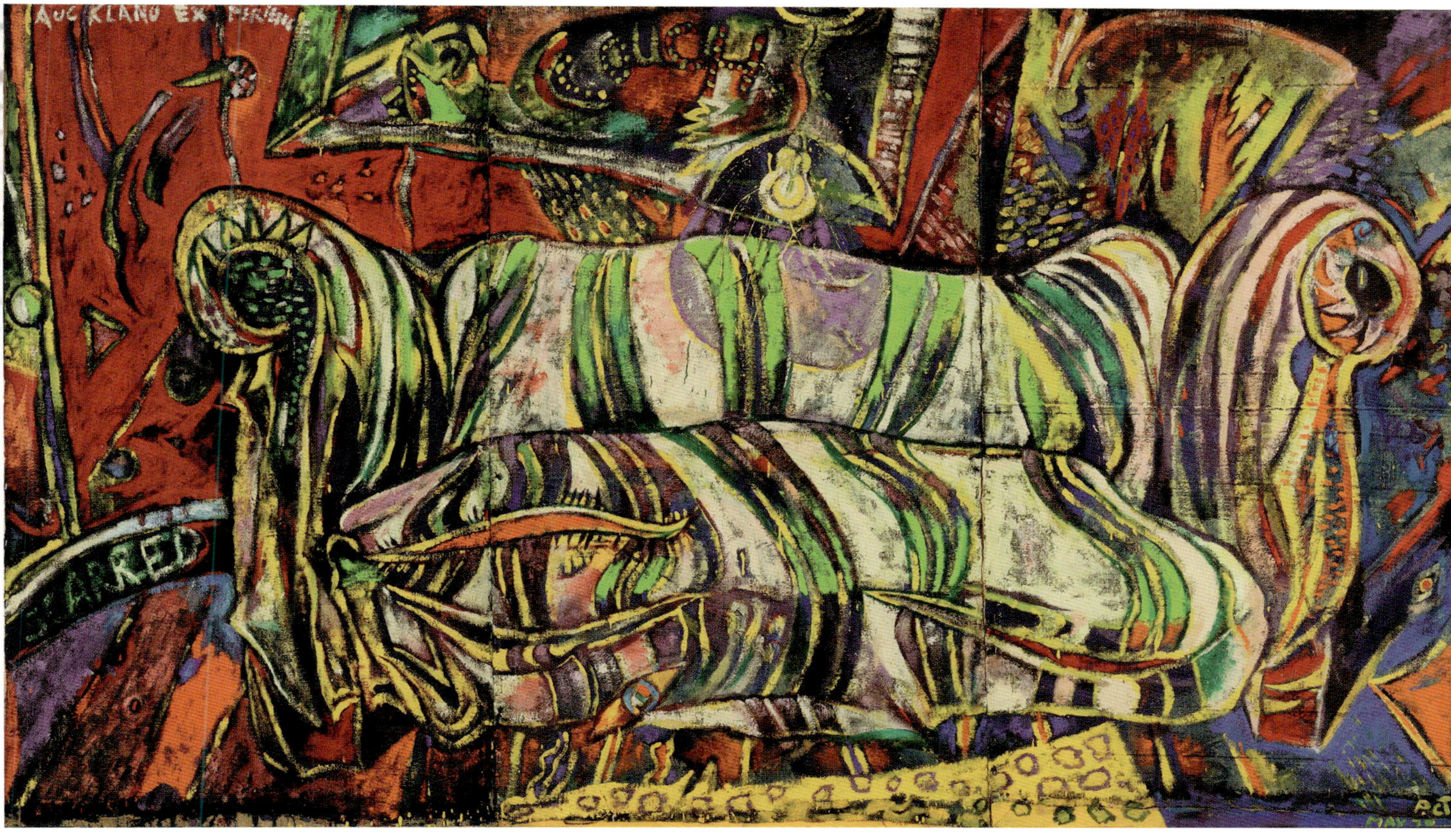

Tony Fomison

The third prop of this wonky easel, and probably the most stable despite the dark and dirty anti-bourgeois act.

Hugely intelligent, dogged with health issues and physical shortcomings, Tony dug deeper into our collective psyche than almost any other artist in our short history. Knowing him wasn't easy – you never knew if you were going to be thanked or insulted for some act of generosity – but it was worth it just to be there. Just to sit in the corner and watch him paint, brushing it on, brushing it off, rag in one hand and big hardware-store house-painting brush in the other. Chuckling at his own jokes . . . such a peaceful performance interestingly at odds with the dark content of the painting.

Of the after-work shenanigans, legends abound – most of them true – but he did have a big heart, a secret life, and I haven't the space to go into it here but the love was there. Just look at the paintings, and be bloody glad we had him for a while.

Tony Fomison
The Fugitive
1981–1983, oil on hessian board
1230 x 1830 mm

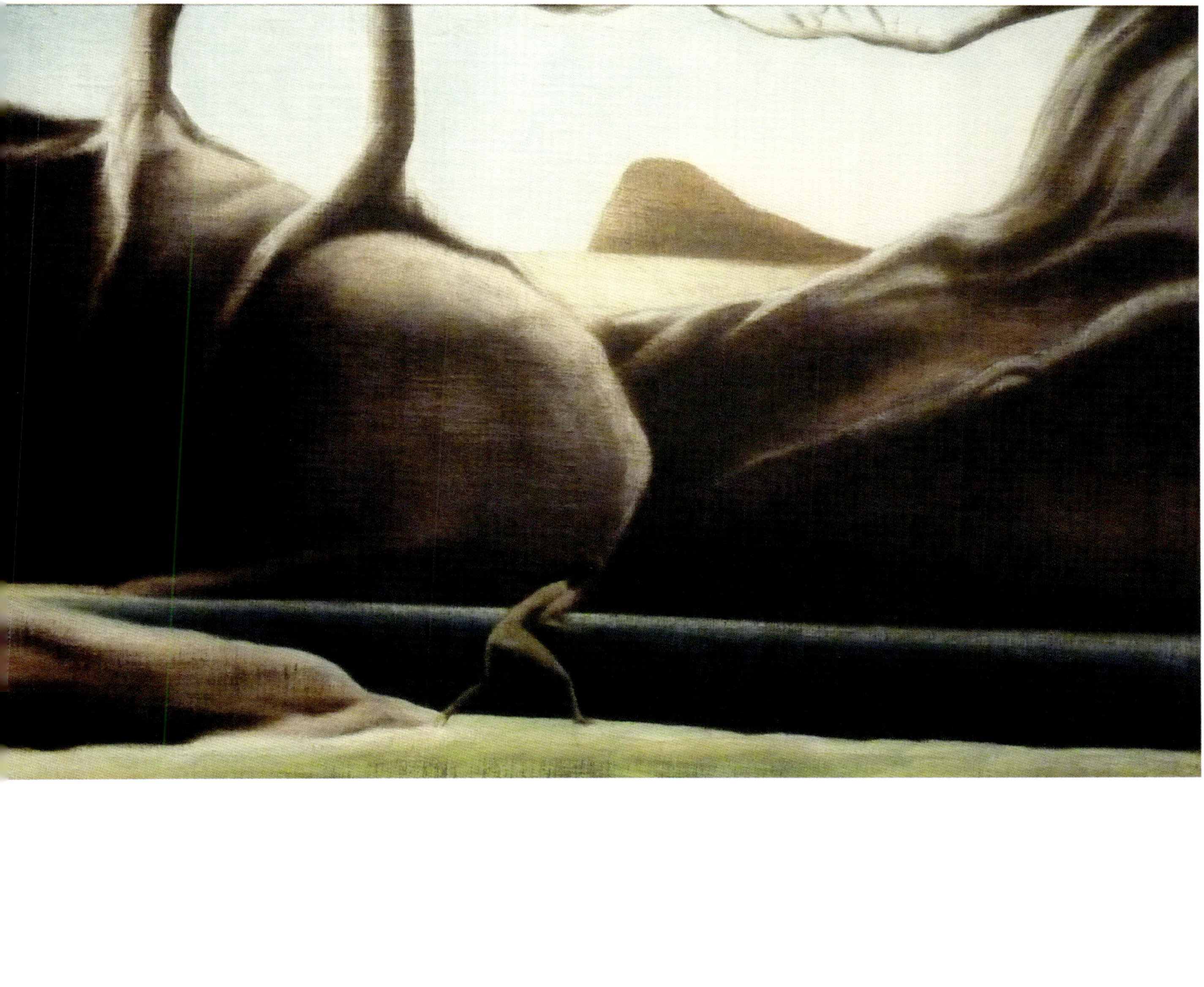

Jeffrey Harris

I don't want to insult Jeffrey's intelligence by speculating like this but he did appear to come from a very unusual position. Initially he seemed to be 'just' another naïve art discovery, painting on a relatively modest scale scenes of domestic life in the recognisable style of the genre – raw colour, dislocated perspectives, awkward junctions of foreground and background.

And then, somehow, because of an epiphany or a mentor, I don't know, he suddenly upped his scale massively with all the corresponding mark-making and compositional structures to match. And the themes opened out into primary-coloured images of extreme anguish and despair. Most wondrous of all, this raw and graphic assault chimed in perfectly with an international movement booming out of Europe at the time, called either trans-avantgarde or fauve nouveau, and Jeffrey suddenly had a context for his aggressive and messy narratives.

There was nothing fake or manufactured about all this, whatever the context, and Jeffrey somehow caught up with his new role and became The Artist Jeffrey Harris, buried deep in his dark themes, piled about with empty paint tubes, turps-soaked newspapers and paint-clogged brushes, living the life, and painting jewels like this.

Jeffrey Harris
Magdalena in Front of Bach, French Farm
1996–2010, oil on board
312 x 406 mm

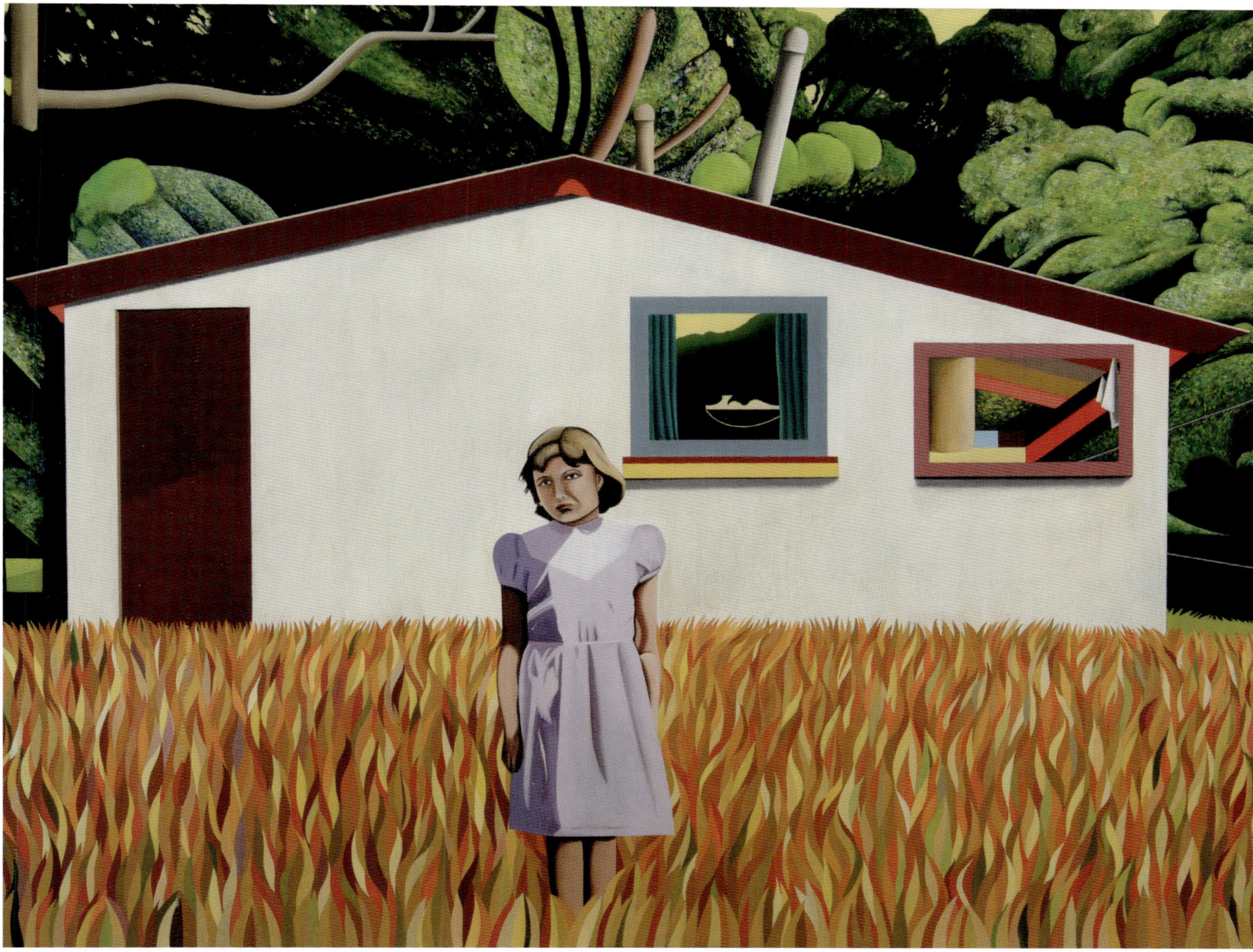

Philip Trusttum

Phil is a painter’s painter . . . as the saying goes, ‘He could paint the phone book’, and he probably has. Anything and everything from his world gets hauled out onto the canvas, though you have to do your homework to decipher most of it such is his endlessly inventive way of bending the subject to his design needs. Points of view get radically flipped, scale shifts psychedelically and form takes flight in fluid zig-zagging pattern.

The thing that ties all this jazzing about together is Phil’s fantastically intuitive understanding of composition and colour, and his transformative touch with the medium, with the paint.

We watched it pouring out of him at art school, and it’s still pouring out! You say to him, ‘Have you done enough yet, Phil?’ and he just laughs.

Philip Trusttum
William Under Bucket
2004, acrylic on loose canvas
1870 x 1870 mm

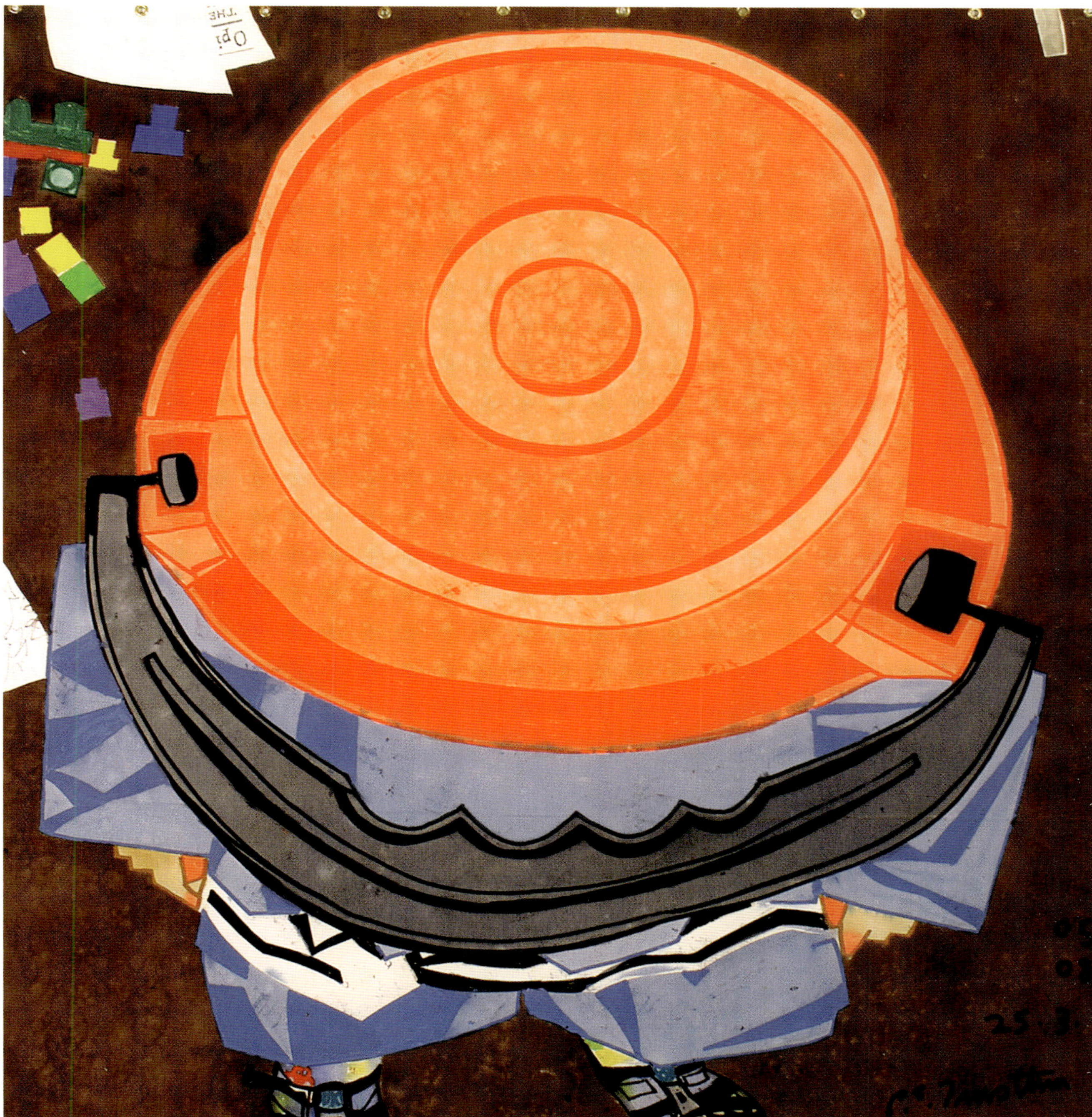

Michael Smither

I must be getting old, I like this guy. I've seen enough, more than enough, really, to be convinced, despite not being a huge fan of his biblical narratives and his (to me) plain bonkers music/colour theories.

A lot of Michael's oil sketches and still-lifes have been appearing at auction lately, and I'm impressed at how impressed I am by them! You have to seriously know how paint and colour behave to be able to flick it around like that.

I chose to illustrate this early work because it's been a favourite of mine for years but I could have happily used any number of paintings (like *Hapuka Head on a Plate* or *View of the White Gate Kaitakis)*. It's his manic intensity that gets him there I think . . . a Quixotic ambition to arrest the physical world, one painstakingly glazed pebble at a time.

Michael Smither
Mokau
1967, oil on board
770 x 1110 mm

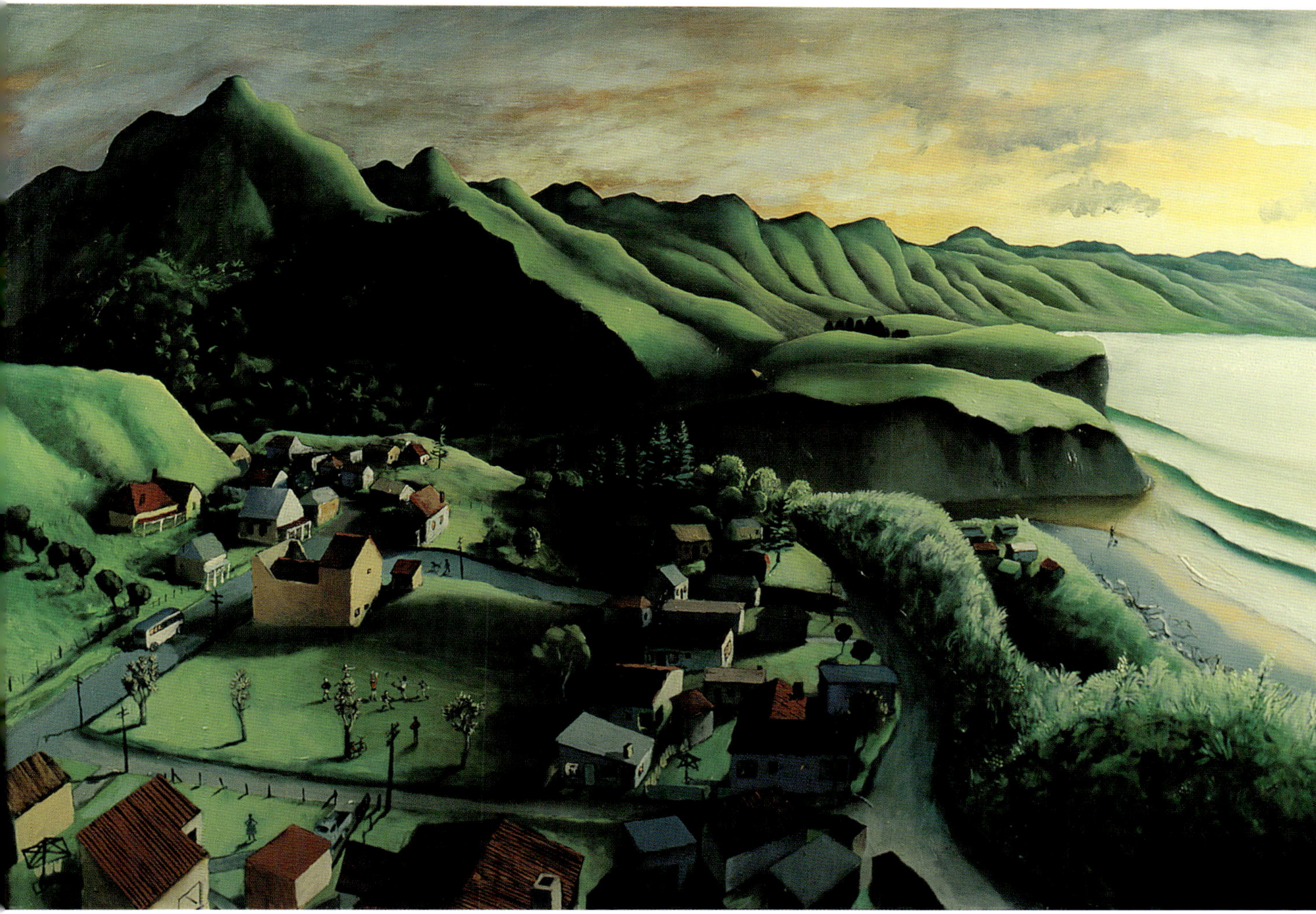

Grahame Sydney

In as much as New Zealand is hardly big enough to bring forth more than one of everything, Grahame is the painter who does this: immaculate reflections of his love for the South Island landscape inspired by a genuinely deep dedication to the region.

A true regionalist, he brings a focus to his environment that is as diamond bright as the land itself, a perfect marriage of motif and method.

In a long and consistent career Grahame has produced some truly iconic New Zealand images. *Slow Sign* is a particular favourite of mine; four square and slightly off-centre, it works both as an arresting abstraction and a compelling narrative loop.

Grahame Sydney
Slow Sign
1975, egg tempera
558 x 609 mm

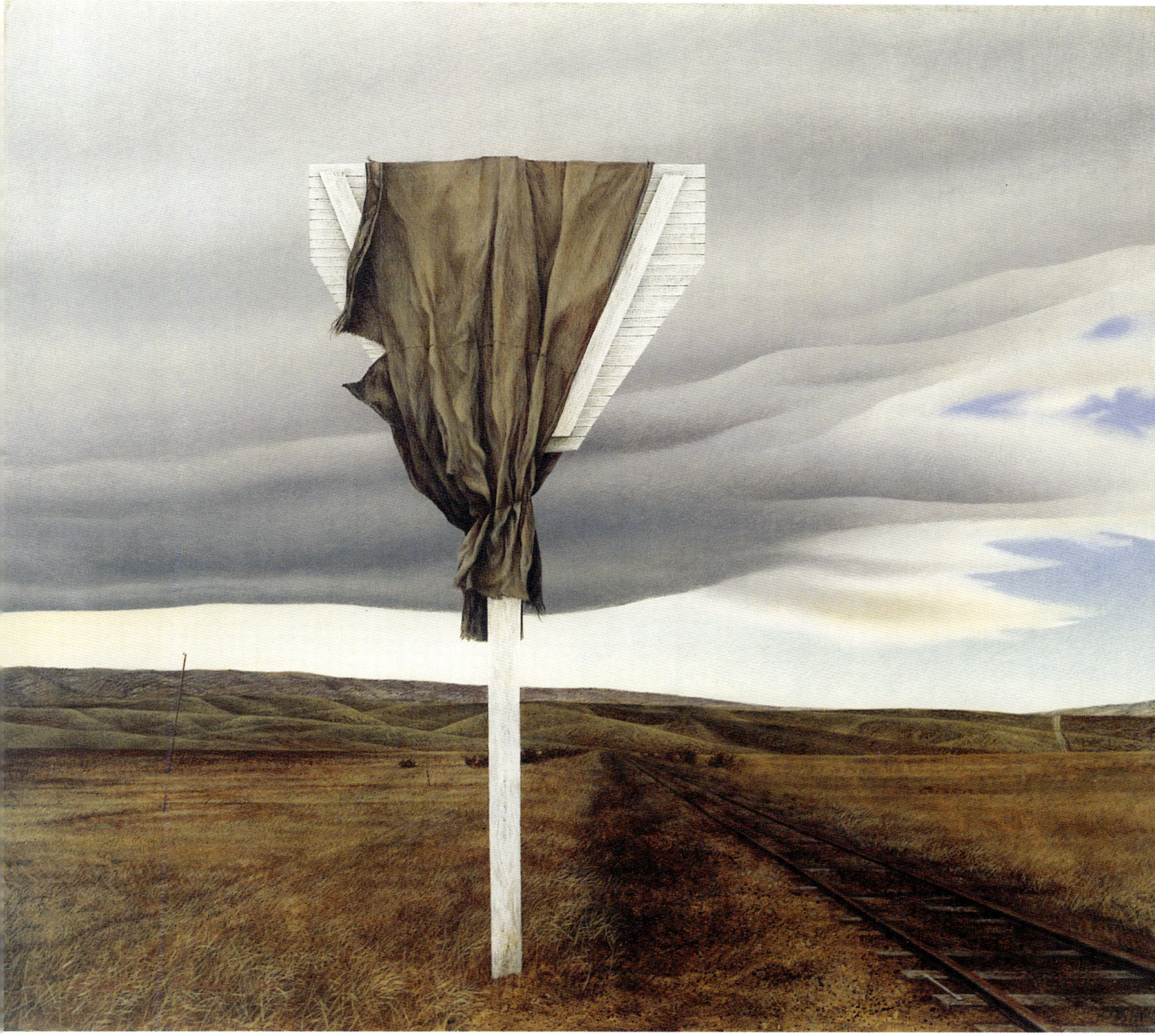

Juliet Peter

I came to Juliet much later than I should have. I was aware of her *School Journal* work of course, because of my own involvement, but I was unaware of the painting and the prints somehow. It was quite a revelation when I found that there was much more to her practice.

The thing that impresses me about this image and the others that I subsequently tracked down, and this is the reason why she's in the book, is her unusually high professional level of draughtsmanship and formal design. I find her deep absorption of mid-twentieth century modernism, albeit in an understated British way, strangely uplifting and always feel I've had a small 'overseas experience' whenever I see her work.

Juliet Peter
Untitled
1951, lithograph
370 x 460 mm

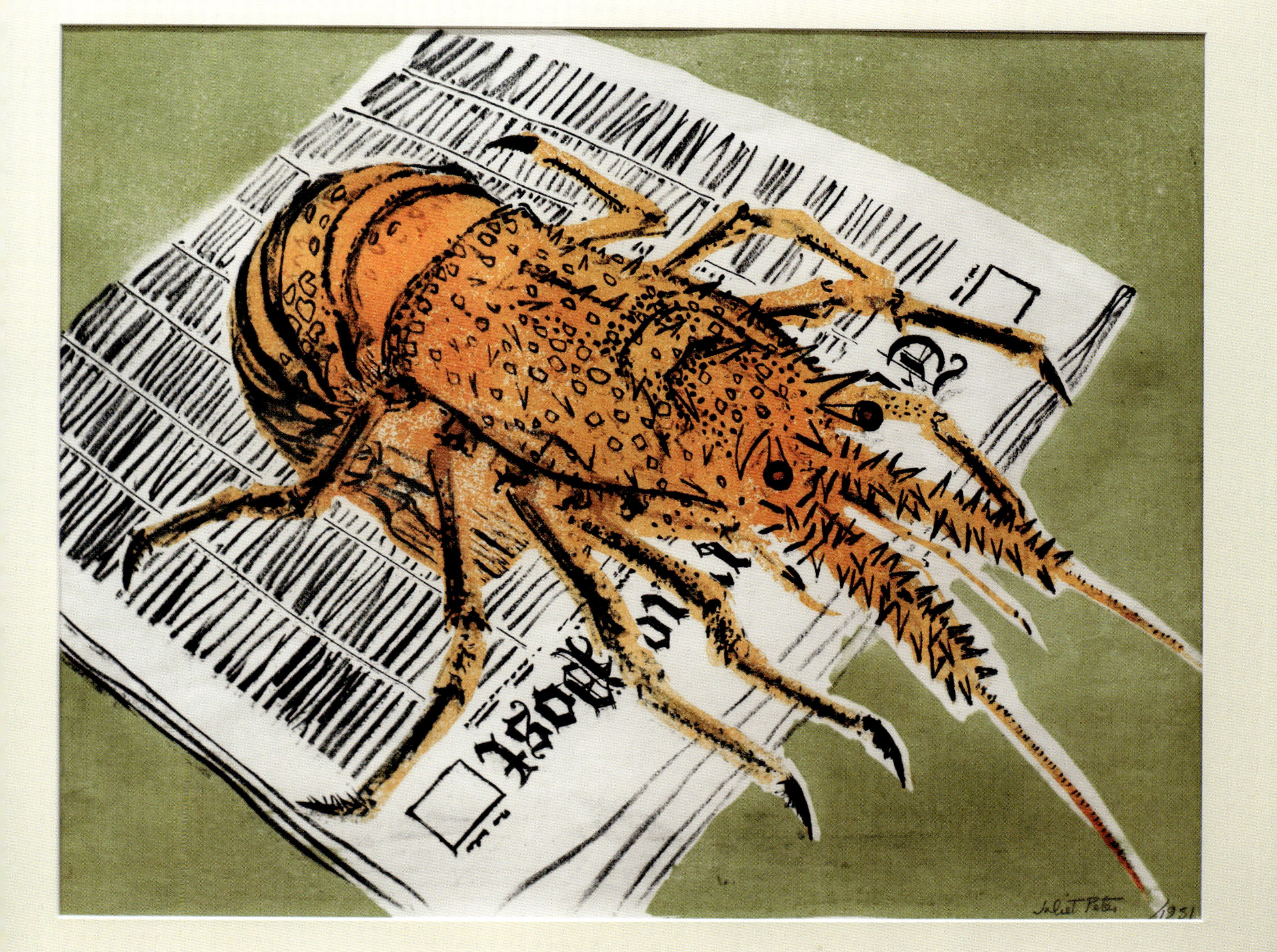
Juliet Peter
1951

Jacqueline Fahey

Jacquey is one of those painters/draughtspeople who seems to paint as freely as she writes. It just seems to pour out.

I'm sure she has her share of heartache but the torrent of deft and skilful rendering with which she shepherds her images onto the canvas leaves me wondering about the unfairness of it all. And, yes, yes, I know skill isn't everything but you'd have to admit that it helps.

And it sure helps Jacquey! But she's much more than that of course; boldly going where she felt it was necessary to go she produced a vivid body of fiercely intelligent feminist icons, never once losing sight of the fact she was making paintings first.

The sheer joy and exuberance evident in the production of these works ensures that they'll still be great paintings long after the message is history.

Jacqueline Fahey
With French Paint Use Protection
1992, oil on board

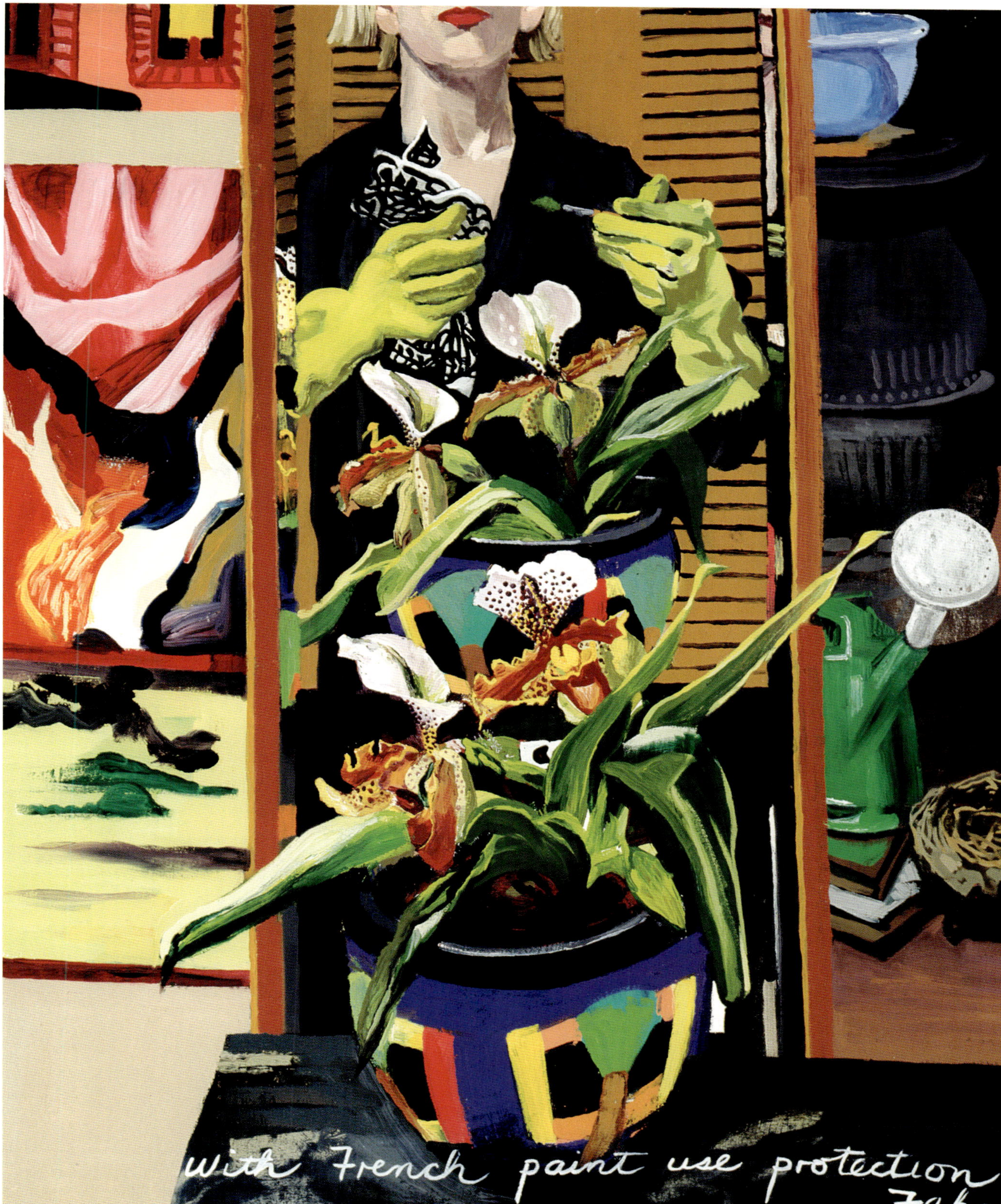
with French paint use protection
Zahe.

Paul Hartigan

Paul was a member of that group of like-minded individuals, the New Image movement, that I refer to in the introduction. Paul and my pop culture interests run pretty much neck and neck, and in all the years since the late 1970s we've been playing catch-up in our respective endeavours, nudging each other on.

Always keen to explore a wide range of mediums, Paul consistently brings a bold and uncompromising strength to whichever direction he takes. His understanding of the relationship between the thing being expressed and the vehicle that's doing the expressing is always impressive.

Whatever the latest technological advance in this business of reproducing or generating an image, Paul seems to have an empathetic relationship with the process, and can always produce a body of work that illustrates the potential of the technology while at the same time making the most of its limitations.

Anyway, it's not the medium that's the issue, it's what you do with it. I was thinking about this the other night when I drove past his neon mural *Colony* at the University of Auckland's Faculty of Engineering. Paul always hits it with a wide-open and unequivocal faith in the power of a straightforward and unfussed idea. Thinks of it, isolates its most expressive profile and does it. It takes a lot of nerve to cut through like he does.

Paul Hartigan
The Bitter End / Pie Guy
2008, H-type canvas
1600 x 800 mm

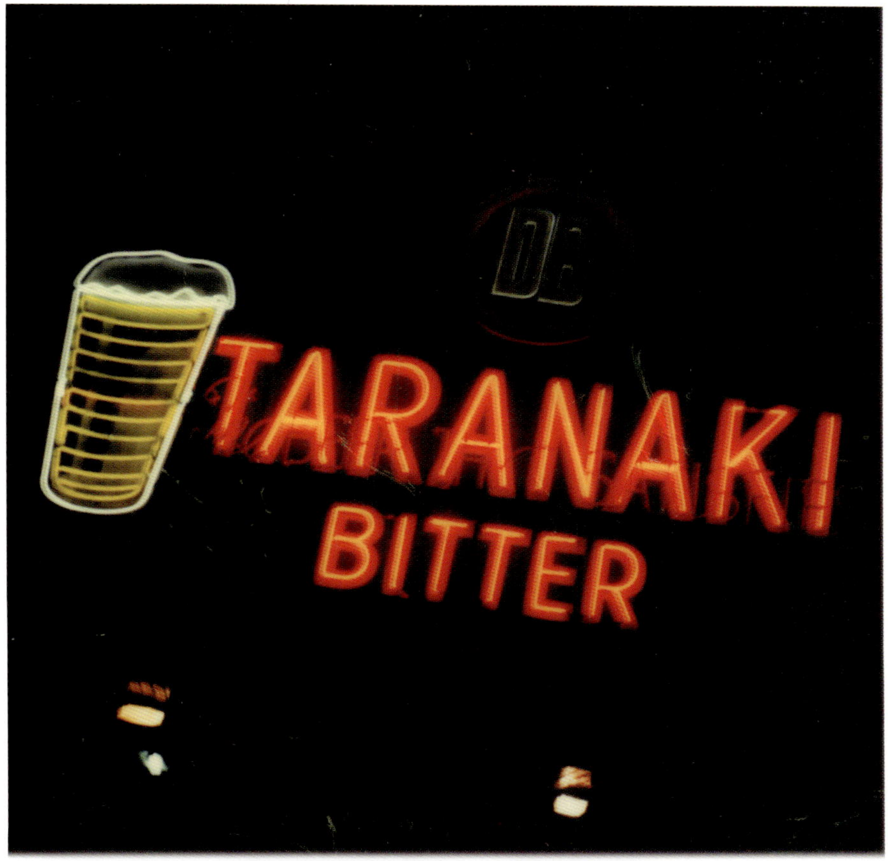
DB
TARANAKI
BITTER

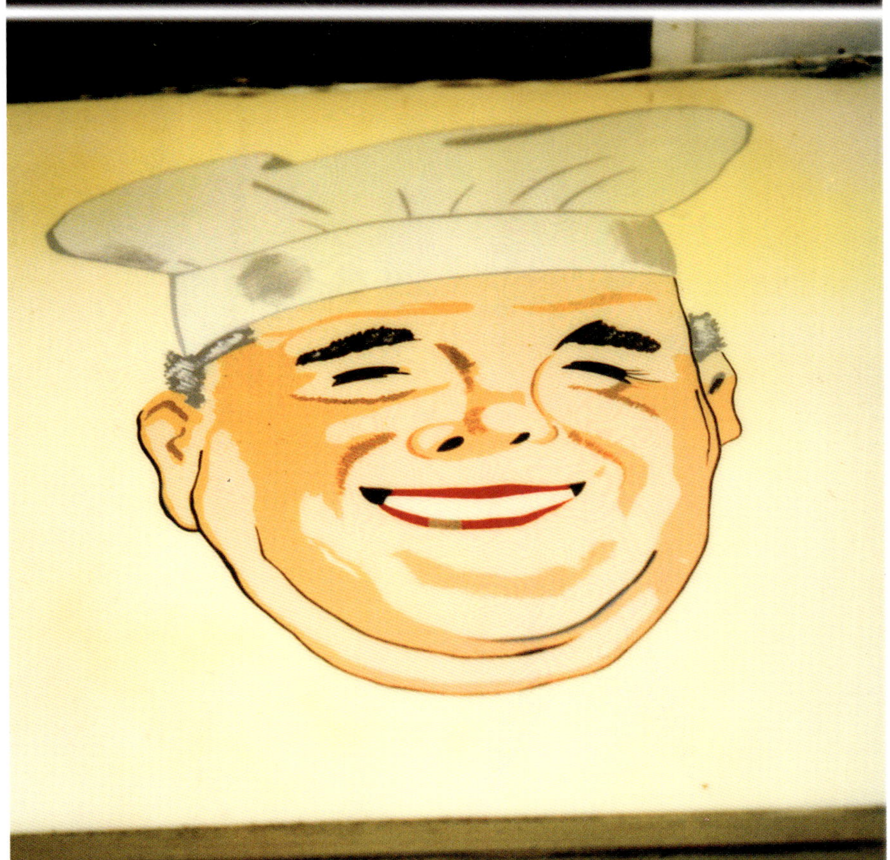

Tom Kreisler

Look at this painting; it's a painting waiting to happen, waiting to be turned on. So typical of Tom. A statement of the screamingly obvious and the frustratingly evasive. Tom had a system of non-painting that used to drive me insane. He was acutely aware that painting at some level is a complete nonsense, as soon as the brush hits the canvas it's a cliché.

So how to paint without actually painting and giving the game away?! I suggested he hold the brush a millimetre or two above the canvas.

Tom's response to this dilemma was to negate as much as possible. He used brushes so clogged with paint he could've been using a chewed stick. He painted with veils of reluctant colour that could've almost been the dirty water from the paint jar (though he was an absolute master with colour when he did decide to let go). And so on through to the non-content of the painting's subjects. He was one of our best and his early death was a huge loss to all of us.

Tom Kreisler
Tap
2000, acrylic on board
690 x 595 mm

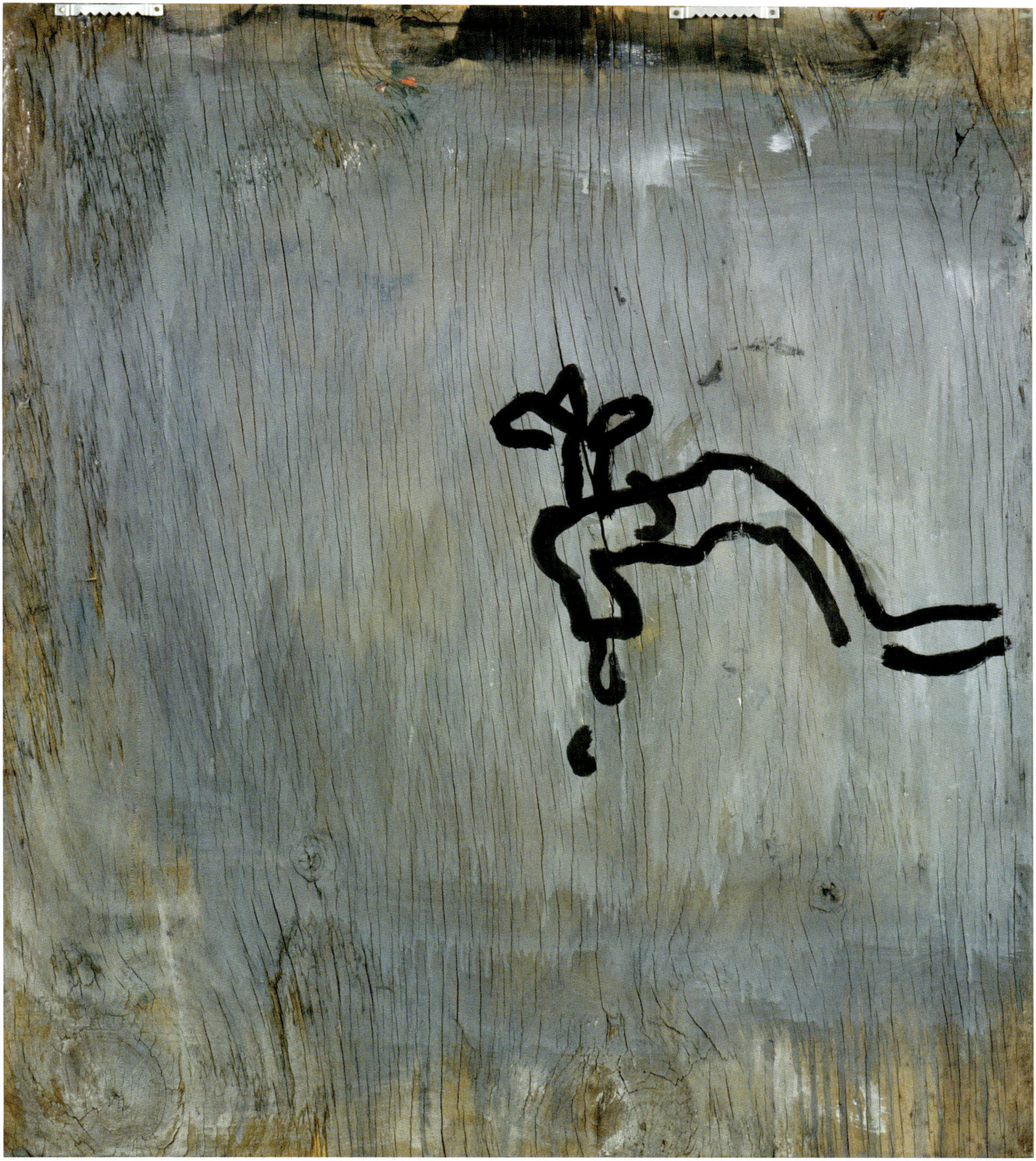

Denys Watkins

Denys has been with me on this adventure from the get-go, by which I mean post-art school in the mid-1960s, so he was always going to be in my book. But even if we hadn't been so close he would've more than earned his place.

His light touch, both with his material and the actual material of painting, has always been an inspiration to me and a nice counterpoint to my often more bombastic approach. Over the years we've propped each other up with a shared interest in guitar music and the imagery of popular culture – two California dreamers.

I can always rely on Denys for 'news of the new'; he has an uncanny knack for knowing what's going on at the front. Whenever I want a catch-up or to swap stories about the latest cultural outrage I can rely on Denys for an interesting insight.

His technique, especially as it has evolved in recent years, has always held an element of 'How the hell do you do that?' which fascinates me. If it's possible for a colour or a wash to have a gentle self-deprecating wit then Denys is a master of it.

Denys Watkins
Man-o-the-woods
2006, acrylic on linen
1820 x 1220 mm

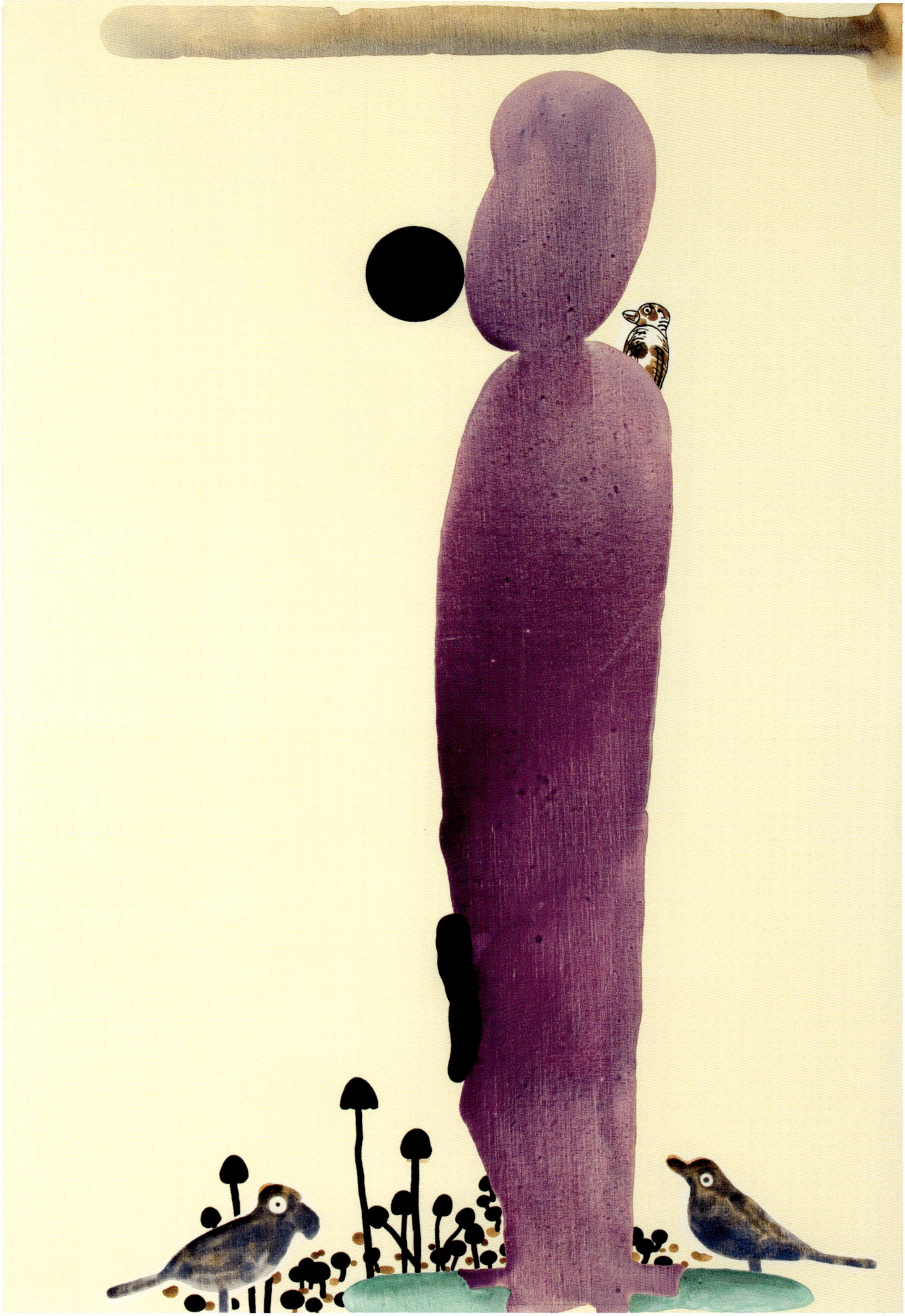

Gavin Chilcott

Ah, Mr Chilcott, where do I start with you?

I can't begin to express the love and respect I have for this man. I don't think I'd be where I am today without his example of daring and reckless behaviour to egg me on. (I mean studio behaviour, not man-about-town behaviour, though whoever writes the Chilcott book had better know a lot about the hospitality business!) Full speed ahead and damn the torpedoes, there's always some pinhead out there keen to make themselves feel better by disapproving, but why would you let that slow you down?

Compelled to set art free of its laboured assumptions, but reluctant to inflict more stuff on a world already up to its neck in it, Gavin has evolved the lightest of imprints. Working almost exclusively on paper with a woodblock, a couple of stencils and a lick of acrylic paint he makes perfect sense day after day. You should buy one immediately!

Last time we visited him in his mountain hideaway he was working on the carpet design for the Government House refurb, working with pinking shears on a motif that looked like a spray of kowhai blossom. In anybody else's hands it'd be craft but in Gavin's it's art, a-r-t, art.

Gavin Chilcott
Untitled
1990, watercolour
and acrylic on
Gregory Flint Gallery
letter paper, diptych
290 x 420 mm

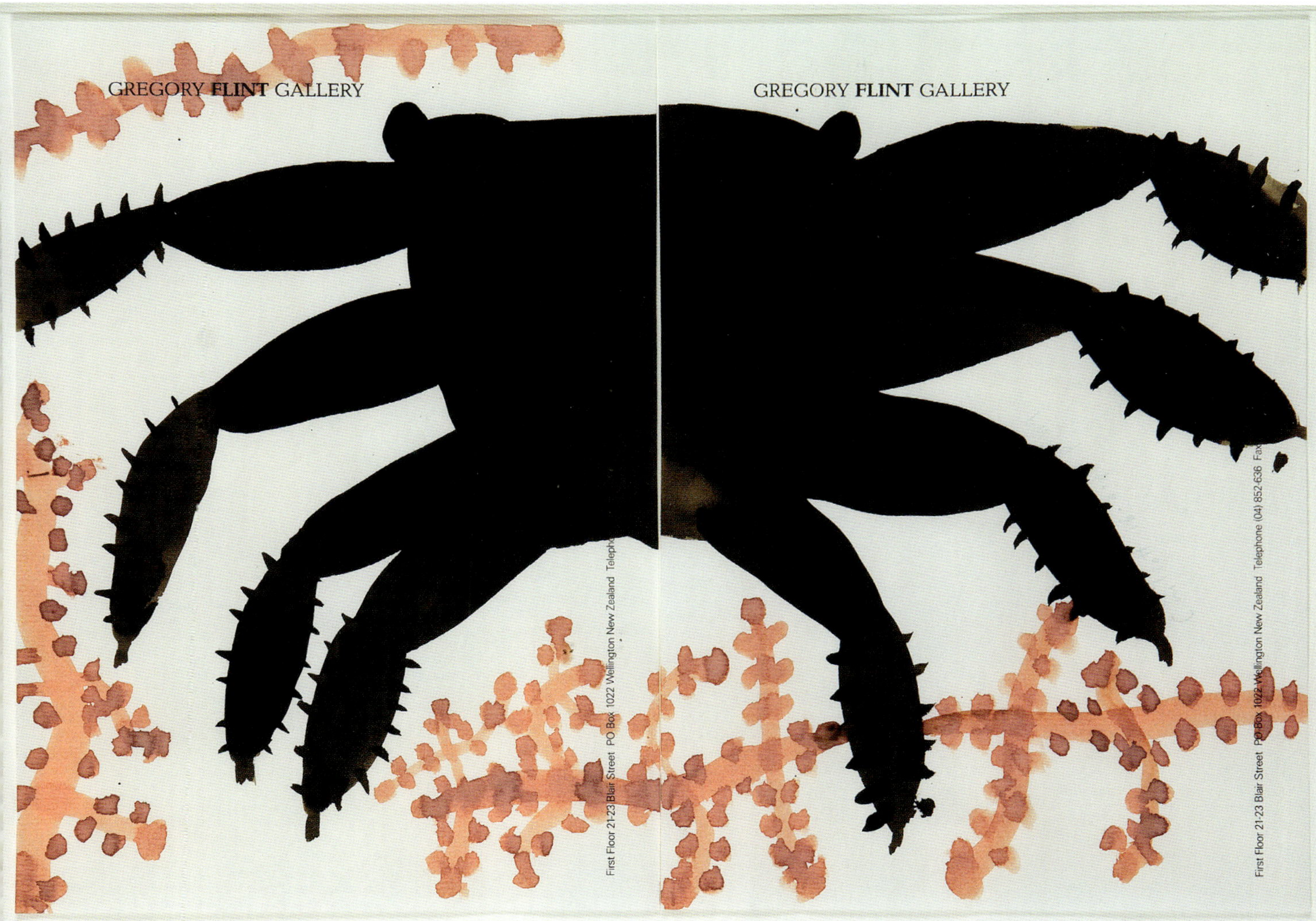
GREGORY FLINT GALLERY
GREGORY FLINT GALLERY
First Floor 21-23 Blair Street PO Box 1022 Wellington New Zealand
First Floor 21-23 Blair Street PO Box 1022 Wellington New Zealand Telephone (04) 852-636 Fax

Dick Frizzell

Enough said, I think.

Dick Frizzell
Hot Water
2009, oil on canvas
500 x 705 mm

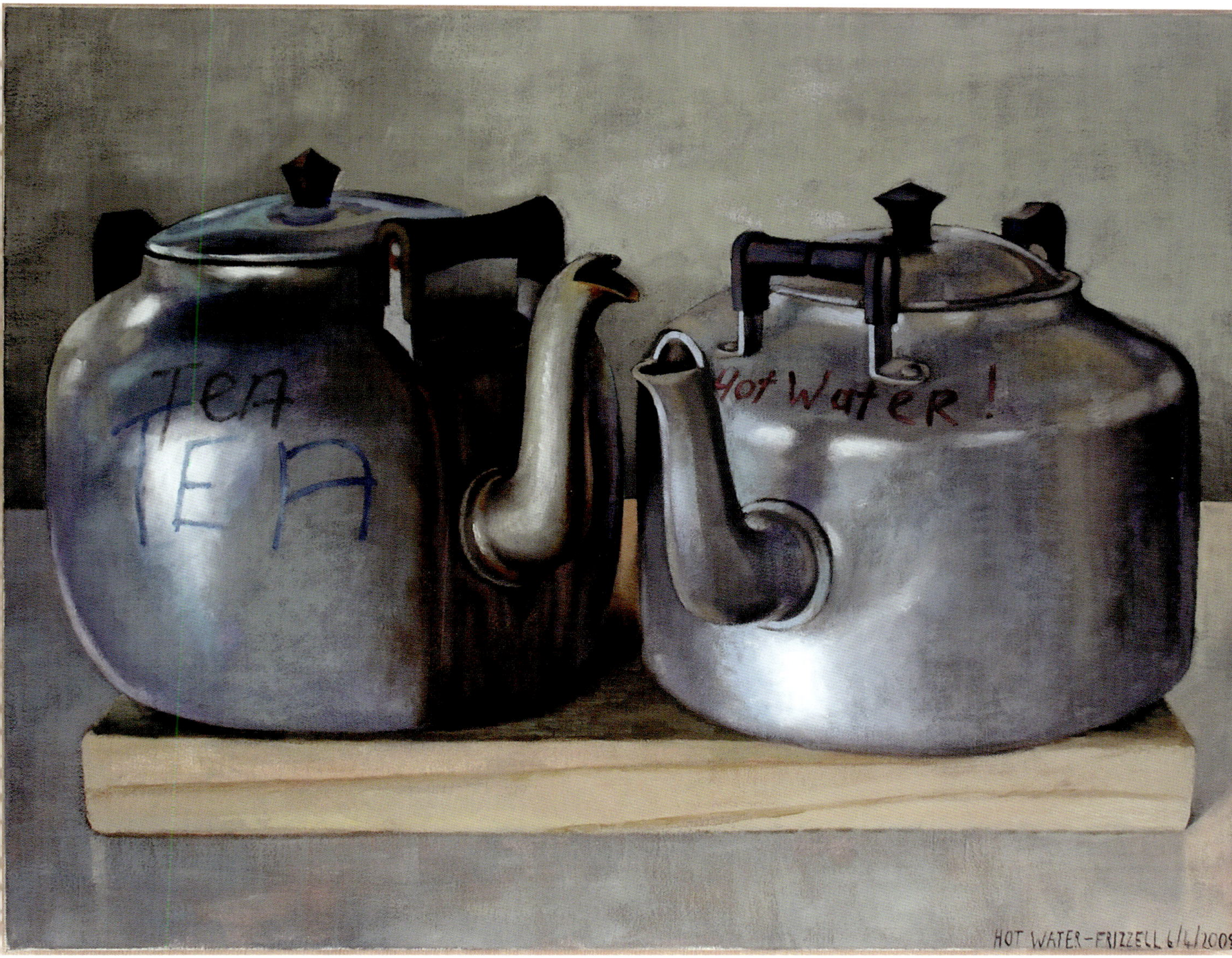
Tea
TEA
Hot Water!
HOT WATER-FRIZZELL 6/4/2009

Max Gimblett

Ah, Max. 'At the height of his powers,' I read the other day, and the new work certainly would seem to prove that. Practice makes perfect, or as they might say in New York: 'Stick to your schtick.'

I have to say I wasn't a big fan of his early cool-minimalist work; somehow the formal purity of the paintings didn't quite gel with the guy I was looking at. The austerity of the work looked a little forced . . . says I, who finds minimalism a bit of a bore after the rationale's been absorbed.

Anyway, Max worked through it. And worked, and worked. Finding and refining, getting out the bucket and mop, going crazy as a mountain monk. And now he's producing work like this.

These are very modern paintings: open, generous, taking on all comers. I quite frankly applaud his mad courage and determination! Instead of fading away, Max gets noisier and noisier.

Max Gimblett
The Silver Chariot – After Kandinsky
2010, gesso, acrylic and vinyl polymers, epoxy, aqua size
40 inch quartrefoil

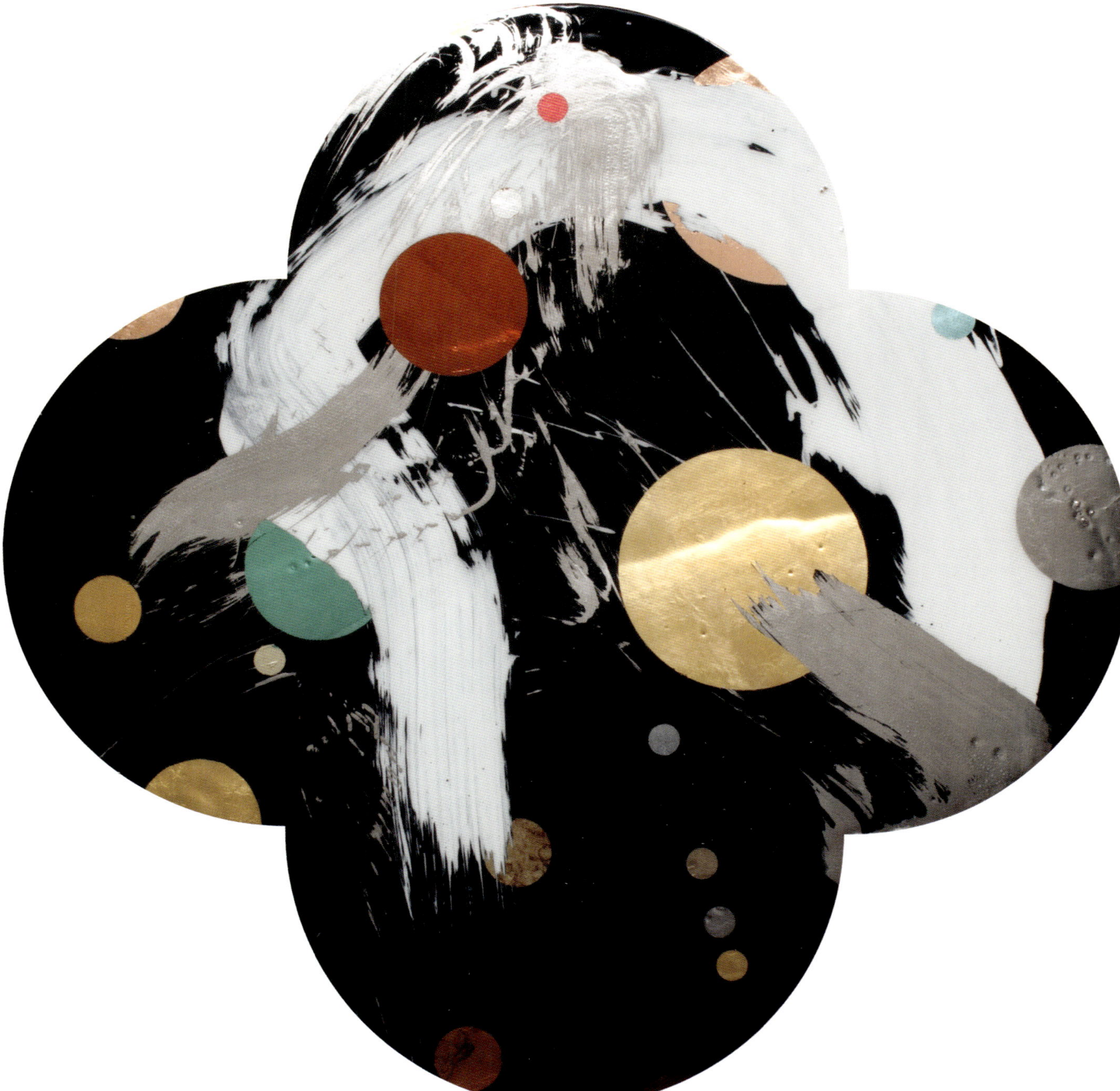

Bill Hammond

Ah, Bill, what weird alchemy is this? What exactly is it about these peculiar paintings that has such a hold on people's imaginations?

I'm not sure if he'll thank me for this but I think it's a sort of grown-up version of what I call sixth-form surrealism. A universal layperson's idea of what art should be, a fruity Dali-esque mindscape, a literal metaphor for creativity. And not only has Bill managed to capture that corner of the market, he's managed to inhabit it with an original New Zealand folklore that's a million miles from Kiwiana but couldn't be from anywhere else.

His are also the most structurally free paintings I know. I asked him once how he puts them together, and he said he stares at the blank canvas until something, like an imperfection in the weave, sets him off. His answer was probably apocryphal and maybe did happen once on a perfect afternoon but it's as good an explanation as any.

He hardly even paints! Bill more or less draws with the paint, calling attention to a certain 'painterly-ness' by allowing it to run down the canvas, and not a dribble here and there but to such an extent that these solemn avian conversations seem to be happening in some oppressive tropical thunderstorm. He really has made an astonishing virtue of just about doing everything wrong.

Bill told me once not to trust anyone who uses too much blue, and he could've gone on to tell me not to trust anyone who relies too much on anthropomorphic birds and cellos. And then he goes and paints this thing opposite, a greenish blue bird playing a cello – and it's terrific.

Bill Hammond
Predator Rock
2006, acrylic on canvas
1000 x 600 mm

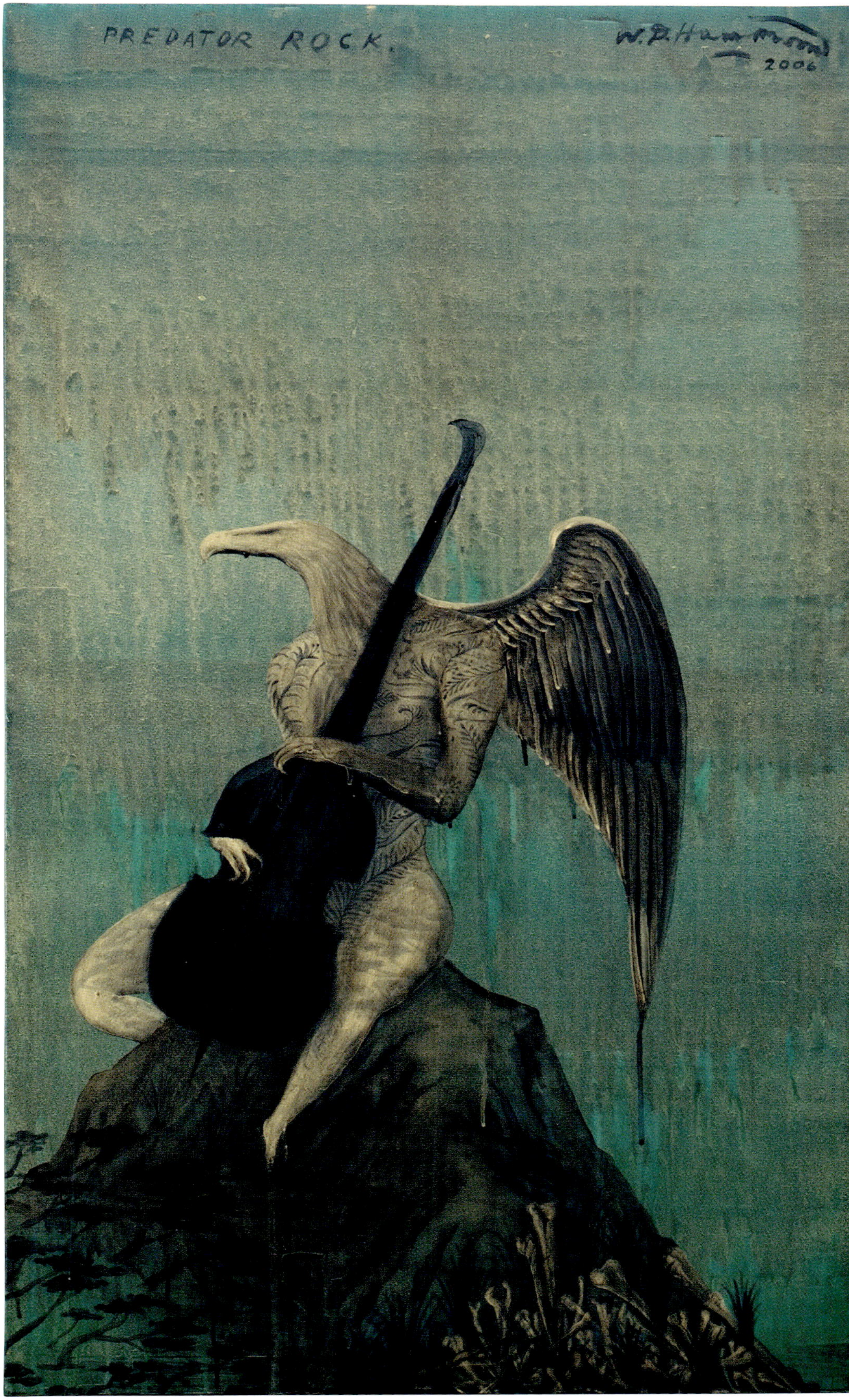
PREDATOR ROCK.
W.D.Hammond
2006

Tony de Lautour

Tony was one of the class of '88 out of Ilam art school. Part of what I once heard described as the 'pencil case' school because of the preponderance of scribbling and doodling in the work, like the mangled lids of those school pencil cases.

I suspect Tony's work was a major contributor to this definition. I first read about his work in an article about the group that talked about this dark young punk painting on comics – not painting comics or from comics, ON comics – and that caught my attention. Tony gunked up the pages with thick white oil paint and then dragged his spiky images of drug-crazed and rocket-propelled kiwi birds into the wet paint with a point-one sable brush.

This painting will surprise people familiar with Tony's 'landscaped logos' and altered op-shop paintings but I was intrigued when I came across it in the Hamish McKay Gallery, and even more intrigued when Hamish told me it was Tony's! This restless level of curiosity and reinvention is what it's all about to me.

Tony de Lautour
Black Spot 2
2011, acrylic, collage on paper
510 x 405 mm

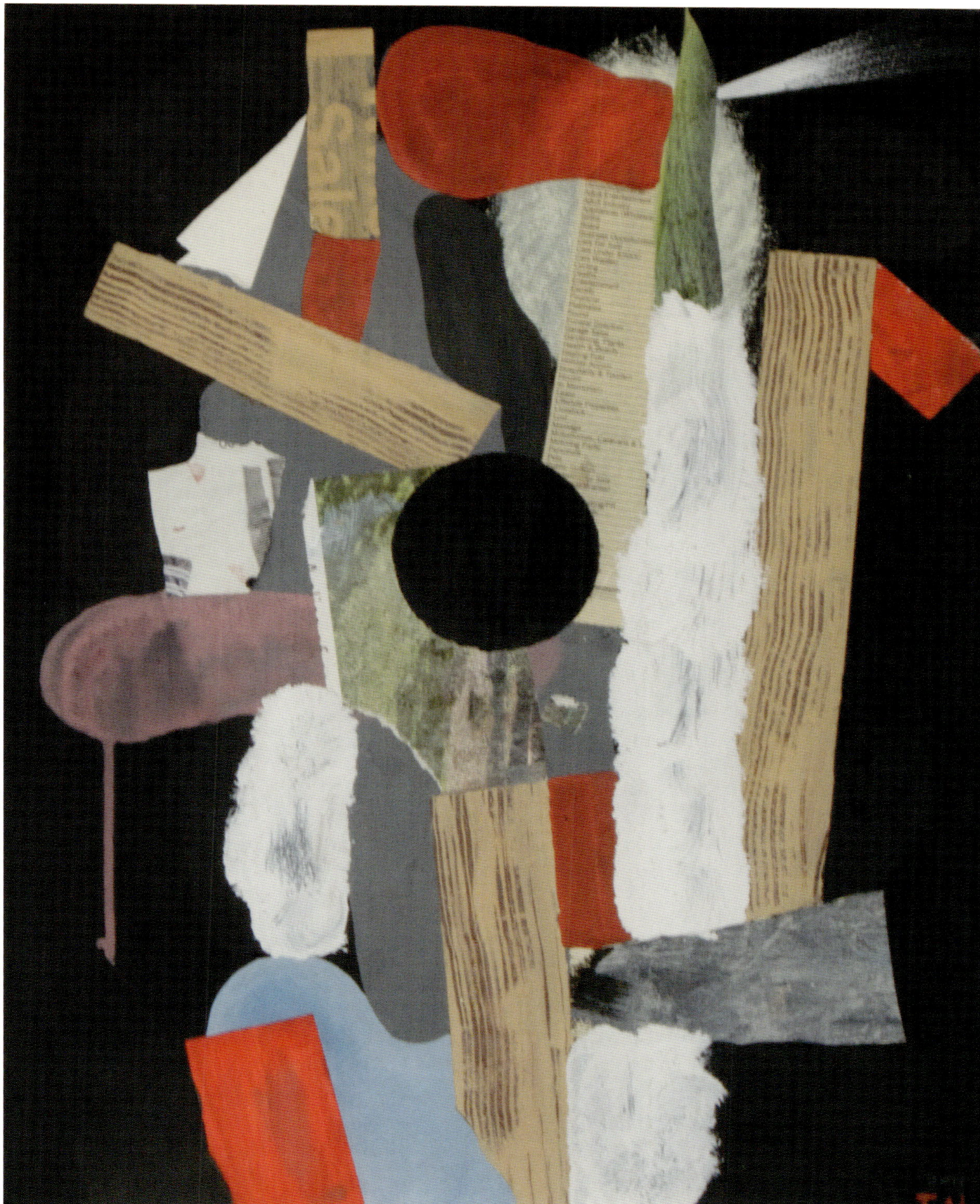
TDL

Tony Lane

Tony's had an interesting career, ticking along okay with his elongated stigmatas when, almost overnight it seemed, he invented the look he ultimately became known for. The pearls, the teardrops, the Giotto-esque deployment of space, the burnished surfaces and the gold leaf.

Pretty sexy stuff, and combined with the elaborate frames folding into themselves and extending the painting outwards from the support, they make for an intensely singular experience in the unfashionably lambent. A sort of secular religiosity hovering on the edge of the mystic. Bit like Giotto, actually, pulling heaven down to earth without muddying the holy water.

Tony Lane
From the Ida Valley
2011, oil paint on linen
375 x 380 mm

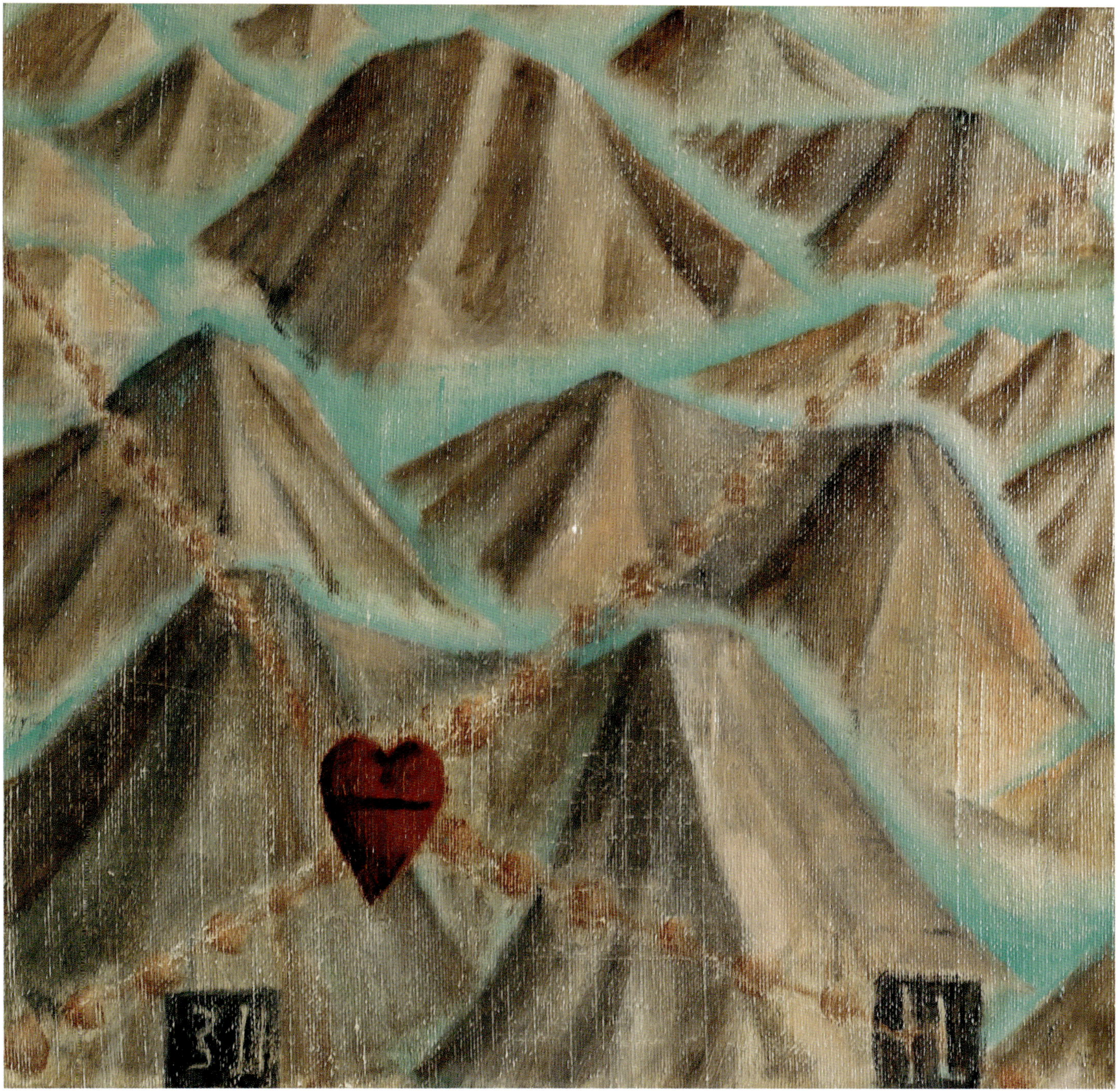

John Reynolds

Not a lot I really need to say about John, such is his ubiquity. I missed him by a year when I started at Elam in '79 but his presence was definitely being felt. I don't think I'd ever heard of a young artist being so socially organised. He very quickly wove his radical social manifesto into the urban fabric of Auckland city, with his famous Diner and his, hell, I don't know, everything else basically. Functions, happenings – John and his posse led the charge. 'Private viewings' in his and Julian Dashper's studio, with selected entry and Julian glaring out from behind the door. This was a whole new energy, which had the art to go with it of course. A new 'adaptable' art that could spring from the studio wall to a fabric, to a boutique mural, to just about anything – sky-writing if you wanted it.

In fact it would be fair to say that John was there at the beginning of what they're now calling 'convergence', the free-for-all between art and design that I wrote about in the intro. And he's still there, tearing back and forth from project to project, spreading the word.

John Reynolds
Trouble [with words . . .]
2009, oil paint marker
on canvas
150 x 150 mm

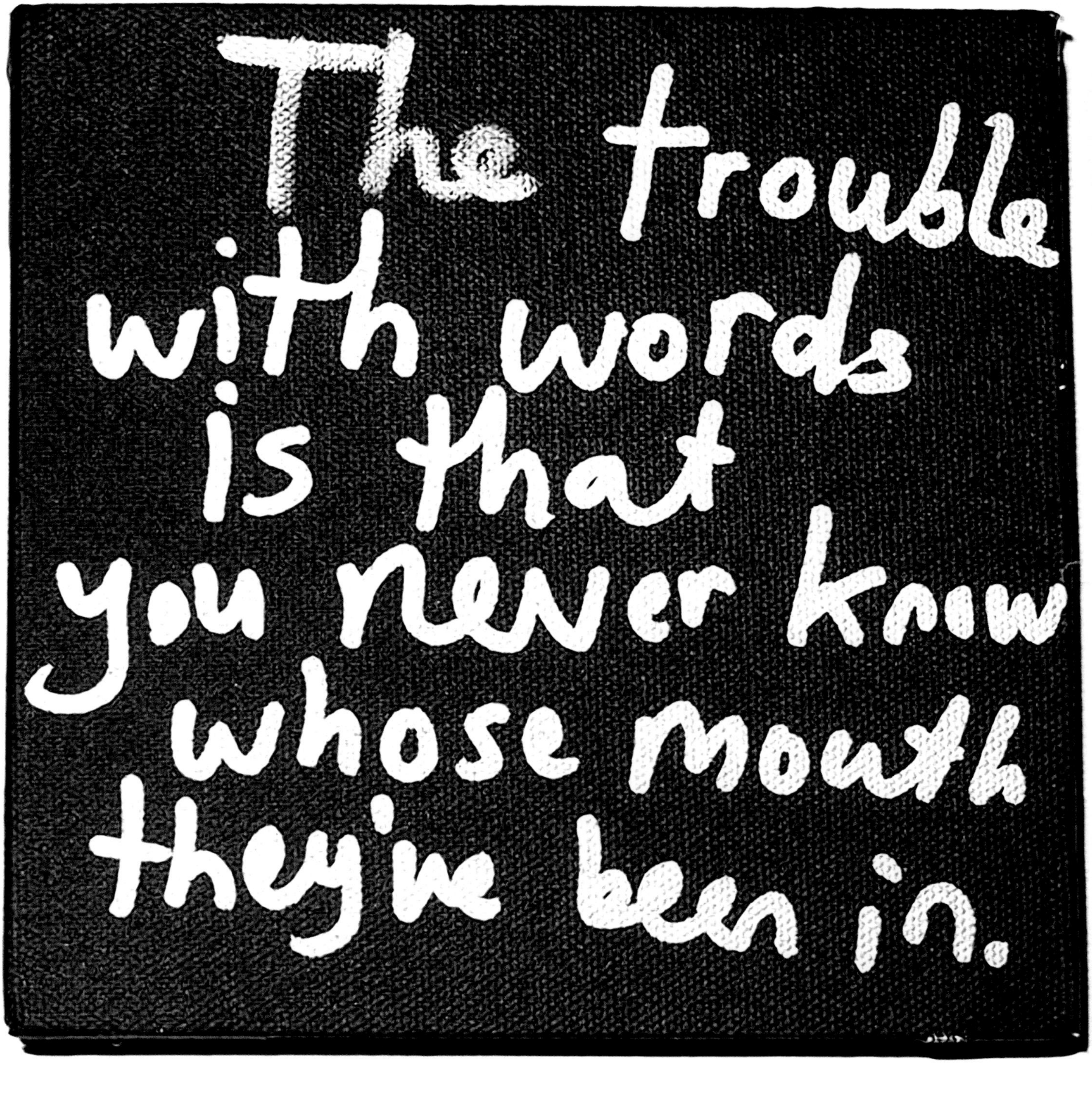
The trouble
with words
is that
you never know
whose mouth
they've been in.

Julian Dashper

Julian was in his fourth year when I turned up as a 10-hour-a-week tutor at Elam. My God, but that was a baptism of fire! How do you 'tutor' a young painting animal like that?! Determined to be helpful – to 'tutor' – I'd brace myself and go into his studio (you almost felt as if you should knock) and stand there thinking of something constructive to say as he strode backwards and forwards in a pair of overalls that could have stood up on their own, sloshing enormous brush loads of various acrylic greys at these floor-to-ceiling canvases he had pinned up around the (large) room. Periodically he'd fling himself into a paint-encrusted armchair and brood on these great Motherwell-ish artefacts, often to the point where he had trouble extricating himself as the polymers bonded between overalls and chair.

I love these mad 'velvet' paintings, the unrestrained gusto of their fabulously ad hoc constructions; 'invented' not long after he graduated, and delivered to the world with a confidence and a 'will to power' that was hard to resist. He continued to wield this brazen will to power through the rest of his (far too short) career but in ways that questioned the actual mechanics of the context of the thing rather than the nature of the thing itself.

Julian Dashper
Guy Ngan Mural, Bledisloe State Building, Auckland City 1987
1987, oil and acrylic on canvas, velvet and linen
2600 x 5000 mm

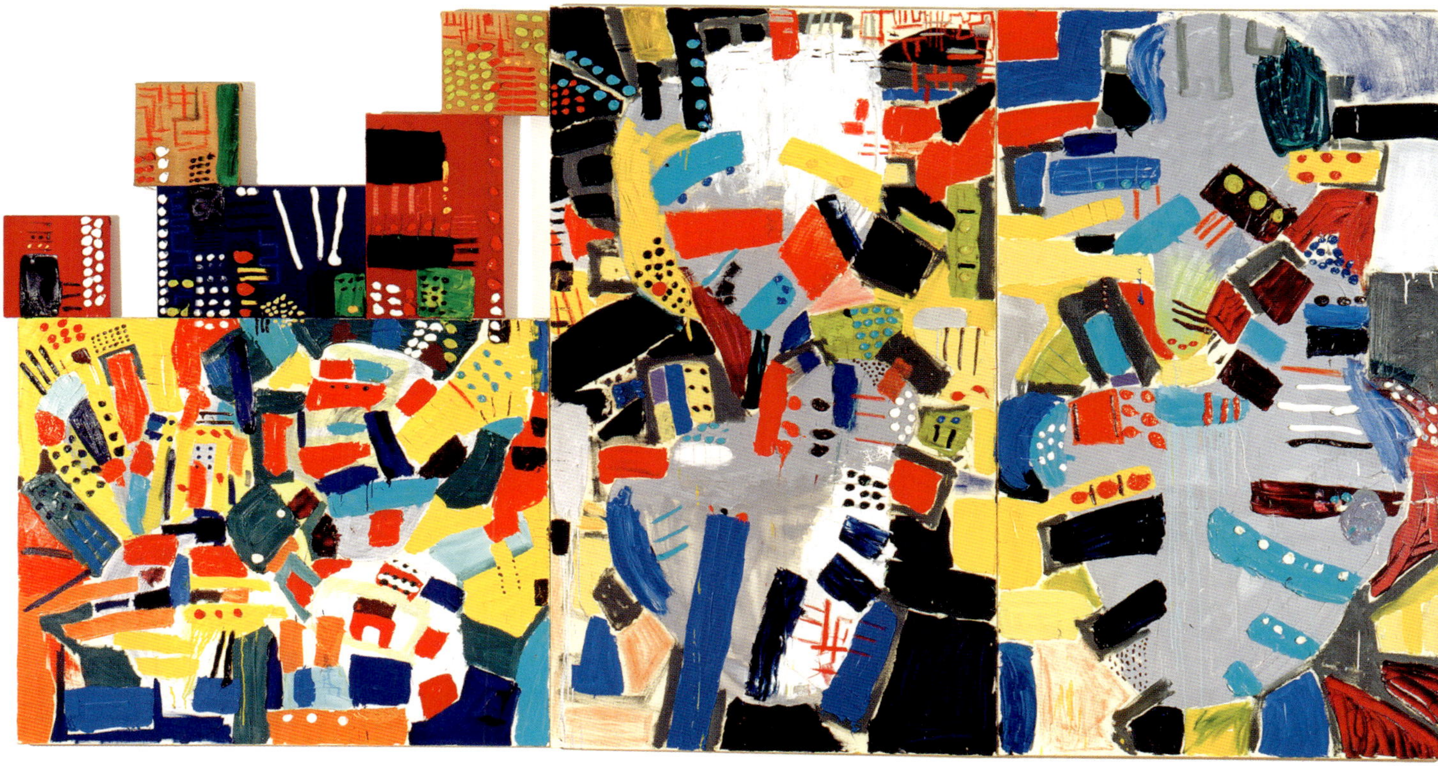

Séraphine Pick

Another one of the 1988 Ilam alumni, Séraphine's periscope popped up pretty early in the piece. Her early scruffitti canvases of sexually ambiguous comings and goings logged themselves into our collective consciousness as soon as they appeared and she has gone on to develop these themes through ever more inventive and ambitious compositions.

Her psychosexual pantheist dream pictures would have been deeply unfashionable or just plain cheesy in anyone else's hands, but Séraphine gets there with an intensity of purpose that makes the highly improbable feel indispensably necessary.

I've enjoyed watching her refining her technique and pushing her ideas harder and harder over the years, always ready to show us that more can definitely mean more, and that she's patient and dedicated enough to actually do it!

Séraphine Pick
White Noise
2010, oil on linen
1650 x 2000 mm

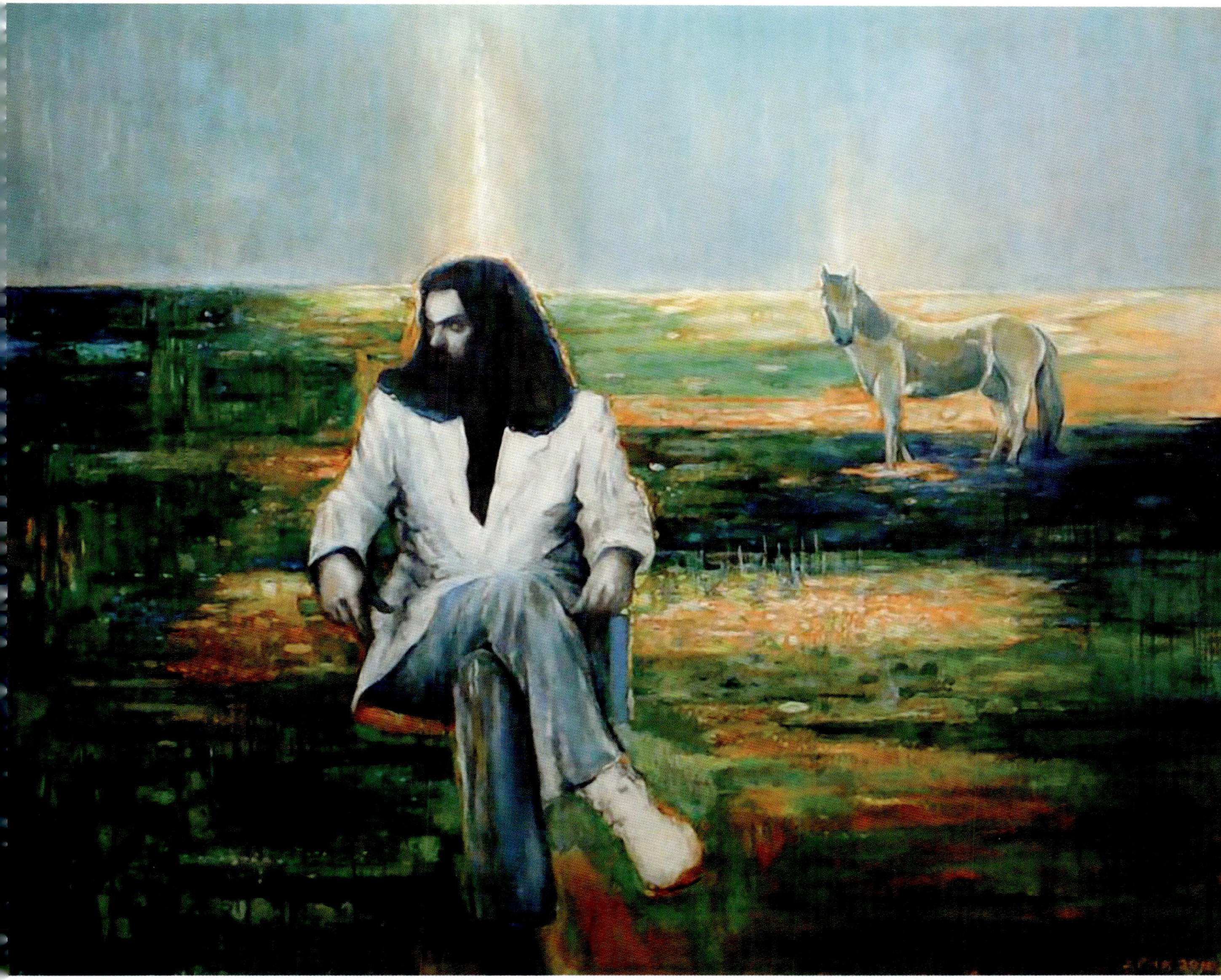

Kim Pieters

A quiet achiever. Kim's paintings would be easy to miss if you didn't keep your eyes wide open; they're so sly and recessive. But once you get in there you're in for a rich and rewarding experience.

Given that they seem to rely on so many accidental and naturally occurring effects – as if she just nails the boards to the fence and walks away, going back and prising them off when they're done, nail holes and all – they maintain a consistently inventive dialogue within themselves.

All her little galaxies of spontaneous doodling and noodling swim blissfully in a space the colour and texture of the icing on animal crackers, small smudges of contrasting and harmonising paint coming and going like stray comets. 'Surreal abstraction' if there could be such a thing.

Kim Pieters
short title *'quodlibet'*
2010, mixed media
on board
1200 x 1200 mm

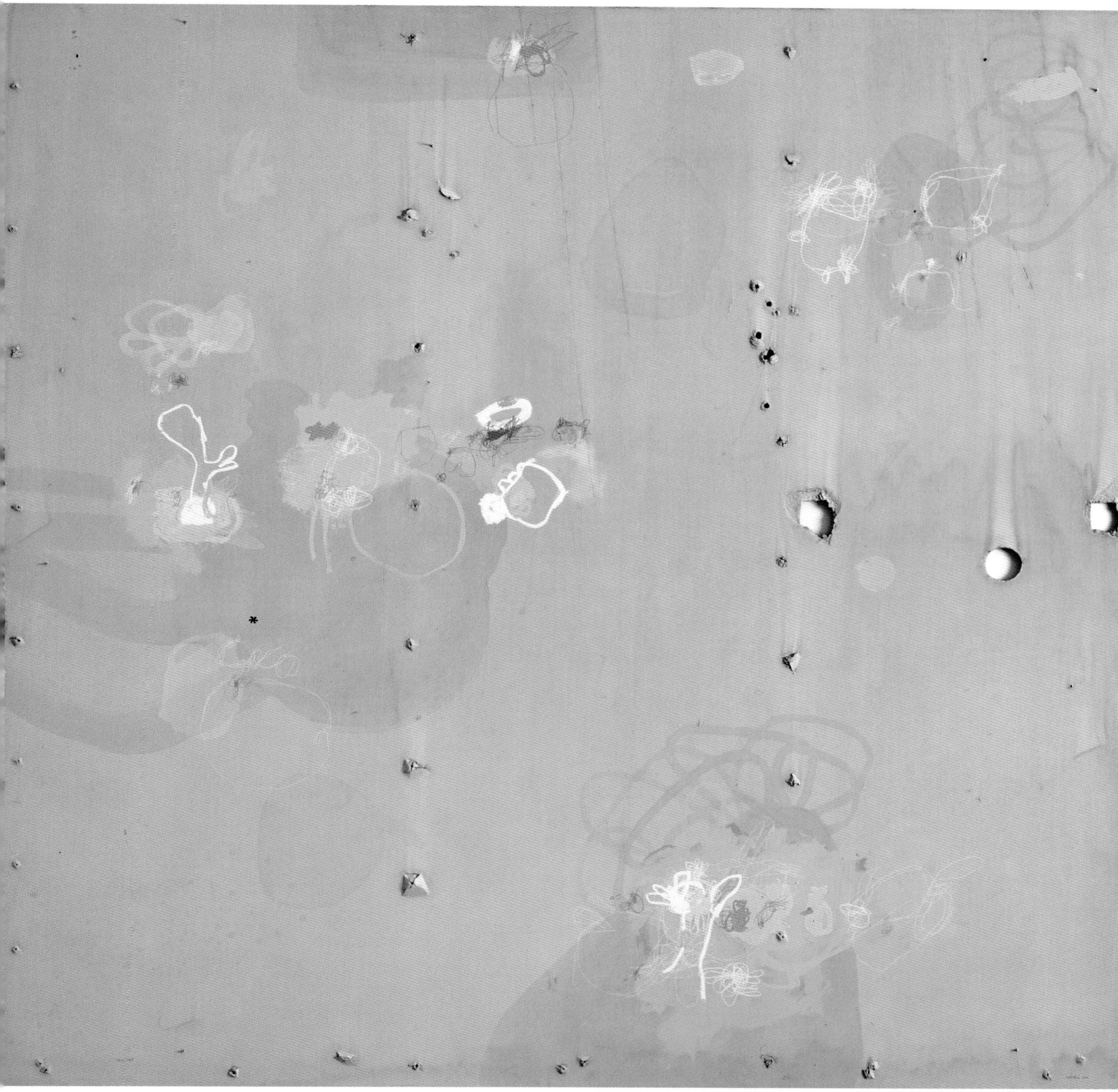

short title 'quodlibet'

long title 'The common translation of this term as "whatever" in the sense of "it does not matter which, indifferently" is certainly correct, but in its form the Latin says exactly the opposite: *Quodlibet ens* is not "being, it does not matter which" but rather "being such that it always matters".'

from 'The Coming Community' by Giorgio Agamben

Richard McWhannell

When the McWhannell book gets written it's going to be interesting leafing through the colour plates from the front to the back. Richard has maintained an unusually consistent course throughout his career, building, refining and extending his skills and technique in a way that graphically illustrates the steady evolution of a central idea.

While the early work has a significant personality of its own it's the way that with time, practice and fierce concentration he has developed a range of tools capable of some seriously heavy hitting.

Despite some very successful forays into landscape, and I was very tempted to illustrate one of his Pararaha series here, Richard's main focus is people and the fascinating business of portraiture.

Quite a hard discipline to parlay into a serious philosophical vehicle, but Richard has done it by an obsessive level of application that goes way beyond superficial things like 'likeness' to a personal narrative that literally exploits the sitter (self or otherwise) to talk about the nature of art, the traditional training of the hand and eye, the possibility of paint, and so on. That he also manages to leave some very good portraits in his wake seems more like a bonus than the actual endgame.

Richard McWhannell
Barbara Ward is: Leonardo da Vinci's 'Lady with an Ermine', 1483–1490, Czartoryski Museum, Krakow
2010, oil on board
535 x 382 mm

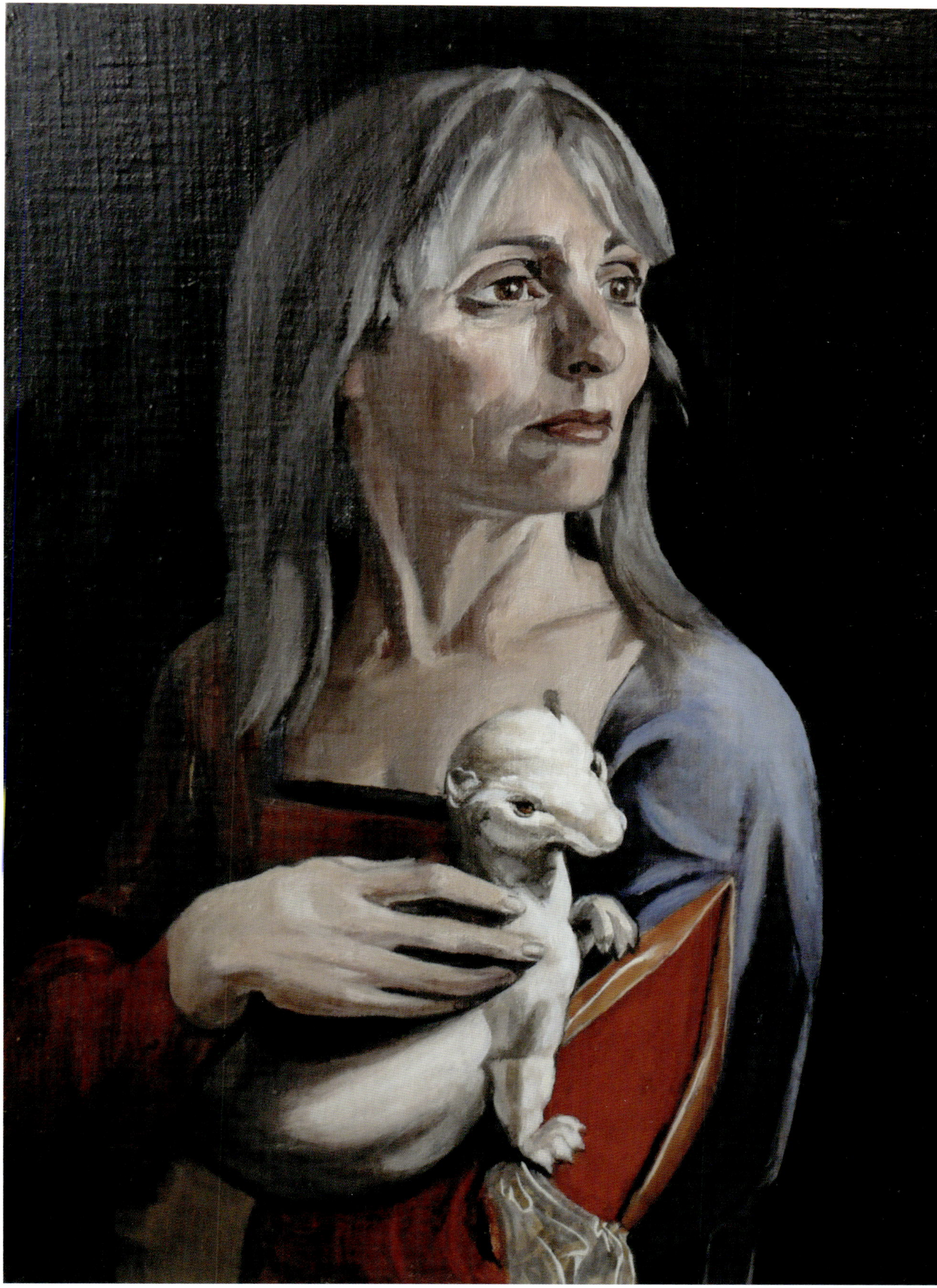

Shane Cotton

Where do you start with Shane Cotton? Another of that 1988 class out of Ilam, virtually a star from the get-go, hoovering up contemporary movements with a clear understanding of the need to cut through your influences and get them out of the way smartly. All this as well as displaying a natural graphic virtuosity that pretty much precluded any chance of failure.

And then he really got going . . .

Despite being burdened with the responsibility of being the new young Maori art hero (and I'm a bit nervous about writing this because I'm not at all sure that Shane's felt encumbered by anything much but I think it has to be said), I know Shane would have succeeded in any context such is the depth of his intuitive knowledge of what art is, what it can do, and how to make it do it.

While talking a lot about issues important to him, Shane has never depended on the polemic to carry the painting but has cleverly woven the stories so subtly into the formal language of the work that they will always be able to be read and appreciated on some level. If the aesthetic ain't right, it ain't worth a damn, no matter how much you might care.

Shane Cotton
Star Eater
2011, acrylic on linen
2065 x 2065 mm

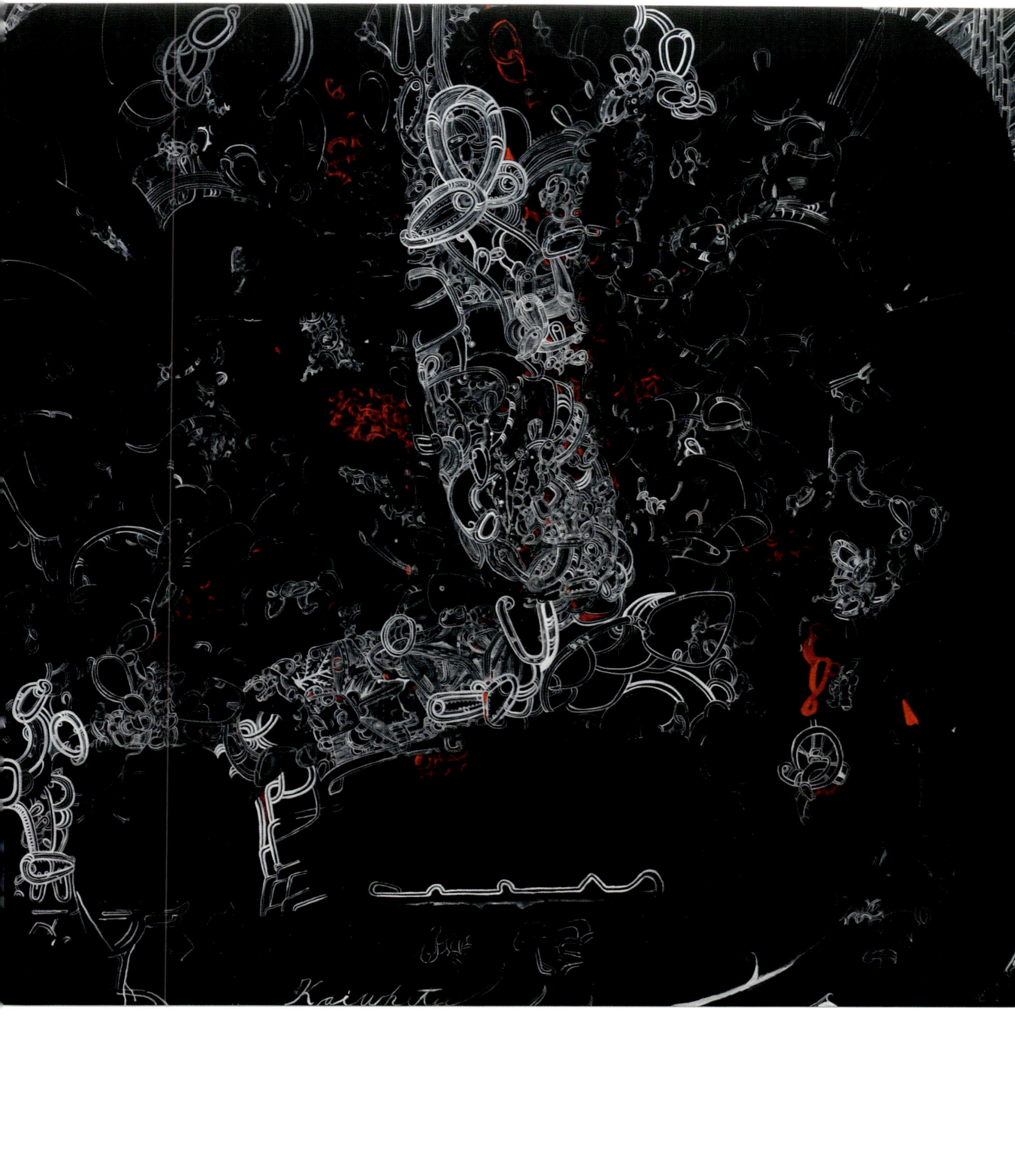

Peter Robinson

I was going to use one of Peter's Big Crunch works here because I love it when art and science conflate perfectly, and I'm excited to see another artist so obviously taken with physics and cosmology. I've always thought that if you were curious about what art is you'd have to also be interested in what life is. Both information systems being essentially expressions of the same thing.

Anyway, after all that, I 'discovered' his new paintings. Thought he might have forgotten how to do it, lost in his big white-out.

This guy moves in leaps and bounds, crashing through walls like his polystyrene juggernauts, sweeping the floor with his big ideas. He must've technically come up to speed in a hurry to slot back into painting mode and produce work like this. As always, Peter hits a whole raft of contemporary painting systems right on the mark, maybe even an inch or two in front of it.

Peter Robinson
The Mushroom Hunter
2009, acrylic, charcoal, ink and enamel on canvas
2130 x 1830 mm

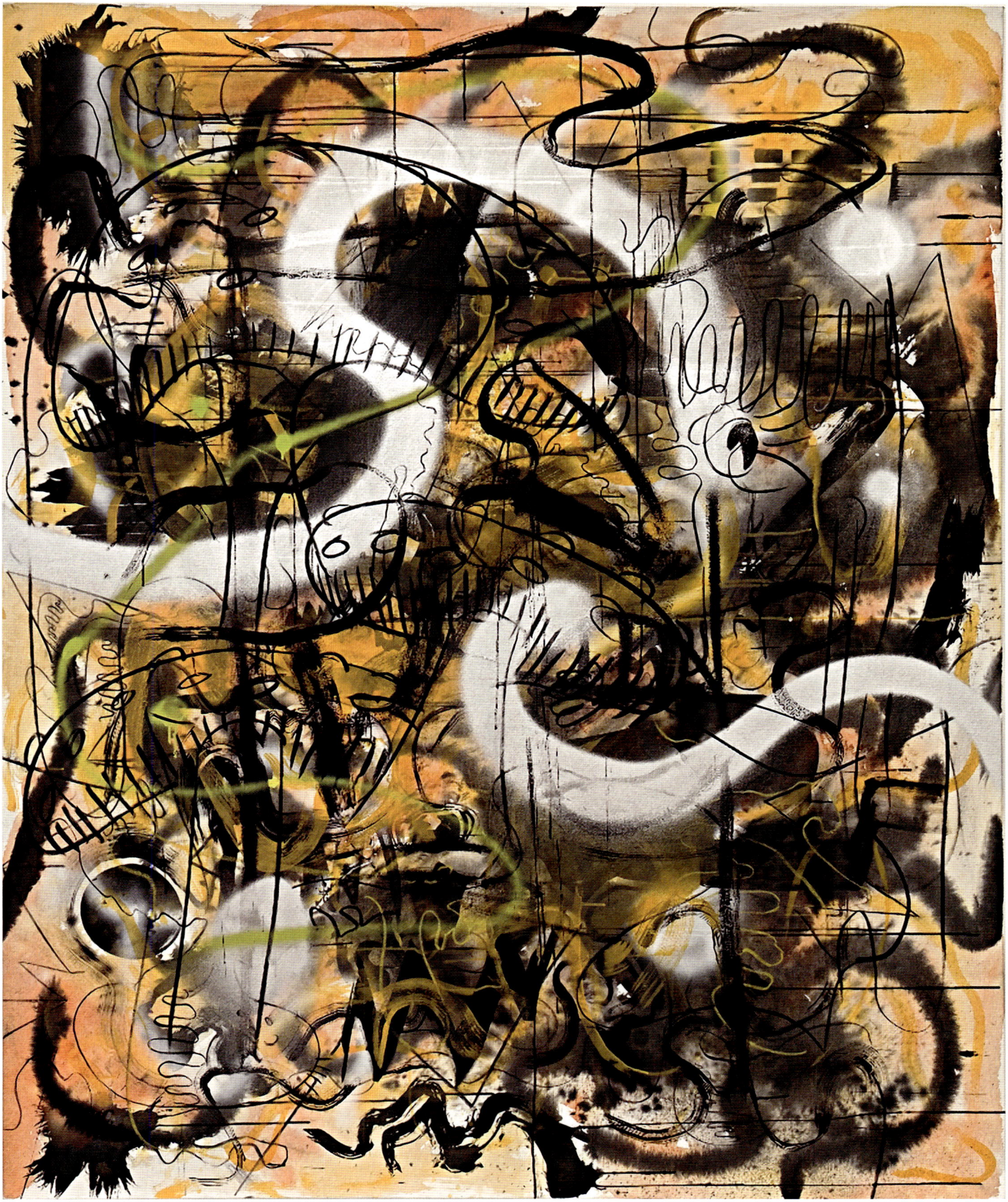

Chris Heaphy

Always in command of a very nice graphic touch and with a sharp eye on contemporary shifts in style and strategy, Chris has produced some sound work over the years, but nothing that prepared me for the recent explosion of invention and application evident in this new work.

Great image collectives, images composed of images, technology put to work in a way that not only justifies the means but glories in it, and opens the way for an exciting exploration of scale seldom seen in local dealer galleries. It's a fabulous breakthrough and I look forward to seeing where it takes him next.

Chris Heaphy
Kingdom
2007, acrylic
on canvas
1900 x 1450 mm

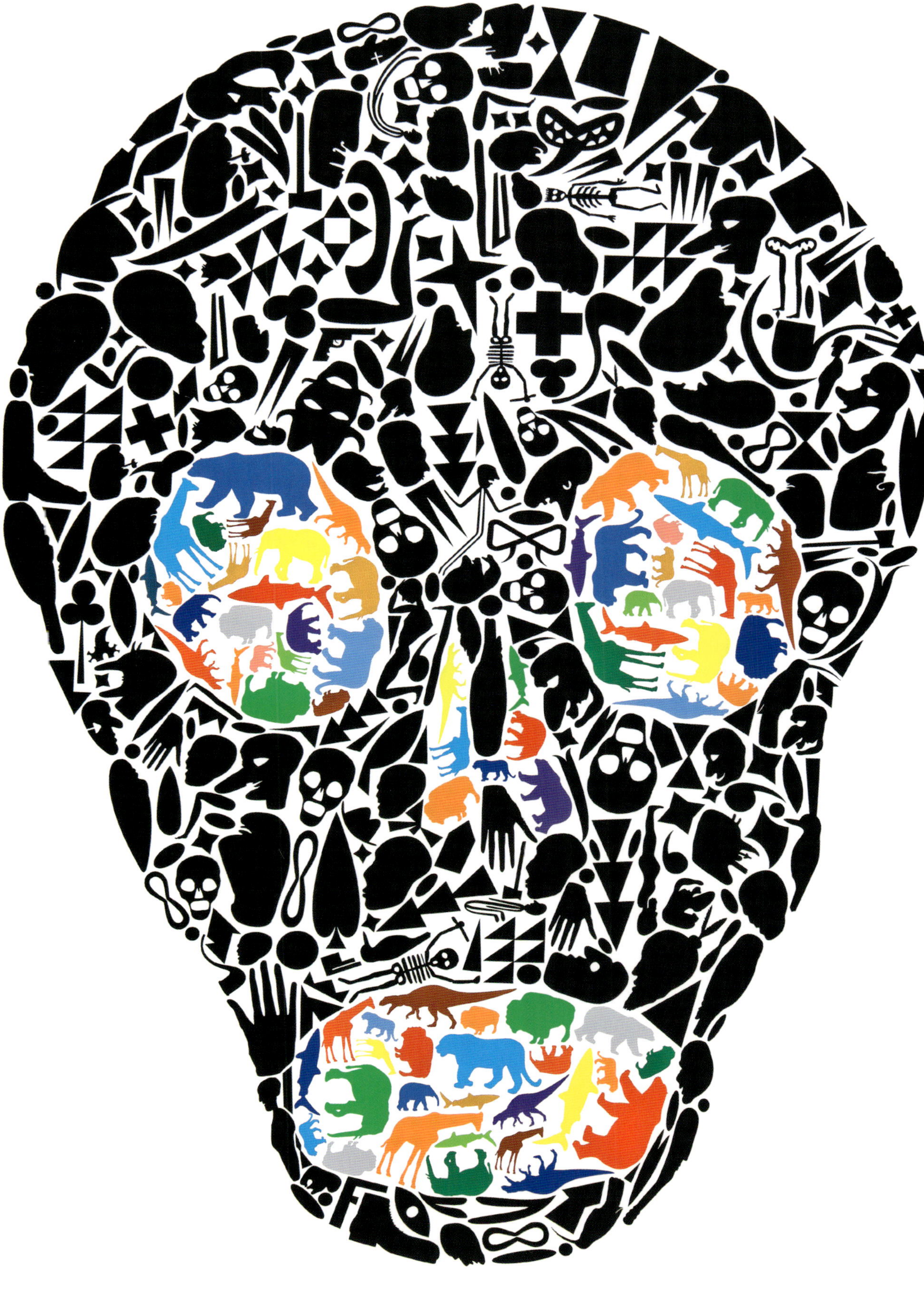

John Pule

The artist/poet, the poet painting his poetry and the painter writing his paintings. John's right there in the middle.

His work's a bold invention, obviously inspired by tapa cloth's symbolic narratives but taken to a whole new level. John's visual poems of Pacific flora and fauna backgrounding episodes of pre-Christian or Christian village life . . . colonial or postcolonial conflict . . . are woven into sophisticated abstract space. All there to be interpreted 'as you wish' or just appreciated as the formal dynamic of busy tertiary detail resonating against organised mass. Everything you'd hope to find in a painting really.

His technique of dry brushing over the half-dry paint of the line work helps to visually bond the tracery of the line with the surrounding void, and takes it one step away from the merely notative. Every new body of work gently extends the possibility of visual storytelling without compromising either the poetry or the painting. Keeping it in the middle.

John Pule
I Will Carry Anything That You Want
2006, oil and ink on canvas
2000 x 2000 mm

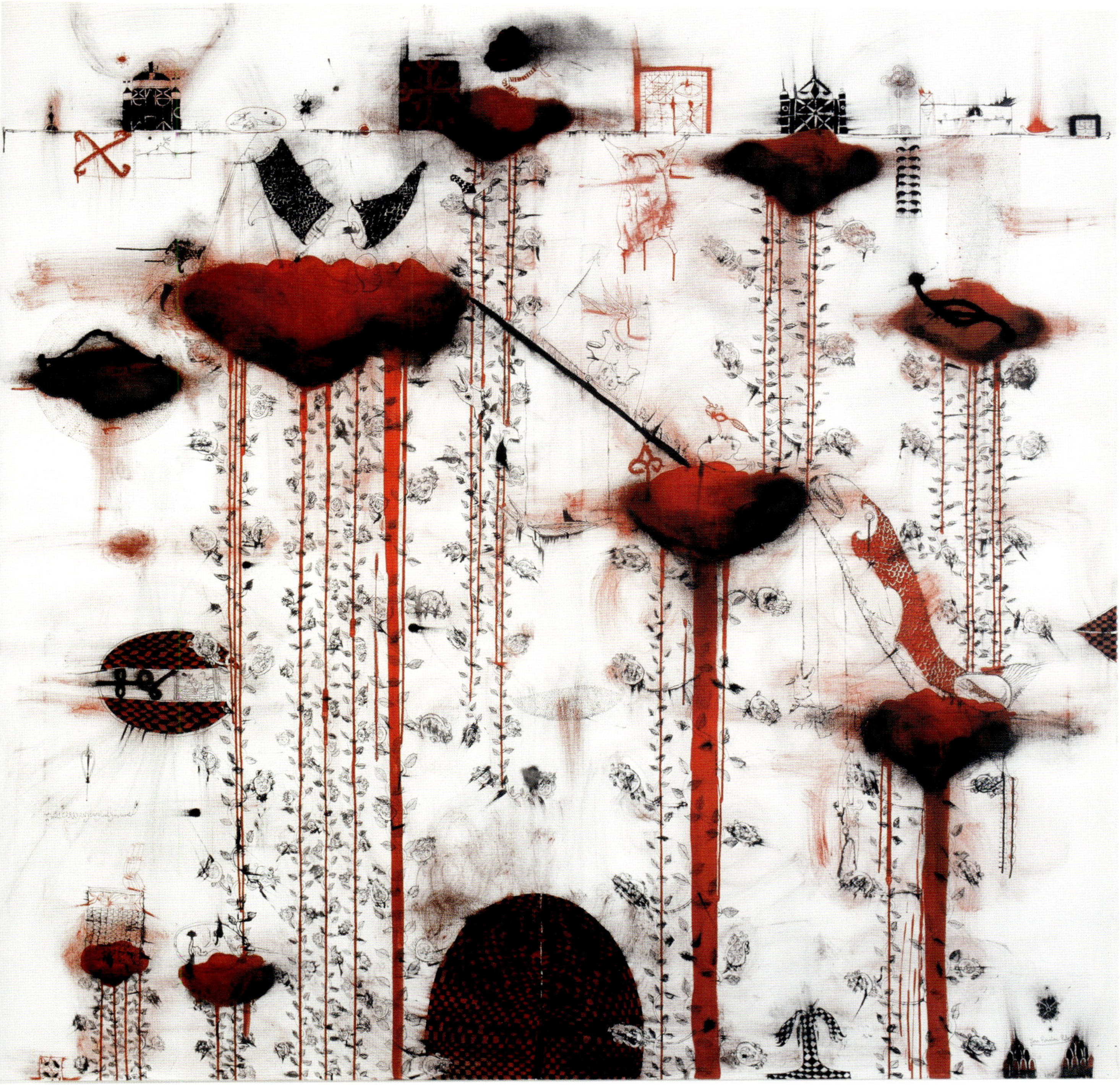

Judy Millar

I take my hat off to anyone able to reinvent the expansive painterly gesture and recapture abstract expressionism without the burden of the macho/psycho subtext.

Evolving out from relatively modest experiments with reductive turps washes, Judy's painterly language has quickly developed and is capable of taking charge of space on a scale seldom seen in New Zealand painting. So cleverly managed is the sense of openness in the weave in the interacting planes of her painting that standing in front of one of these controlled explosions I feel like I could dive in and frolic about like Scrooge McDuck diving into his money bin.

There's a courage and reckless sense of going for broke symbolised in these expansive gestures that I find incredibly stimulating. Don't stand there waiting for any meaning to reveal itself, just jump in.

Judy Millar
Untitled
2010, screenprinting ink on canvas
1350 x 970 mm

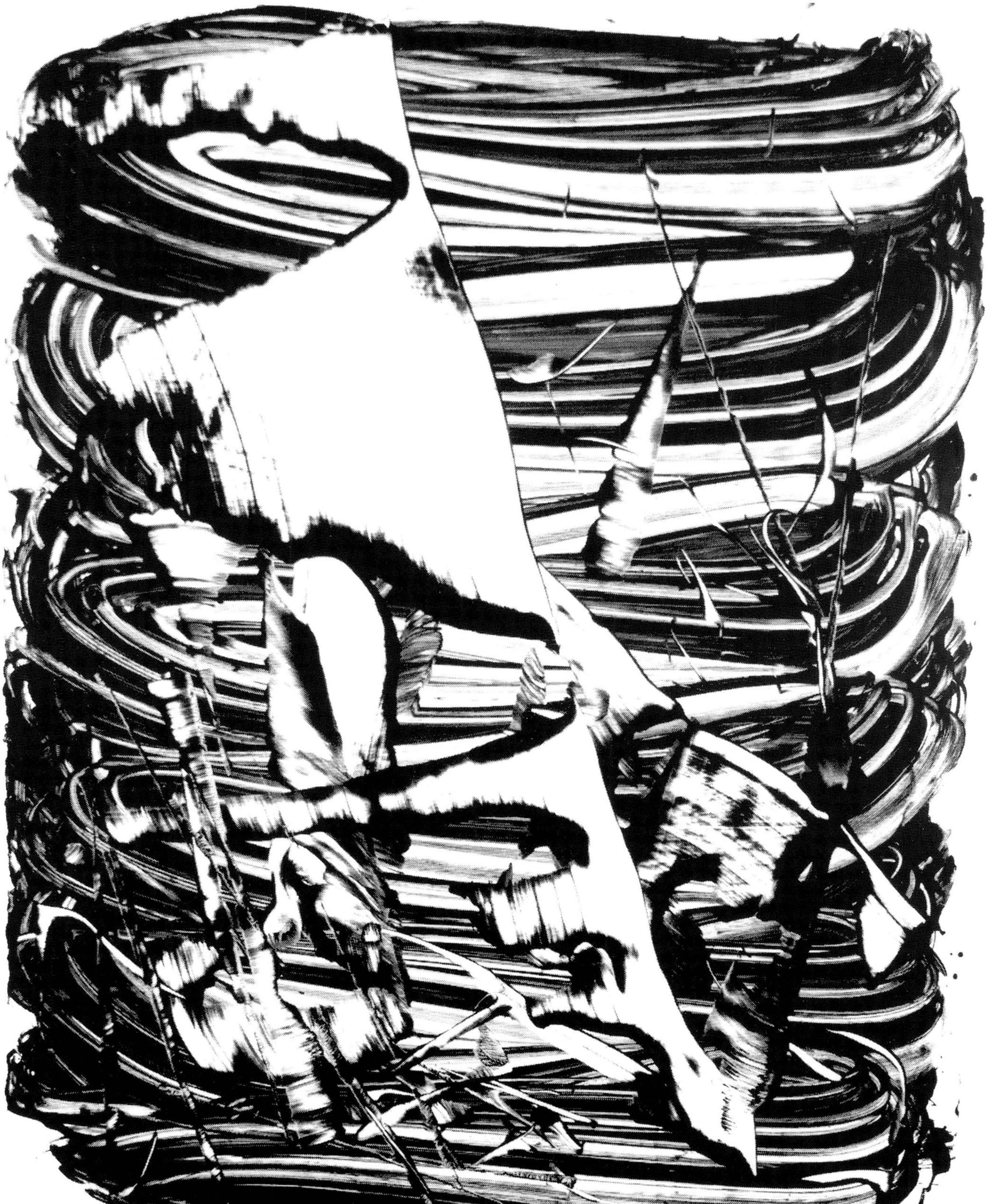

Michael Stevenson

I don't think Mike's painting much at the moment, since massively complex socio-historical recreations became his main obsession, but back in the day when he was painting he produced some truly sublime works.

At art school Mike chomped through the history of twentieth-century modernist painting, analysing it from within, till he arrived at this deadpan rendering of the ponderously melancholic truth of our rural heart.

In the end I guess painting just wasn't big enough to contain the breadth of ideas that he became consumed with but the images he did produce in that short time continue to reverberate.

Michael Stevenson
Two Stacks of Bibles
1987, oil on canvas
on board
446 x 595 mm

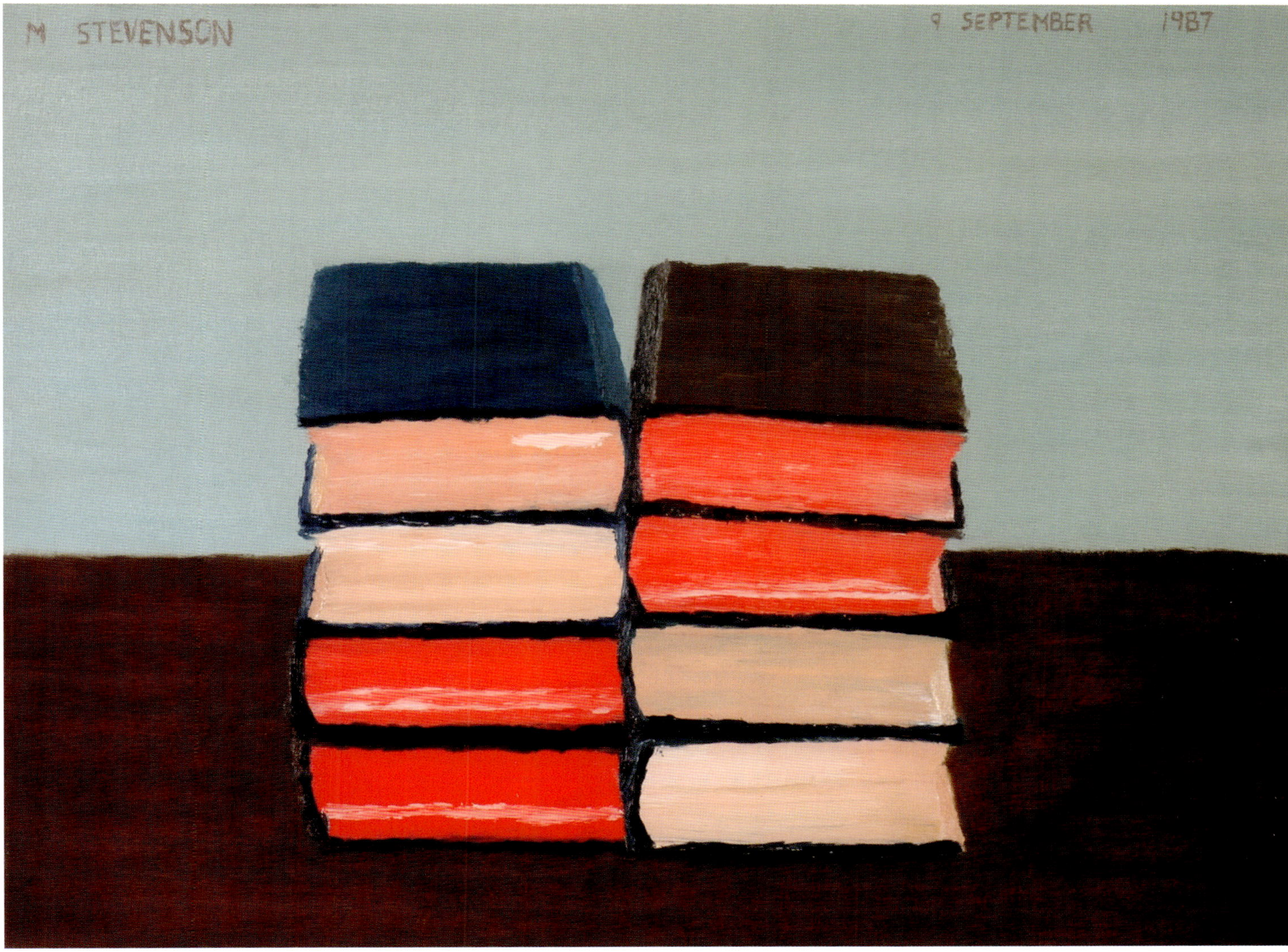
M STEVENSON
9 SEPTEMBER 1987

Karl Maughan

Karl was another student of mine at Elam in the glory days when we all clung to the life-raft *Paint and Be Damned* as it drifted through the treacherous reefs of postmodernism. (What nonsense . . . but it did feel a little like it at the time!)

This is the first painting of Karl's that made me sit up and think that there might be more to him than the crazy student guy. It's an incredibly sustained work of observation and application, and very much a precursor to all that's followed since.

Often accused of not getting out of the garden . . . over time, Karl has proved that his mission is to stay right there and represent nature's limitless abundance, rendered as exuberantly positive as the artist himself.

Karl Maughan
Silver Beet
1987, oil on canvas
1120 x 1830 mm

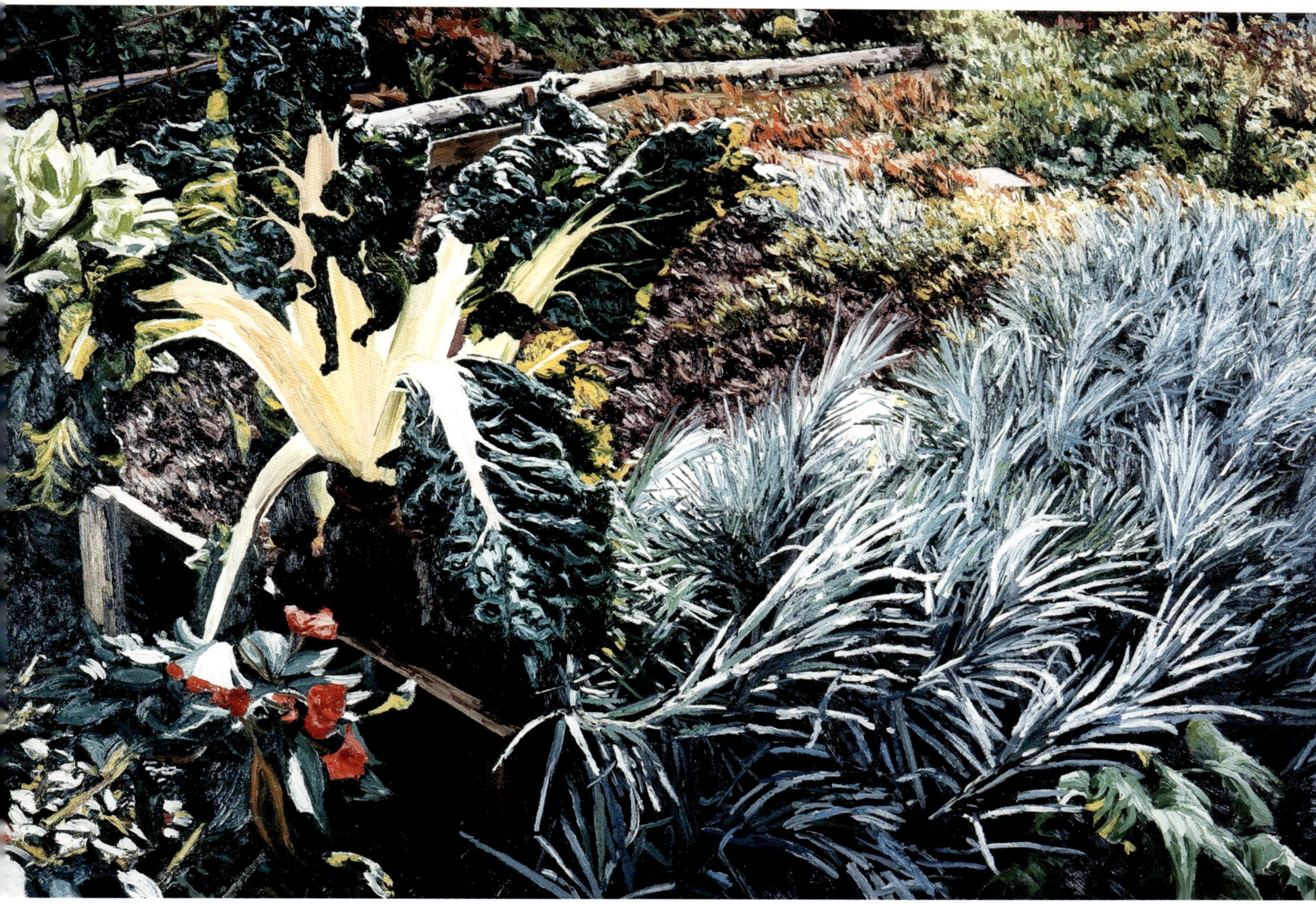

Joanna Braithwaite

Now here's a painter!

I first saw one of Joanna's large (very large) sheep's head paintings in Brasserie Flipp in Wellington many years ago. I had no idea that anyone in New Zealand could control paint, wet on wet, on that scale, and not only paint per se, but paint actually doing something (describing a sheep's head, in this instance) and doing it magnificently, without giving away any of its painterliness.

Her subsequent work has never failed to satisfy, for all the above reasons, becoming less youthfully bravura, for sure, but even more fluidly assured in the process if that were possible. I doubt she'd be able to convince us of her Dr Moreau parables if they weren't delivered with such lush conviction.

Joanna Braithwaite
Ascension
2000, oil on canvas

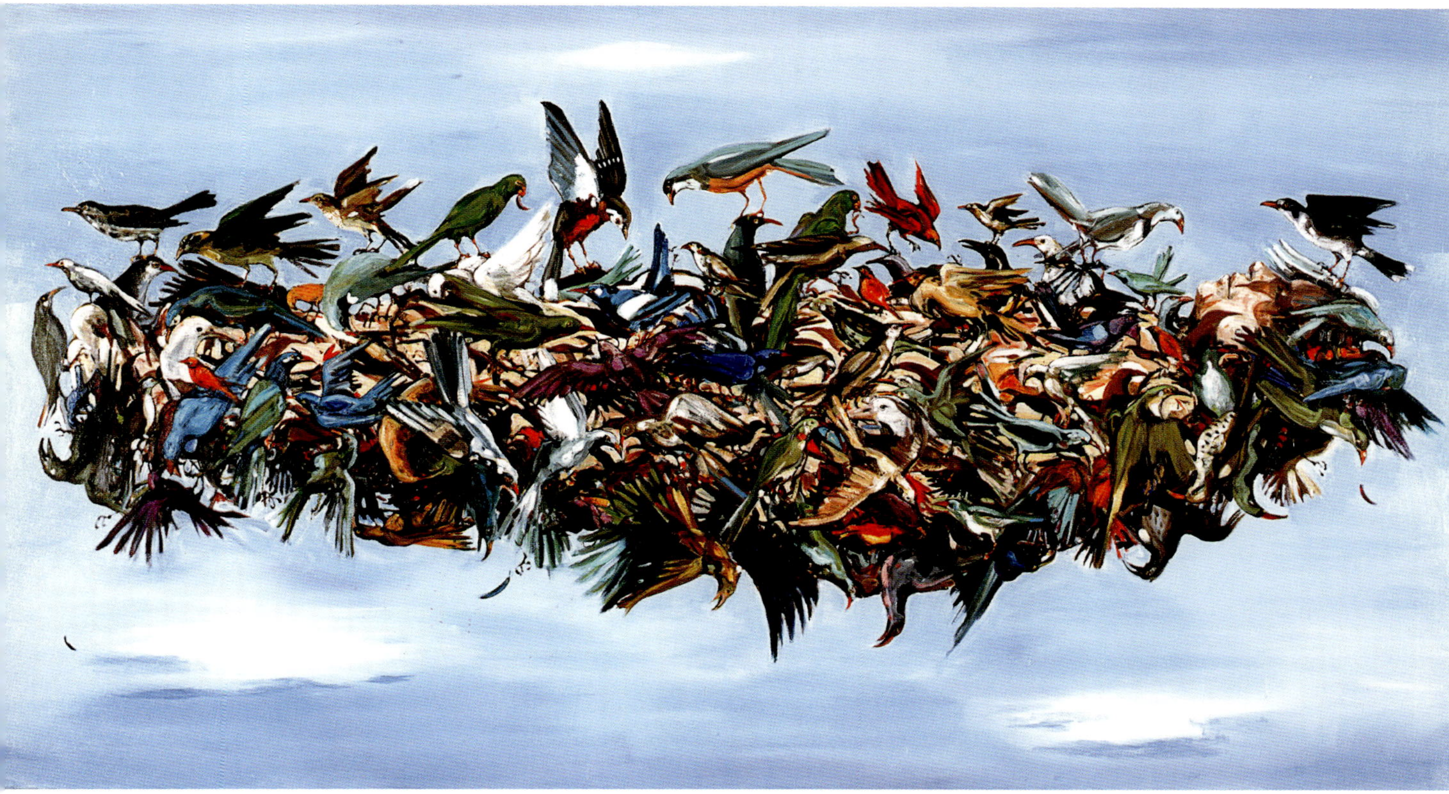

Johanna Pegler

Another quiet surprise. Again it was hard to see where her work was going when she was a student at Elam, working hard down there in the basement, but you could definitely feel it was going somewhere!

Painting in general was going through a pretty difficult time right about then in the late 1980s, everyone getting hammered senseless with postmodernist theory (fun times), but Jo's stoic certainty that there was life in the old form yet was incredibly reassuring to me. In fact her attitude, when I think back on it, went way beyond certainty. I don't think she ever countenanced the idea of painting not being here. Painting was just what painters did and they did it by responding directly to the world around them and, especially in Jo's case, making it a bit of a treasure hunt in the process.

Johanna Pegler
Lake Land
2005, watercolour
on paper

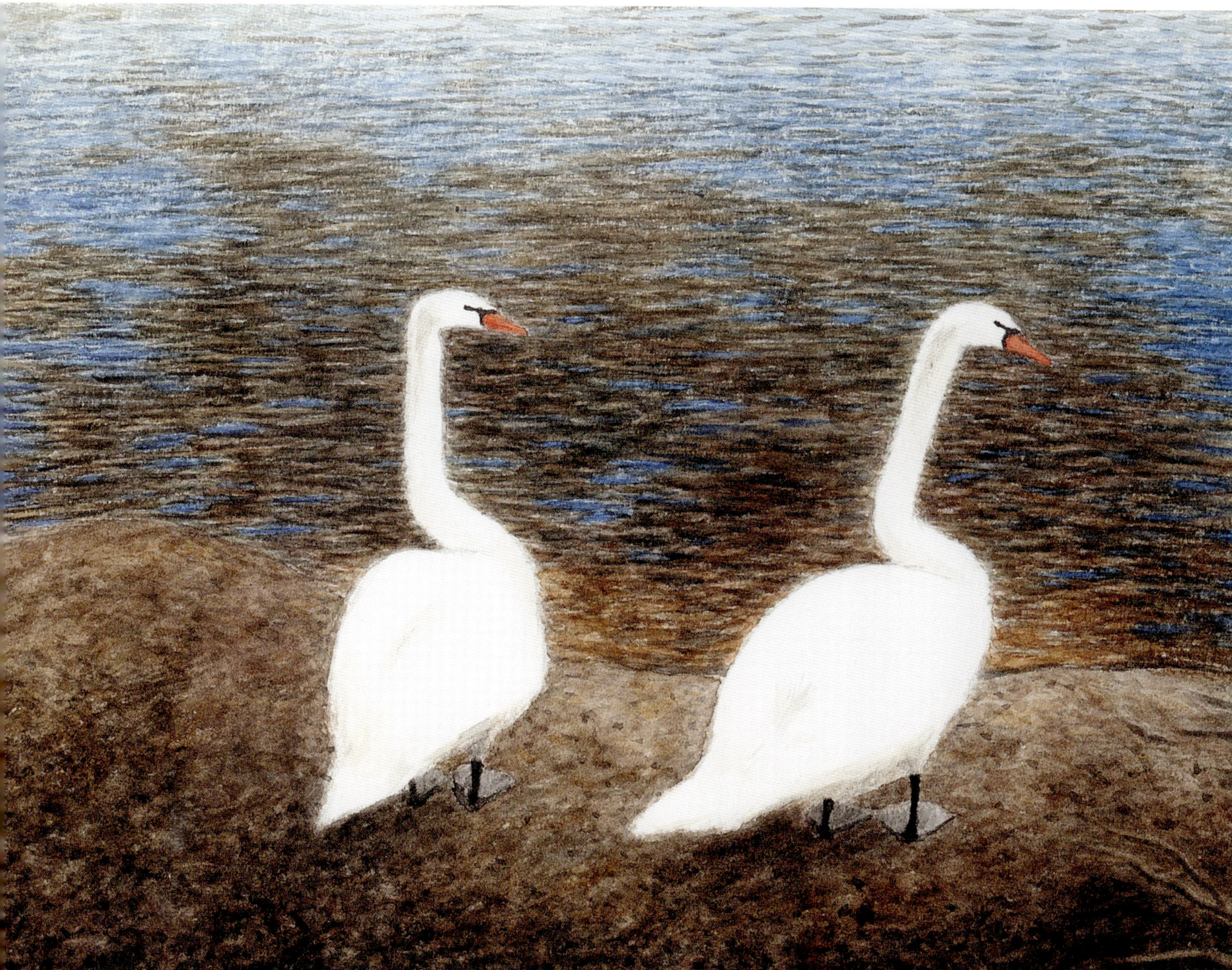

Mark Braunias

I love this boy. I envy him his ability to hit a wall the way he does, scribbling out his Gunk philosophy, colouring in and colouring out till the room is spinning with his strange cartoon universe. Like the Warner Brothers' family put through the mincer, Daffy Duck without his beak, or Elmer Fudd without his, well, without his anything really.

Such is Mark's fiendishly clever parallel iconography that it lulls you into a sense of familiarity until you suddenly realise that you recognise none of it. By then you're hooked, of course, left struggling to connect the dots and to find a way back to the recognisable which always seems to hover only a three-fingered glove away.

His is a fantastically sustained act of invention and I can only begin to imagine the massive amount of research that goes into these 'spontaneous performances'.

Mark Braunias
Study for a Parallel Universe
2010, inks and acrylic on paper
1900 x 1200 mm

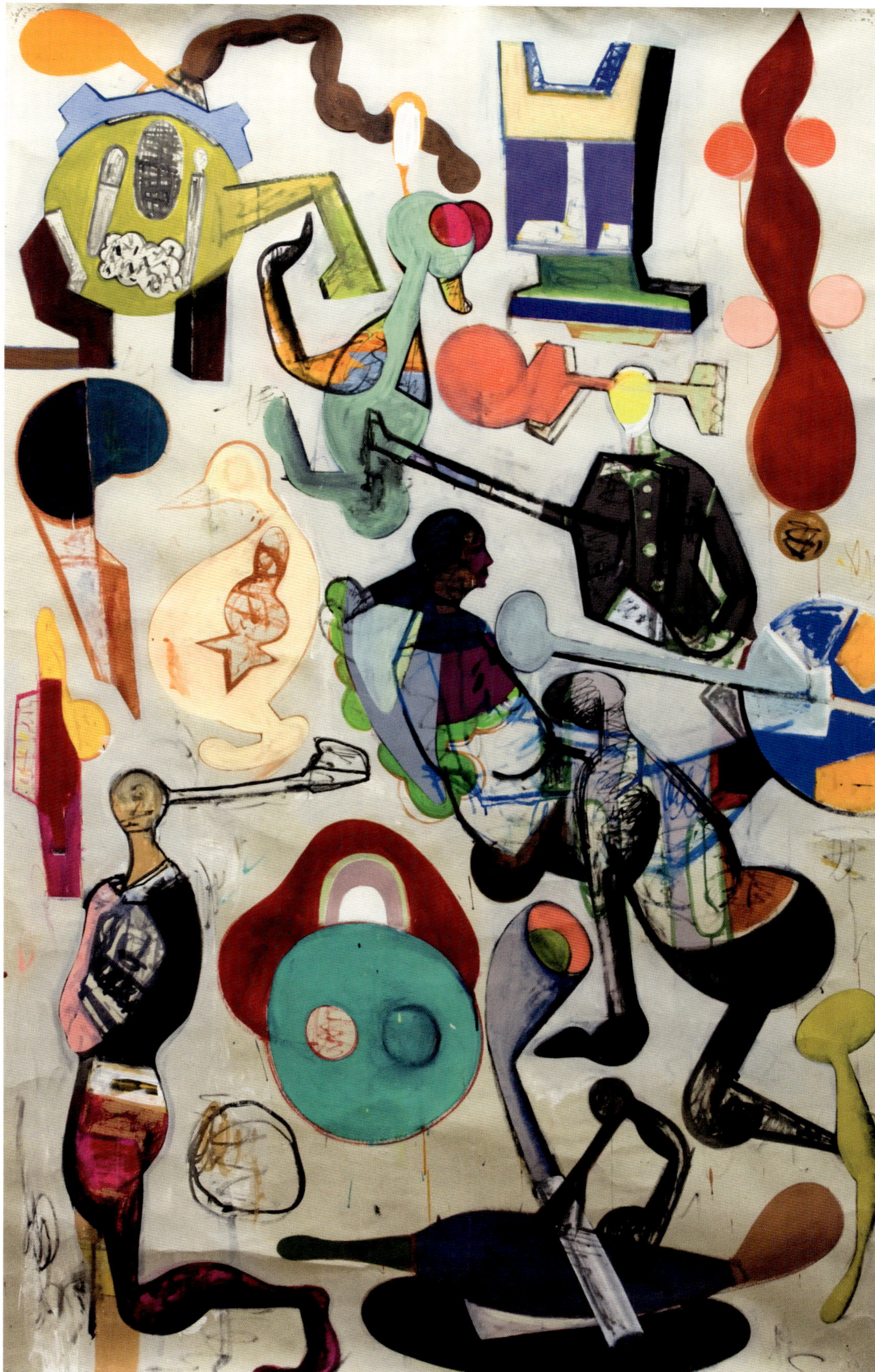

Richard Lewer

I taught Richard for a few years back in the day . . . or I thought I was teaching him. I know I talked to him, and he listened very politely; he was a very polite boy, he still is.

And now to my eternal amazement and delight he's turned out to be a very original and very successful artist! I wish I could figure out how he did it. He certainly had the self-flagellating seriousness, and the discipline, but where the focus and all these crazy ideas came from I have no idea.

I love the way he goes at it . . . no holding back. He welcomes resistance, resistant materials. Paints on Ven-lu-ree blinds, Formica tabletops, acoustic tiles, billiard baize . . . anything to stop the politeness. Shameless in a curious kind of way, he breaks all the rules of serious career management and displays a fearless disregard for the art racket's strange little unwritten protocols. He's too busy recording how bizarre life is, as it reveals itself to his wide-eyed point of view, to worry about etiquette.

Richard Lewer
Mother and Child
2010, enamel on canvas
750 x 750 mm

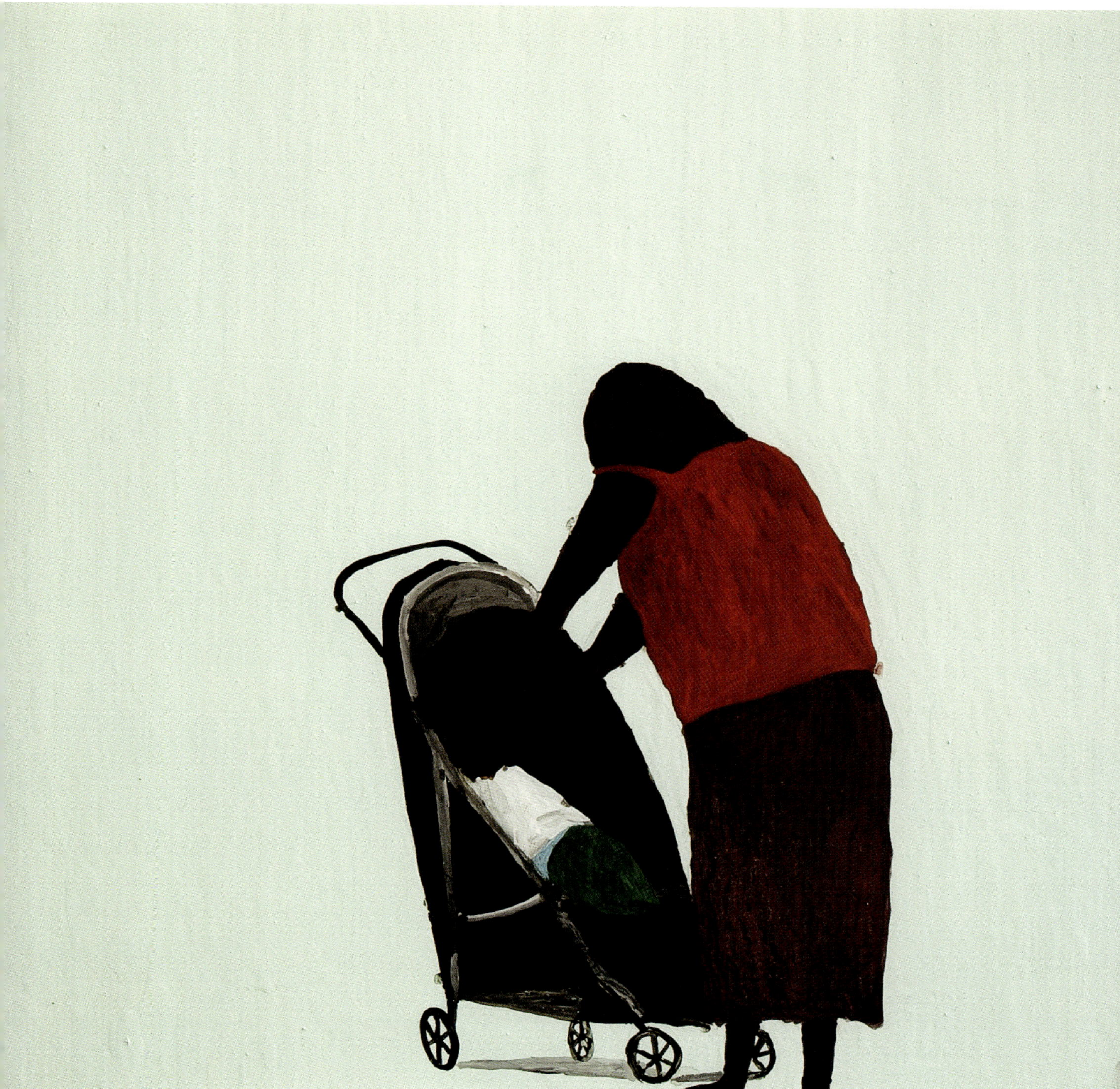

Patrick Pound

Patrick reminds me of the scientists setting out to map the entire human genome . . . Pat seems similarly bent on mapping that unfathomable continent commonly called the 'human condition', a cliché which will undoubtedly appal Pat but seems to be appropriate here.

His 'maps' are vast collections of found images clipped from newspapers, sourced on the internet, discovered in junk shops and filed under increasingly random and eccentric organising principles like 'people eating', 'thumb over lens', and one of my favourites, 'wind'. (Bill Sutton painted the wind and people would ask him, 'How do you do that, paint the wind?' Bill, dry as ever, said, 'Oh, you know . . . flat grass, bent trees, streaky clouds.')

I'm not sure how these collections of Pat's began; did he say, 'Here's a great image of someone with arms outstretched!' and then, 'Oh, here's another one!' And, 'Hey . . . !' Of course there was a lot more going on than that but I suspect he couldn't have imagined from the outset what a self-defining monolith he was beginning to author!

Seeing all these random people united by such tiny individually insignificant actions carries a strange poetic weight, a weight of evidence always hovering on the edge of meaning.

Patrick Pound
Portrait of the Wind – detail
2010, giclee photographic print on rag paper
800 x 1530 mm

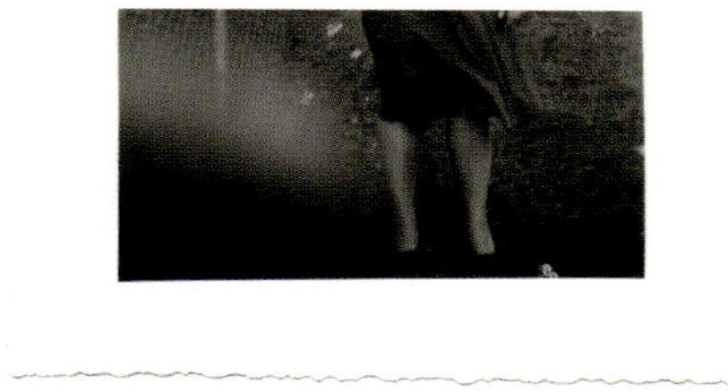

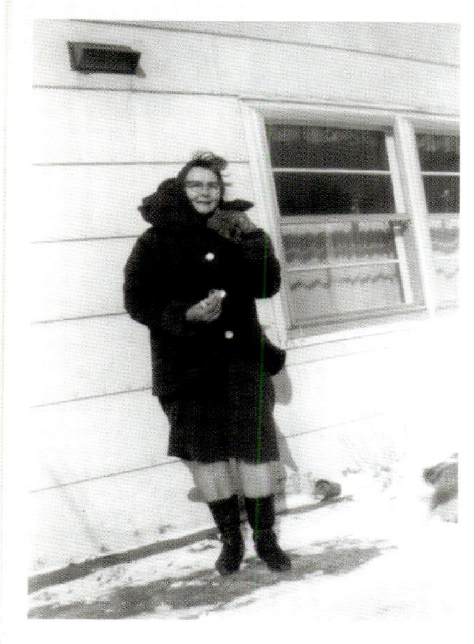

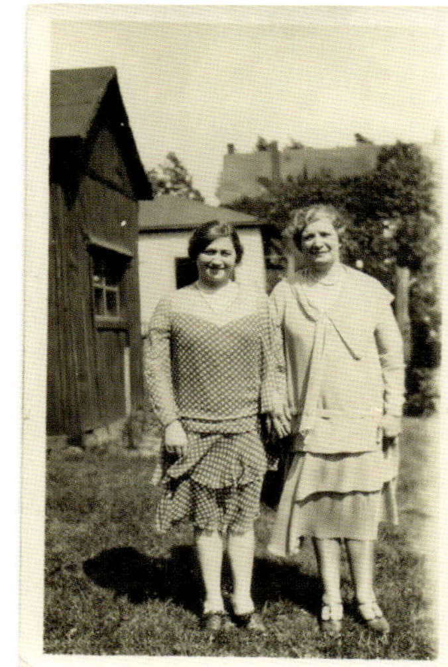

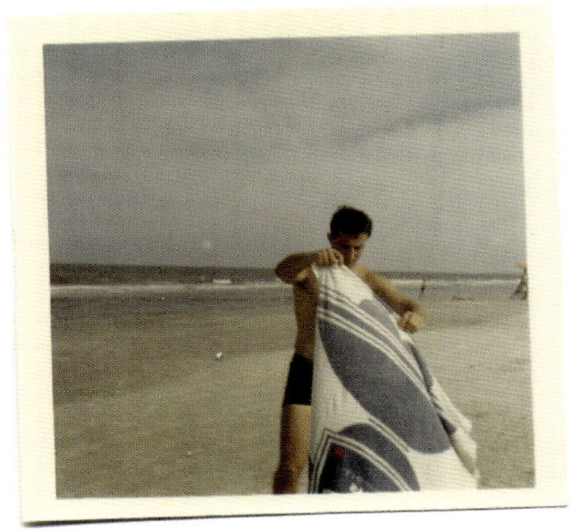

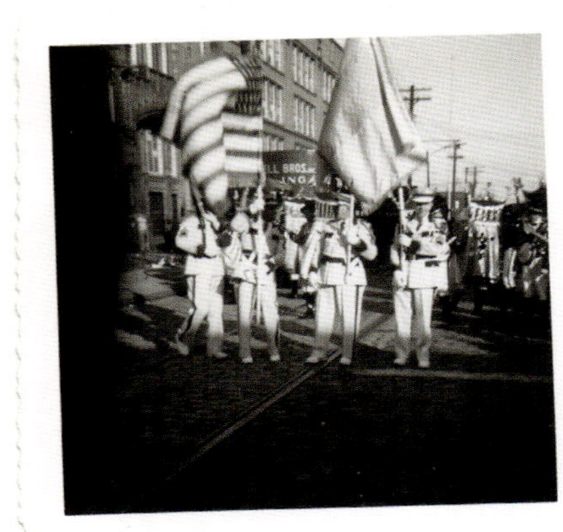

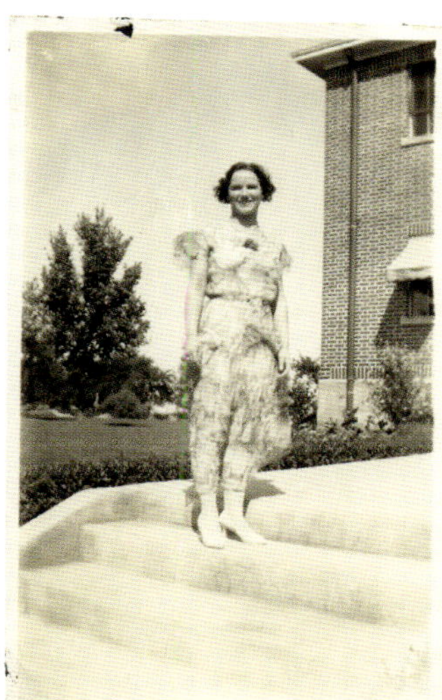

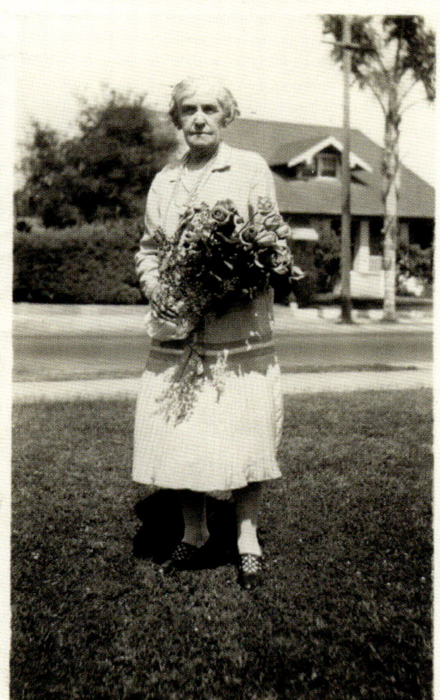

aug. 11 - 1928

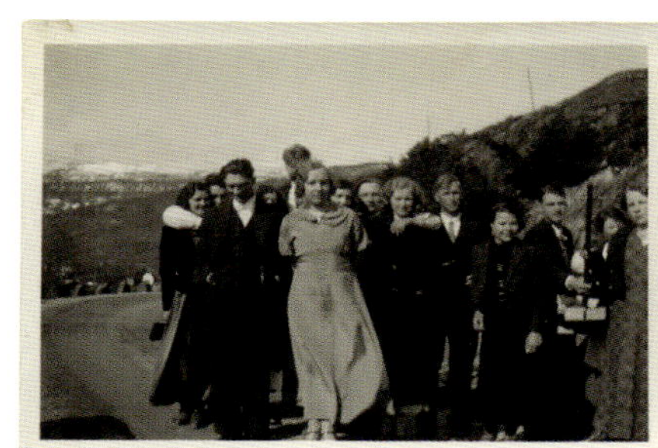

Jude Rae

I met Jude when she came to Elam for a visiting lecturer stint back in the '90s. This was when she was painting the large studies of twisted linen, white on white with a fascinating soft, feathery brushstroke (which didn't alert me to her strong socialist/feminist agenda, a bit of a learning curve for me there!).

We lost touch after that but I've followed her work closely ever since, some of it unfortunately by reproductions because those large charcoal drawings of interiors she did during the Frances Hodgkins residency look singularly impressive.

It's a bit of a challenge deciding on the one image to sum up her single-minded powers of observation and her amazing work ethic. I've gone with *SL 225*, because it's the one my mind keeps returning to every time I sit down to my list. This dedication to seeking the sublime in the ordinary generates a strange feeling of moral uplift somehow, choosing to 'represent' the material world with what I can only call reverence reminds us that this world should be enough.

Jude Rae
SL 225
2007, oil on linen
1370 x 1220 mm

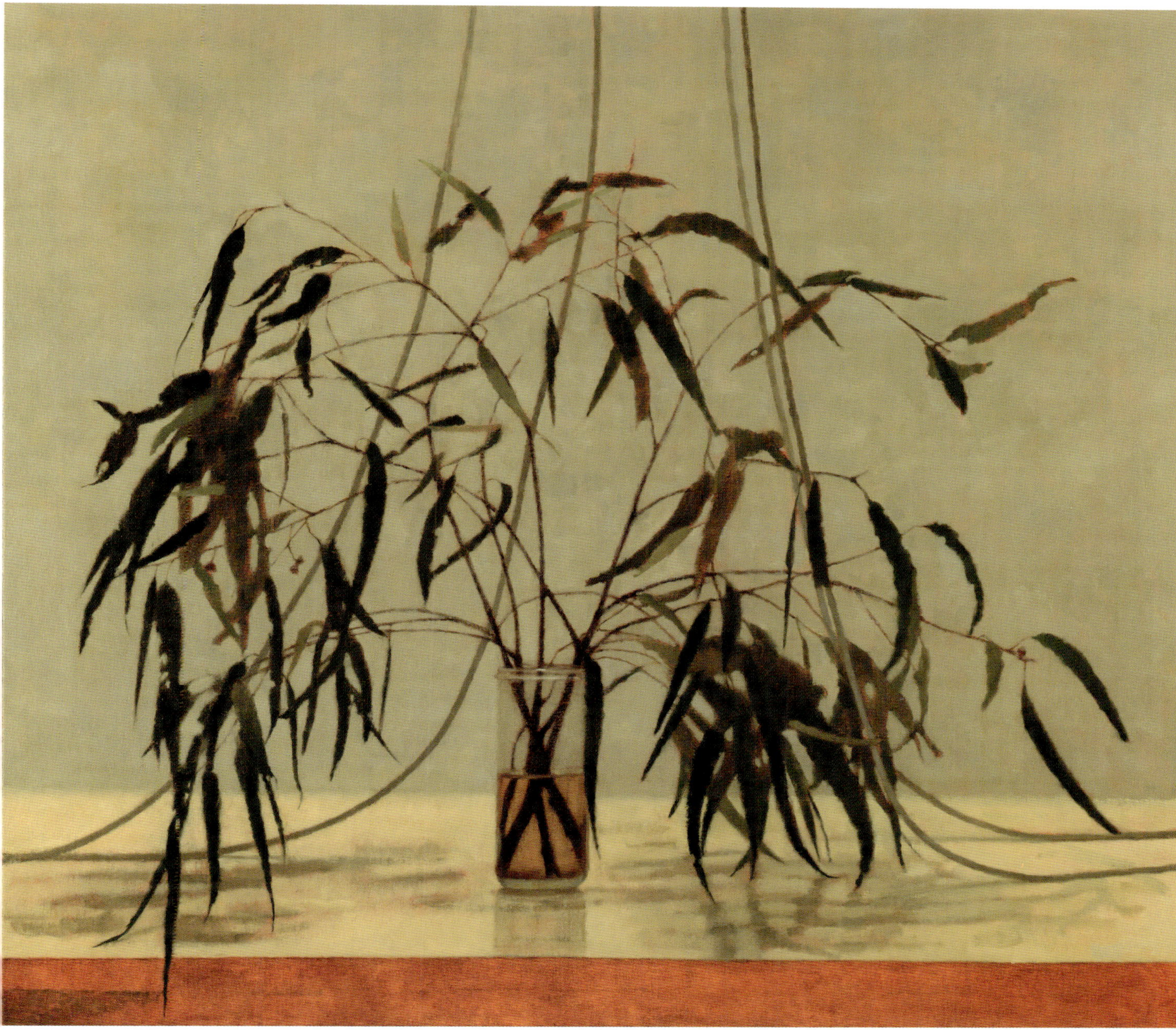

Reuben Paterson

Hell, there's a lot of ex-students in here, but you get that, I guess, hanging around Elam all those years like I did.

Reuben was always a bit of a one-off. Never quite seemed to understand that he was actually in an institution and not in some sort of art holiday camp. Once he enthusiastically suggested that he accompany the staff on their visit to his studio for the end of year assessment, so he could 'guide us through it'!! He was painting with expando-foam at the time and thought we might have a problem understanding it – ha ha! And sometimes it WAS a bit difficult to tell where the studio stopped and his paintings started.

He's still the same . . . serious fun, though now he seems to be a bit more organised. Hell, you'd have to be to accomplish half of what Reuben gets up to!

Reuben Paterson
Estrous
2009/10, glitter and synthetic polymer paint on canvas
2000 x 2000 mm

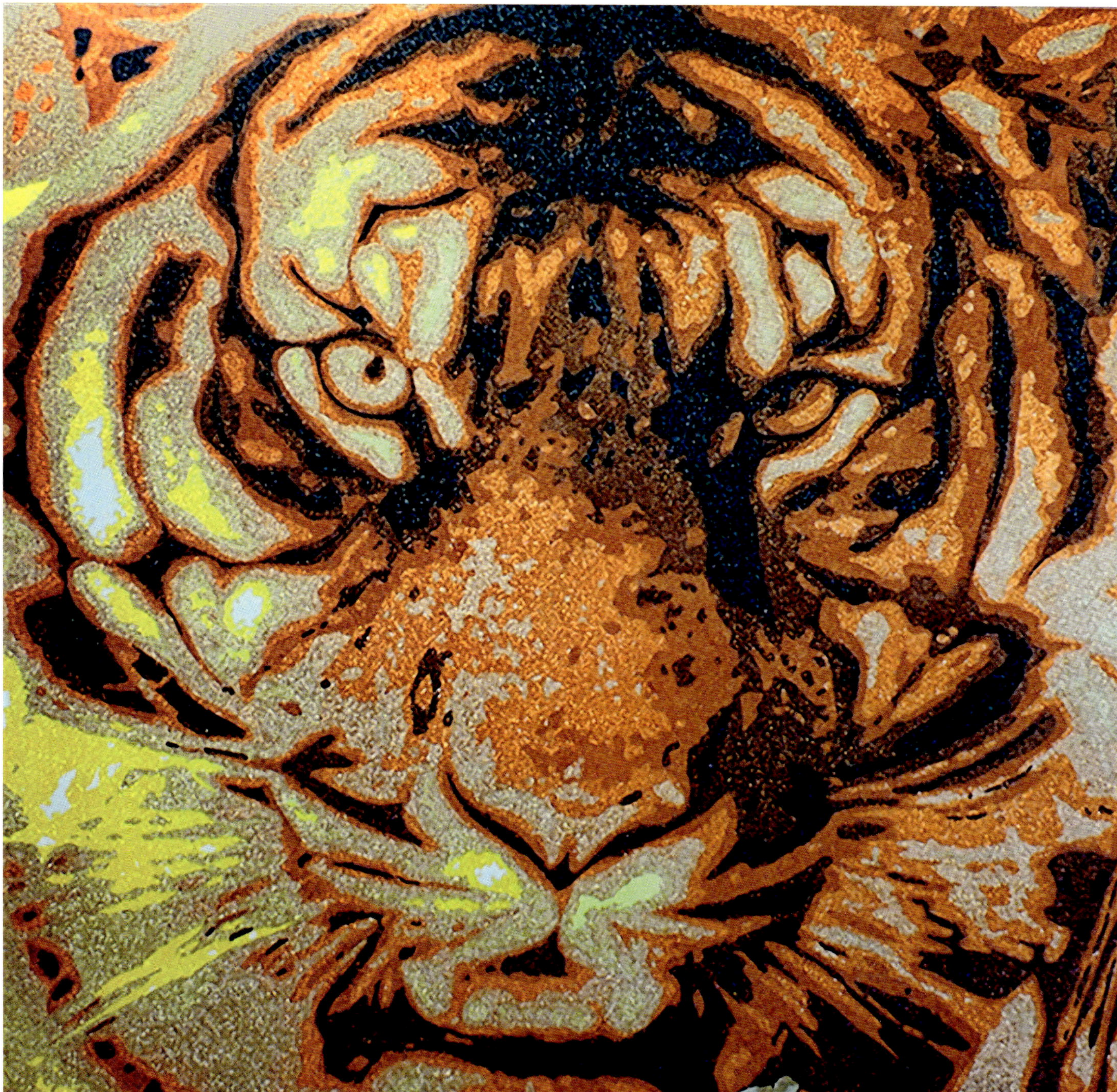

James Robinson

Largely self-taught I think, James came out of a punk/grunge/drug culture that initially alienated more people than it attracted, angst on that level of raw intensity not being particularly fashionable at the time . . . it still isn't!

But James persisted, slashing and hacking, stitching and ripping, plotting and clotting, pouring out his heart and soul. And somewhere in all the paint dribbles, nail heads and tattered diary collages it started to come together as a cohesive and mediated aesthetic. Which it has to at some point because all the passion in the world is no use to you if you can't corral it into some eloquent system, projected with a knowingness that says, 'Yes, I know it looks like chaos, but it's meant to be this way.' There are no accidents.

James Robinson
Traveller
2009, mixed media
on canvas
900 x 900 mm (approx)

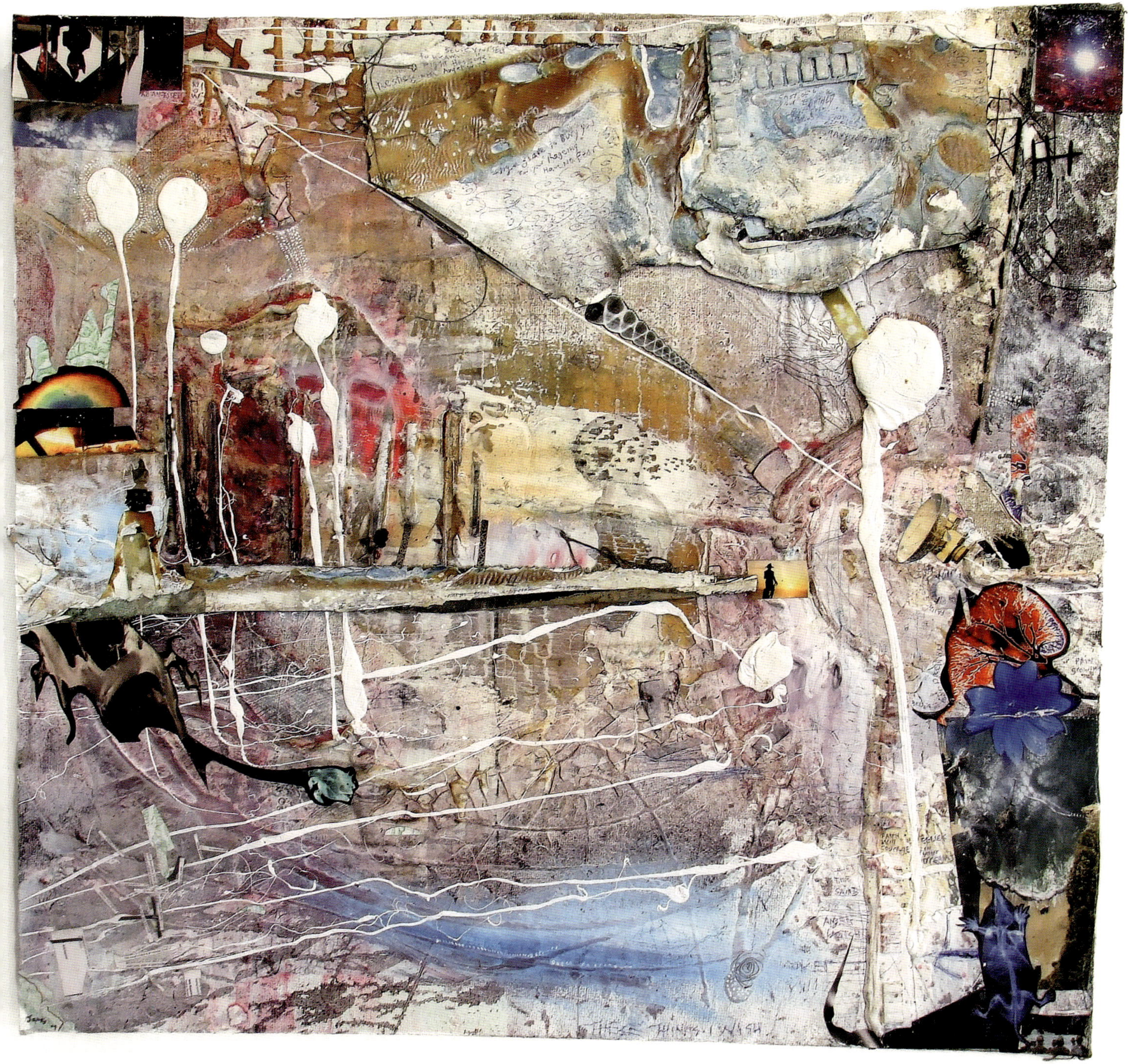

Des Helmore

I was at art school with Des, a couple of years behind him but through mysterious and fortuitous circumstances I got caught up in the heady world of the senior beards . . . got taken up.

Des seemed to be the deepest of all of them, seemed to have already graduated from somewhere else. All that quiet abstract pondering, I couldn't believe he knew what he was doing because I certainly didn't. But I do now.

He crept up on all of us, after a gap of 30 or so years, figuring it out, lost in science and the world of entomological analysis and recording. Honing the skills of observation and patient description.

I love the strangely dense atmosphere in Des's work . . . pictorial noir, a midnight passage through an industrial wasteland without any finger-pointing or admonishing subtext. In fact he seems to prefer this Ishmael-like overview.

There's a little of LS Lowry in Des's works somehow; a completely different formal outcome but the same sense of a hermetic private world that looks like it could be more substantial than this one, but you couldn't possibly imagine how, or if you'd even want to be there. But it's the pondering on all this that gives them their edge.

Des Helmore
String Theory,
2010, oil on board
480 x 617 mm

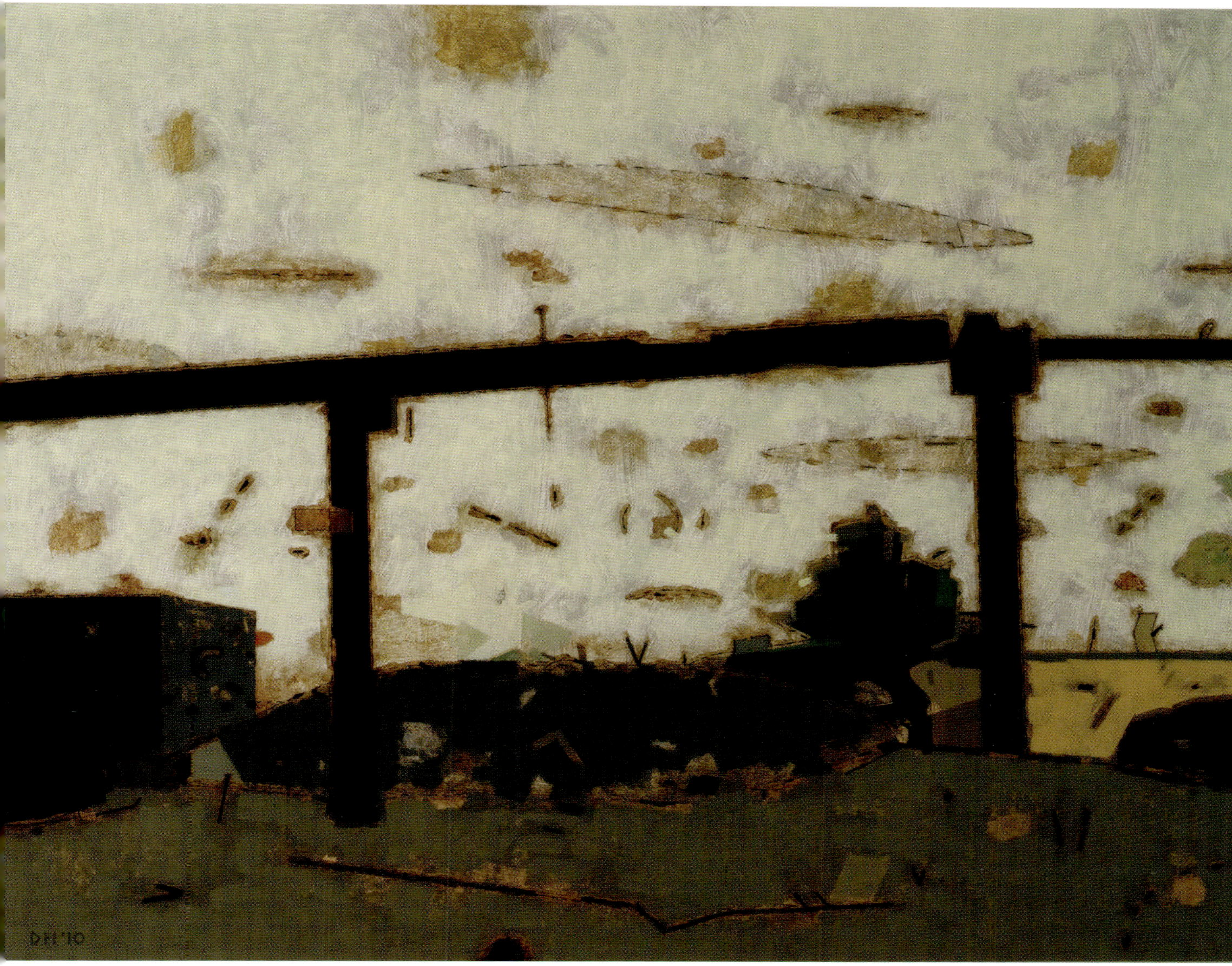
DH '10

Michael Harrison

There's an interesting thing happening at the moment with content and detail . . . with the actual amount of mind-boggling minutiae that a painting can contain. It's an exciting swerve back, almost, to complex and challenging compositions such as Delacroix's *Death of Sardanapalus* where the attention to detail takes your breath away, where the build-up of detail is almost the entire point. Labours of love.

After a very long period where massed detail on that scale was regarded as somehow decadent – 'knitting', as a colleague scornfully called it – it seems to be making a determined comeback. Very large, very complex paintings, painstakingly built.

Which brings me to Michael, not because he does that, quite the opposite in fact, but because his intimate and enigmatic conundrums have been credited with inspiring this fascination with infinite and ambiguous narrative detail.

I find this incredibly interesting, and it actually gives me something concrete to write about here because I find Michael's modest musings very difficult to expound on without somehow betraying their resistance to a reading . . . their ineffability . . . on any level that I can relate to. I mean, I get it, and understand why he generates so much respect and attention, but I don't really get it. And it would take me a whole book to explain what I mean by that, which pretty much explains their significance.

Michael Harrison
Palace of Thought
2006–09, acrylic and pencil on paper
209 x 297 mm

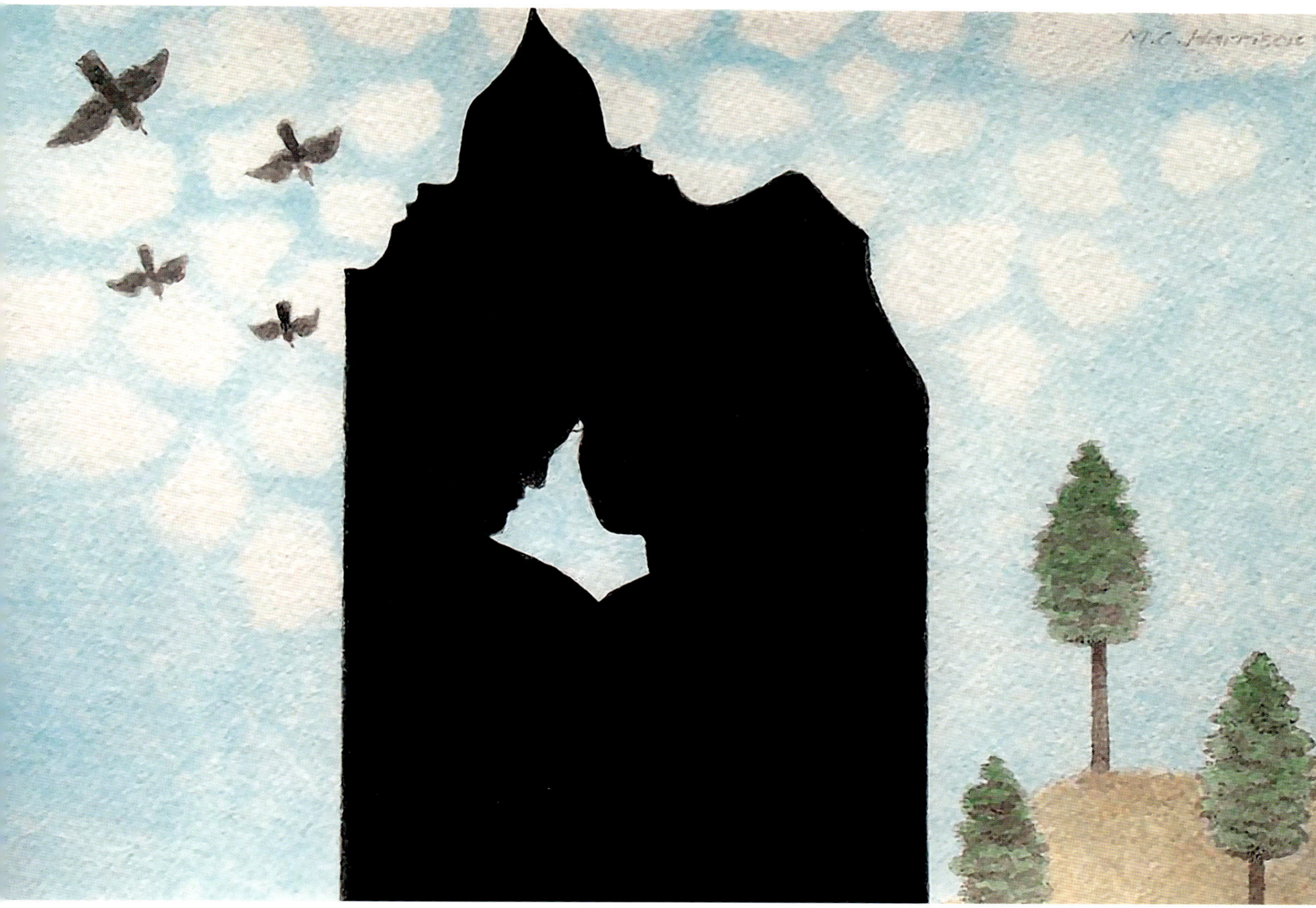
M.C. Harrison

Andrew McLeod

I love newness, not just Toilet Duck brand-newness – though there's a certain fascination in that too – but the newness that emerges in a practice which you might think is entirely mined out and on the verge of total collapse. This occurs when time and space shift significantly and all the raw material rolls over exposing fresh information. It's another manifestation of the laws of unintended consequences – and Andrew is certainly that!

Andrew had a peculiar start at art school, falling foul of a space and numbers game, and ended up pretty much teaching himself in an odd sort of overflow annex 'down the road'. I mention this by way of explaining the strange chewed-over look and awkward tackiness of his early paintings. And I REALLY mean tacky – insects, dust and lint would stick to their gummy surfaces, lending them a sly veneer of 'pulled-out-from-under-the-bed' anarchy. Whether this was circumstance or just plain stance I'm not sure, probably a bit of both, but these props quickly faded as Andrew got up to speed and forgot himself in the sheer practicalities of producing his large and complex compositions.

That sense of newness is still very much there, of course, making the ordinary extraordinary, going where we've been before but in ways we could never have anticipated. I think art's ability to prove to ourselves that we can do this – constantly reinvent ourselves – is almost its primary function.

Andrew McLeod
Seascape
2009, oil on linen
180 x 200 mm

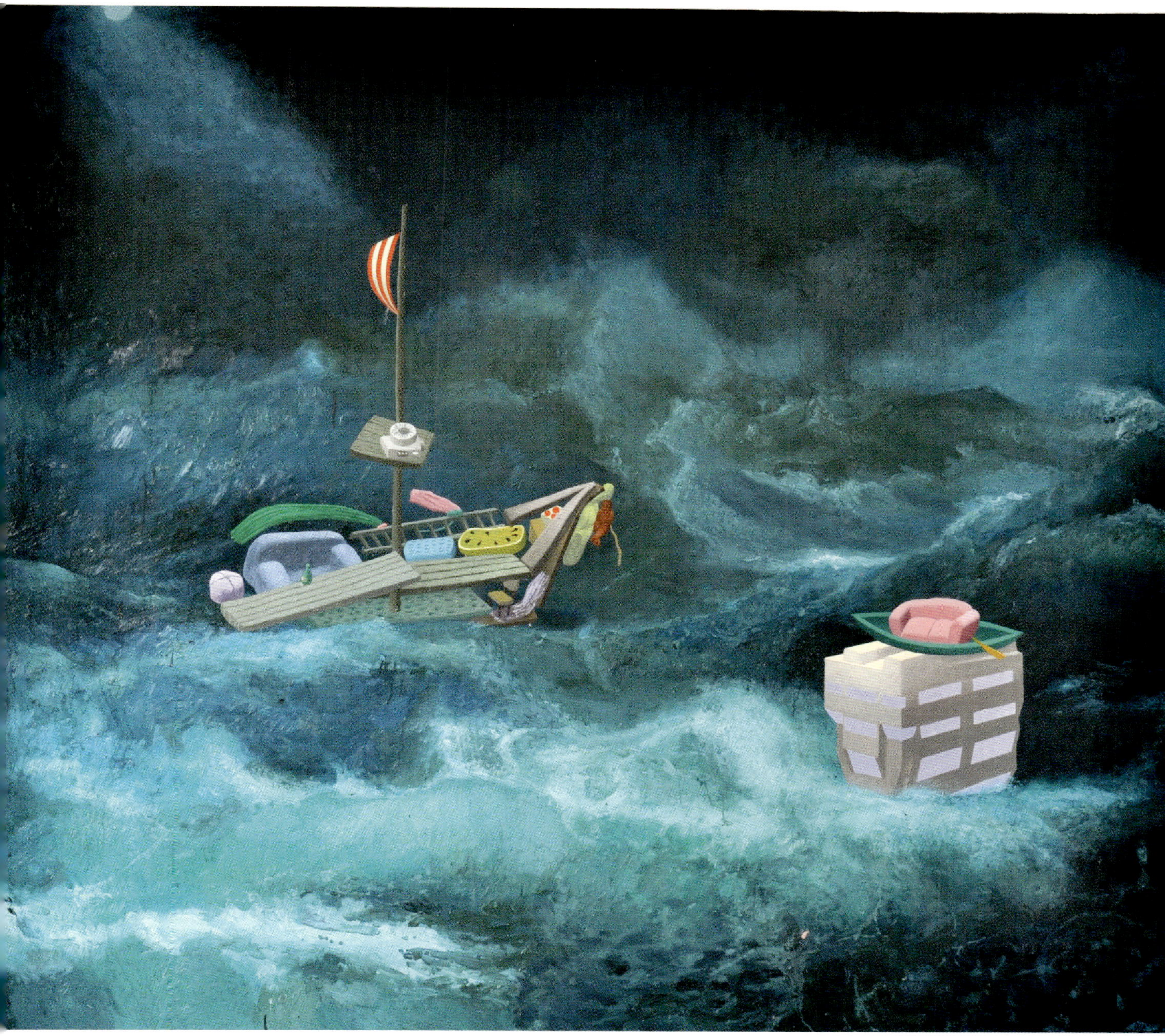

Rohan Wealleans

He's a handful this one, fearless and frightening, pushing his schtick to the point of implosion at every opportunity. 'Too much' doesn't seem to be in his vocabulary.

I made a terrible gaffe one year on a Wallace Award panel when I judged his entry (a large bulletin board collage thing) as a bit unoriginal, clever but not that clever, until a disappointed Rohan informed me later that the entire thing – every bus ticket, power bill and shopping list – was made with paint, not painted with paint, MADE with paint. Insane really, and the work would probably have been a contender if I'd been able to figure it out.

His work is always a surprise, a challenge, and if this book wasn't such a folksy overview I could show you that he can be a right little shocker too. Rohan does incredible things with paint, just about everything in fact except paint with it.

Rohan Wealleans
Squid Shock Demise
2010, acrylic on panel
1200 x 800 mm

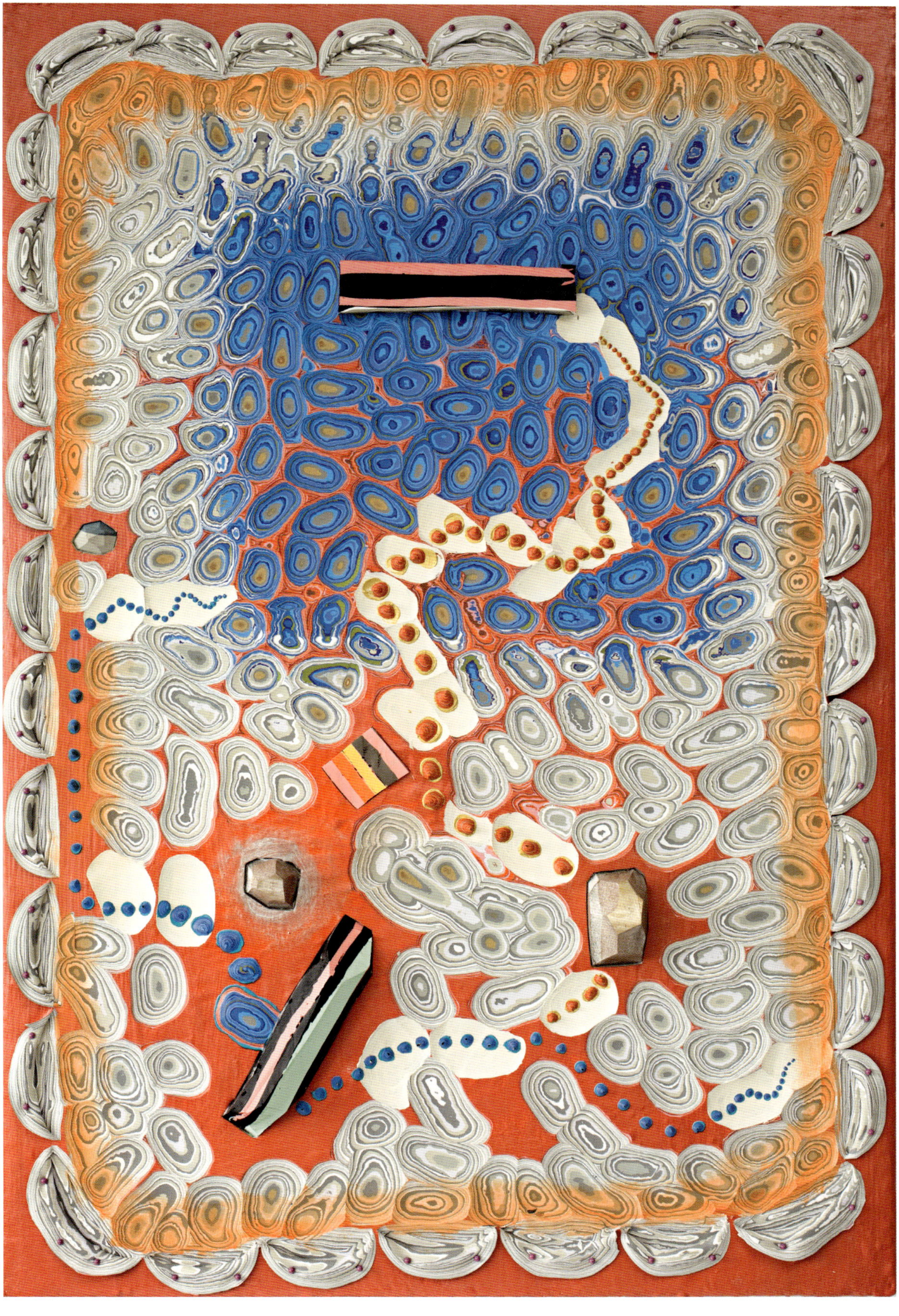

Saskia Leek

Saskia snuck onto the scene in the early 1990s with a knowing sort of op-shop primitivism that was fascinating in its casually projected diffidence delivered with such a tough art-savvy confidence.

Saskia's complete immersion into the character of the enigmatic 'art-waif' . . . easy to copy and to appropriate into fashionable applications but very difficult to carry out with any sense of originality and authenticity . . . was instantly convincing. The are-you-for-real thing being as slippery as the meaning of her faux naïve little folktales.

Over time her work has focused more on the gap between realism and abstraction, the relationship between power and powerlessness, sentiment and cynicism, without losing that curious made-in-the-bedroom quality which distinguished it in the first place.

Saskia Leek
Untitled
2009, oil on board

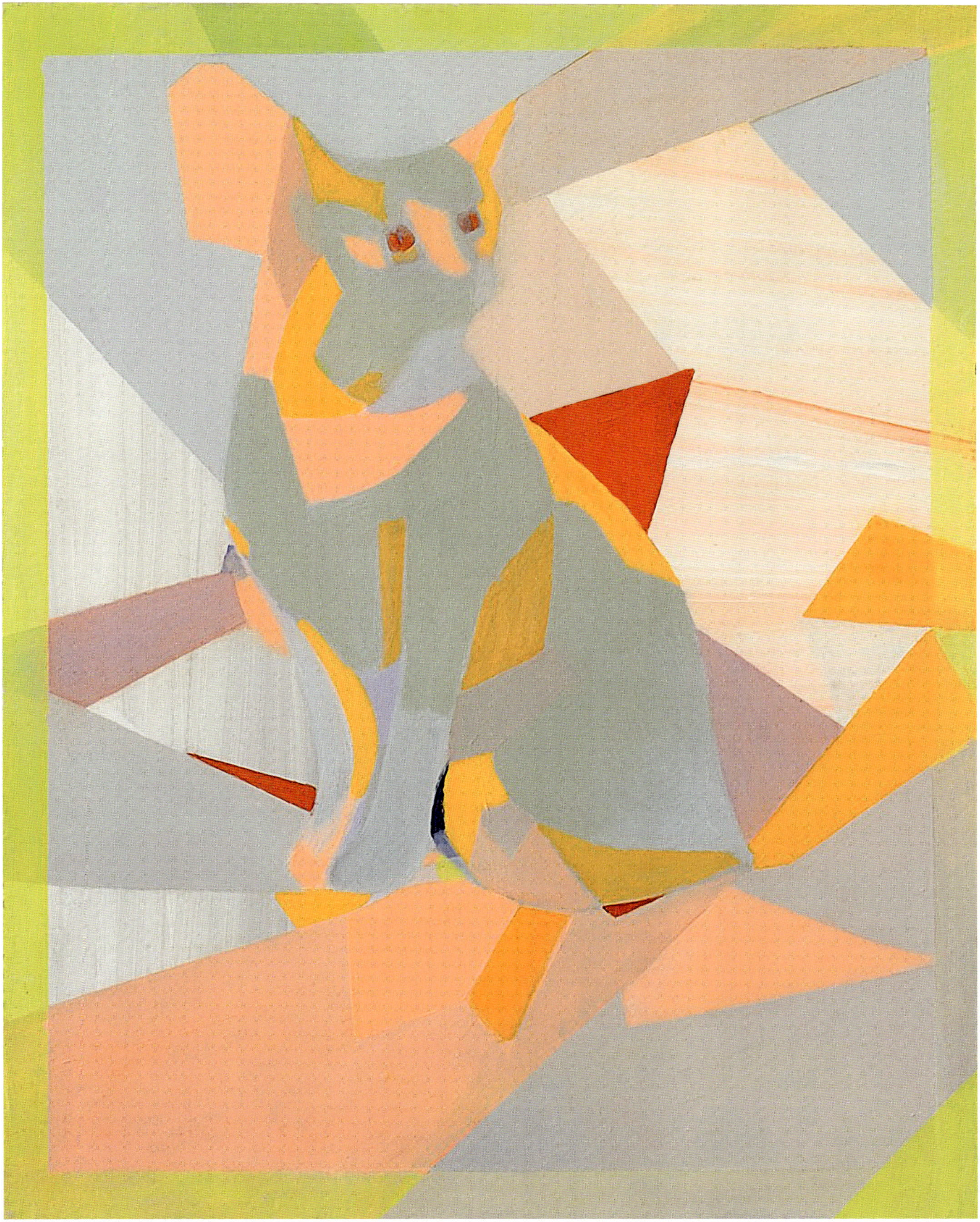

Liz Maw

Here's another artist who seemed to appear fully formed on the scene. And again, she takes the screamingly obvious 'Don't go there' and makes it brand-new.

How you do that of course is a pretty subtle trick and requires a profound belief in one's point of view, and a deep animal cunning that can interpret the zeitgeist and intuit that the context is right for the revamp of a given genre. Again there's a lot of 'moving on by getting it wrong' going on here.

Painters, musicians and designers will often confess to a love for the 'unfashionable' art forms of their predecessors and, having nothing to lose by going there at an early stage of their career, will dive in and make it work through the genuine nature of their enquiry and their natural artistic ability to transmute the material despite its dodgy origins.

And there's no denying the dodgy origins of Liz's references, Westie auto-customising, *Woman's Day*'s trashy obsessions, but she certainly makes it work for her!

Liz Maw
The Immaculate Conception
2005, oil on board
1500 x 1280 mm

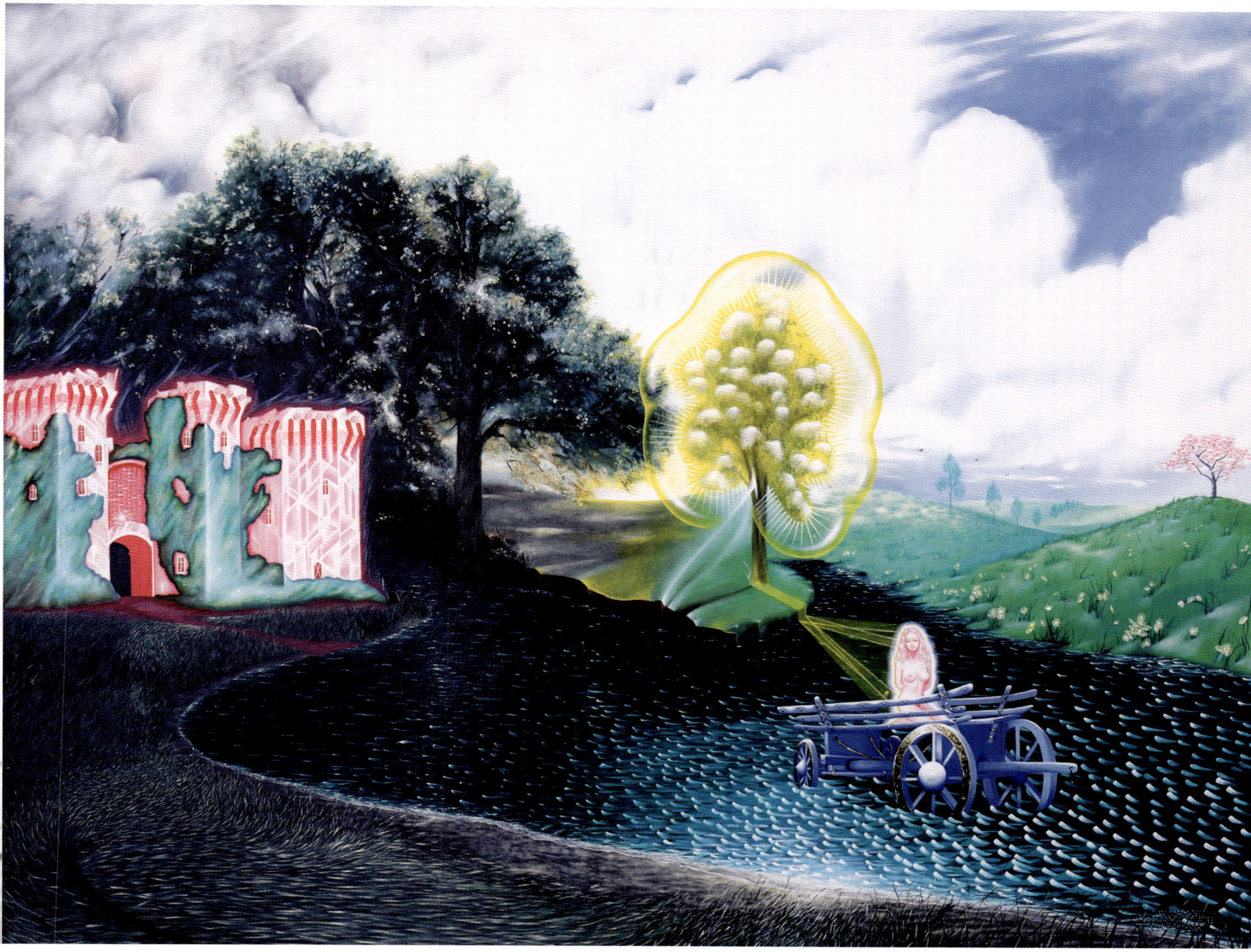

Matthew Couper

Matt must have been Mexican in another life. His immersion in the culture and tradition of Mexican votive painting is so thorough and deeply felt that he seems to have gone way beyond influence and come out the other side with a parallel universe all of his own.

This is a man who obviously lives to work, and he must have one hell of an interior life to be able to draw on such a seemingly endless source of tangled and tortuous narratives. With amazing leaps of scale and a randomly linked cast of characters, Matt moves at a frenetic pace that keeps him one step ahead of the responsibility of explaining himself. Keep moving, so they can't draw a bead on you.

Like the original votives themselves you really need to own more than one to get, at least, a 'sense' of meaning out of them. I can understand why he published a book on his work, even calling it *The Museum of Inherent Vice*, because you have to become part of it, you have to be a club member to enter. And, unlike Groucho's famous comment, 'I wouldn't want to join any club who'd have me', this is one institution that would definitely be worth the ticket.

Matthew Couper
Half and Half
2010, oil and collage
on canvas
1680 x 1280 mm

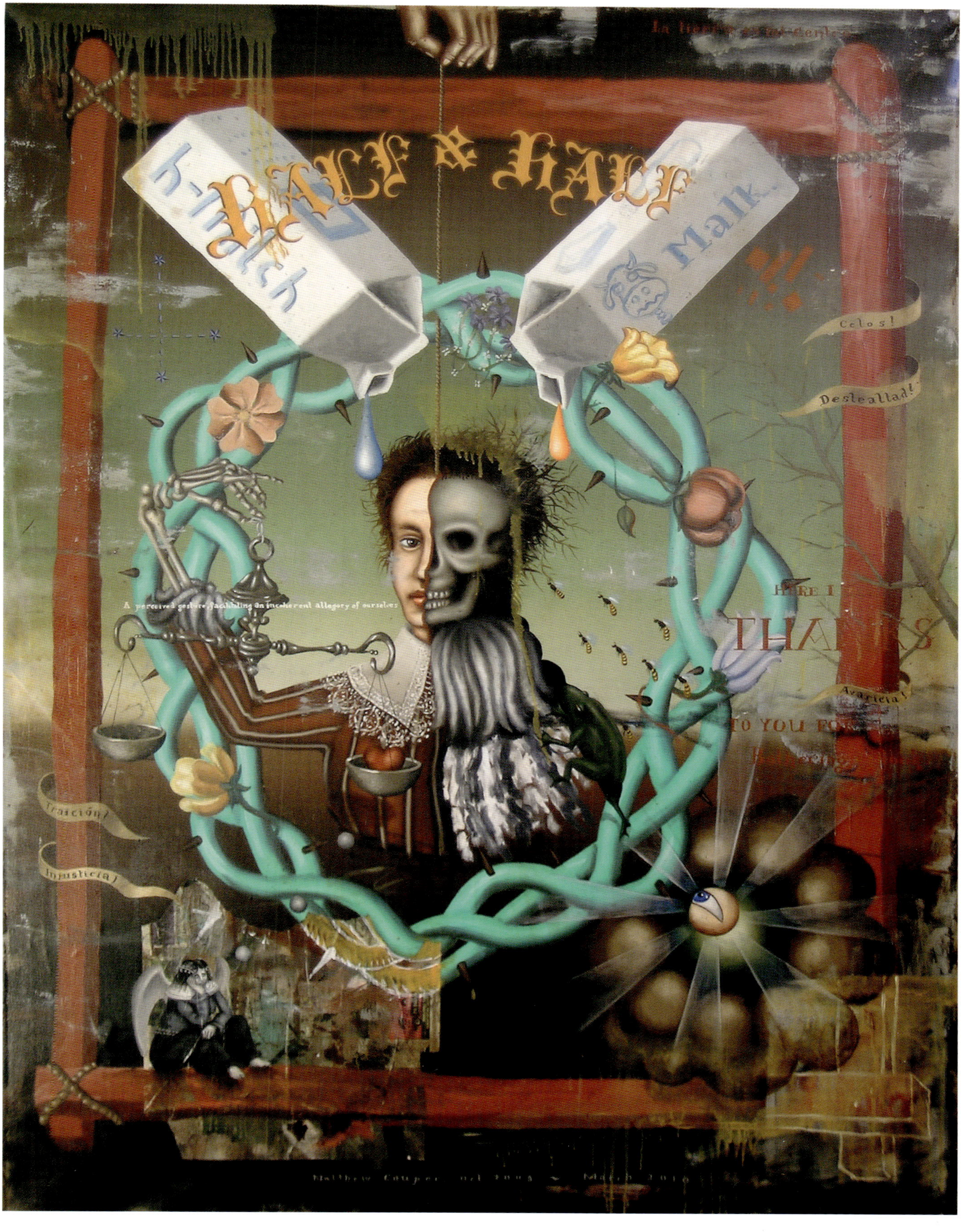
HALF & HALF
Malk
Celos!
Deslealtad!
HERE I
Avaricia!
Traición!
Injusticia!
A perceived gesture facilitating an incoherent allegory of ourselves

Heather Straka

Sometimes you have to wonder about this business, how it works, how it all just keeps on coming. I remember Heather at Elam, hiding behind her fringe, not giving much away. And then they graduate, slip away into the 'real world'. Some fade away, and some come back and surprise you.

Heather first surprised us all with her immaculately rendered crazed-porcelain toilet stalls. I thought they carried a slightly forced metaphor but they boiled with enough sexual subtexts to keep the writers happy and put Heather on the map.

She followed her plumbing portraits with a much more, to me, substantial exercise in postcolonial power fudging and the curious role of ancestor portraiture. Are they paintings? Or does their secondary role as historical aide-mémoire render their actual plastic values redundant?

But these 'plastic values' are what shone through more and more as Heather went deeper and deeper into the phenomenon of illusion and 'mood'. Of course I had to include this work because of the obvious link back to that Tretchikoff I talked about in the intro. Dangerous stuff this, flirting with sentiment and craft. Fortunately Heather's naturally subversive and perverse point of view means she'll always be long gone when the trap is sprung.

Heather Straka
Still Life #23
2010, oil on canvas
470 x 600 mm

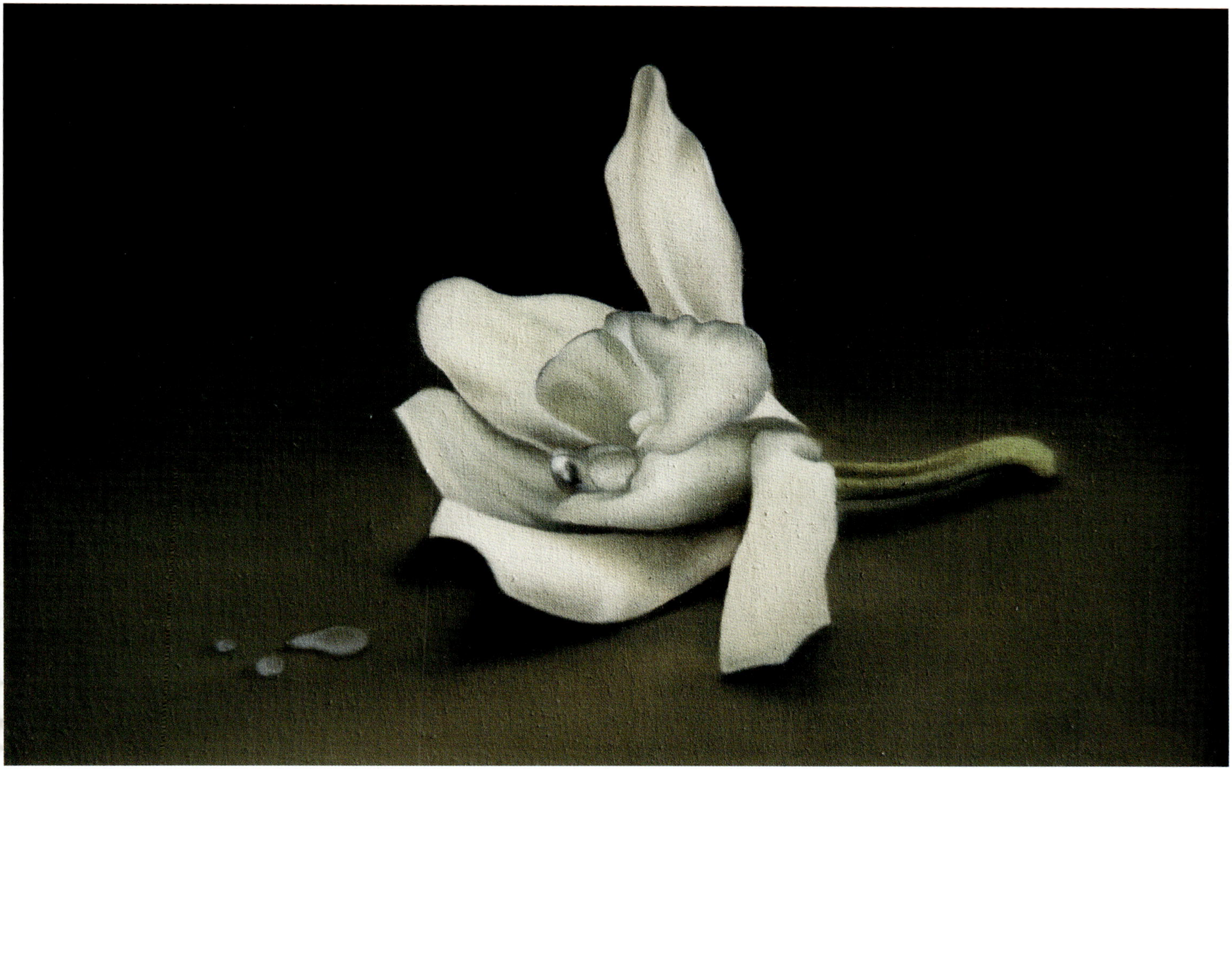

John Walsh

John fell into this 'enriched turps wash' technique early in the piece and has parlayed it into a very impressive means of communication. By perfecting this 'apply and remove' method of ragging and brushing on slick surfaces, he has evolved the perfect vehicle for expressing his own exploration of the myths and legends of Aotearoa. I say 'his own' because by extrapolating the received information out into a mythic universe of his own making he has managed to avoid the trap of mere illustration.

By hovering in this personal space, one step away from the literal, John has been able to elevate his atmospheric compositions to a point where they don't rely on any given source to provide them with meaning, while at the same time creating a narrative hook by appearing to do just that.

Here the meaning resides in the execution of the image as much as it does in the image itself.

John Walsh
Motuhia te Pito
2003, oil on board
1185 x 1440 mm

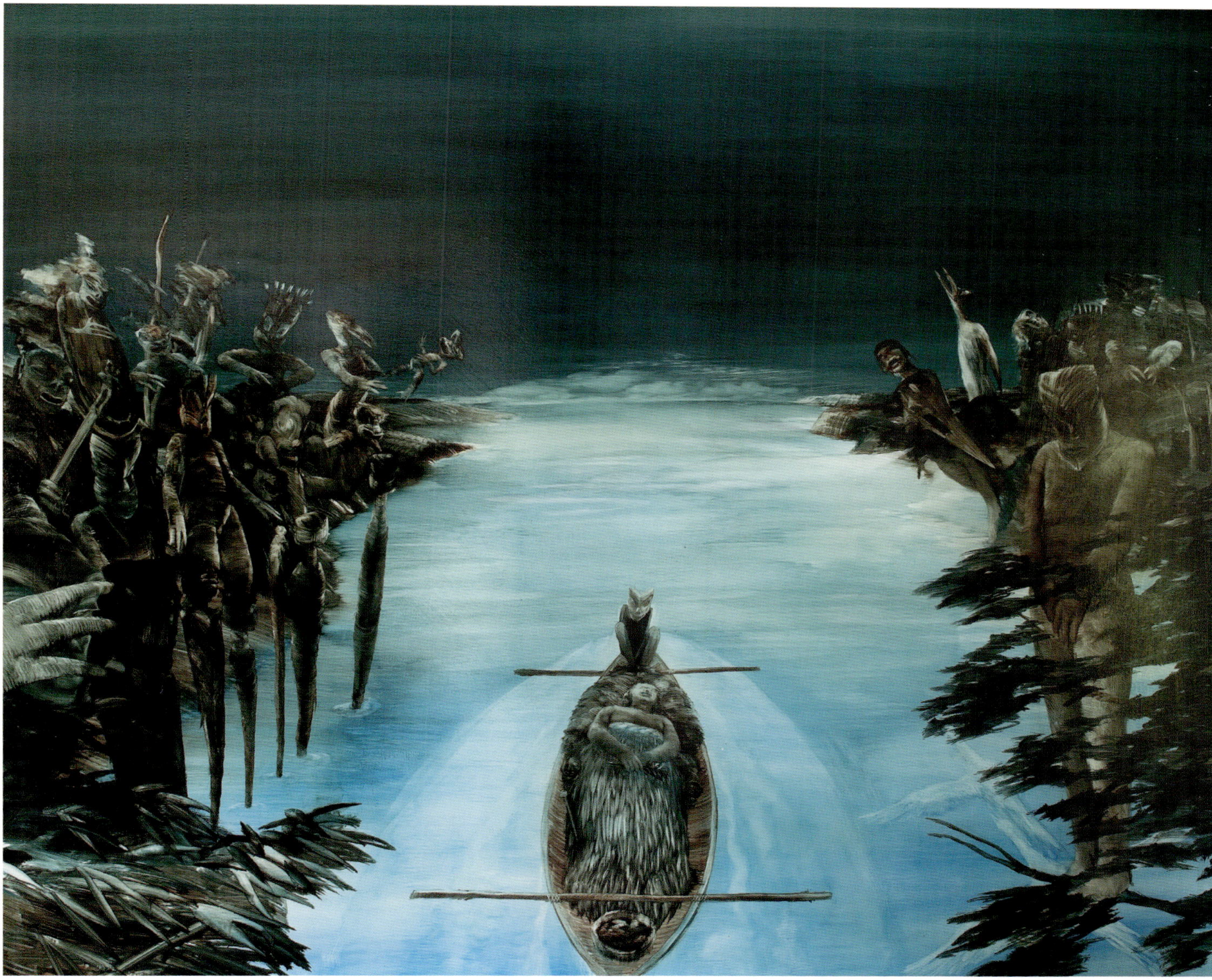

Michael Hight

Here's another intriguing career swerve. Michael appeared on the scene back in the 1980s as a very precocious young man, gluing wheelbarrows to large trans-avantgarde canvases . . . pouring on the pitch. Slowly he tightened them up, calmed them down to very tasty abstract collage/ constructions using resins and found materials.

Having got that nailed, he started flipping over to traditionally rendered landscapes, going there to see how it felt, I suspect. Then someone commissioned him to paint every beehive in New Zealand, and by the time he'd finished that his skills, and no doubt his reference files, had become so sophisticated that he seems to now be on a mission to render the whole ball of wax, reclaim the picturesque, one rusty truck in the long grass at a time!

Practice makes perfect. Be careful what you wish for, Michael.

Michael Hight
Awatere Valley
2010, oil on linen
1115 x 1825 mm

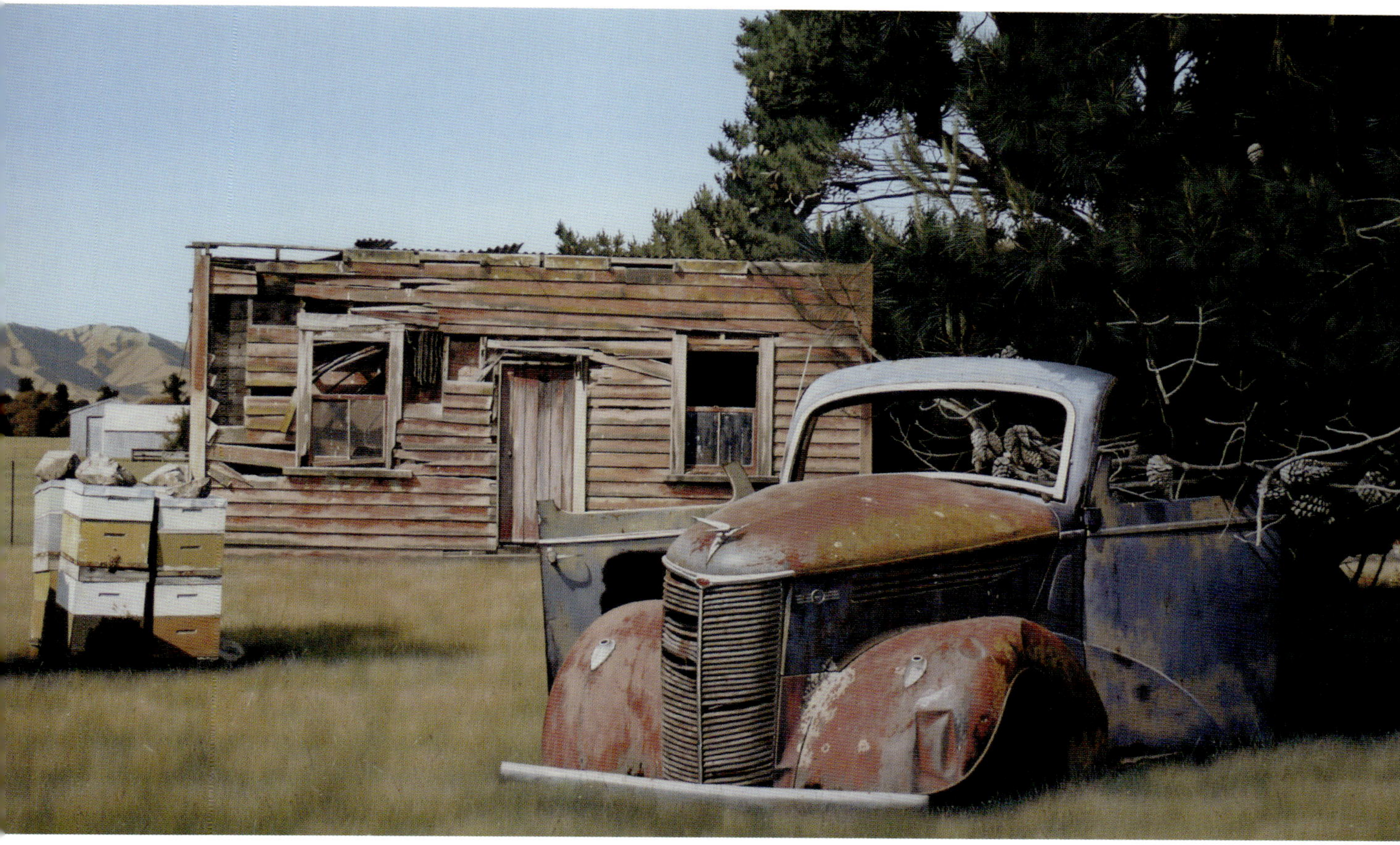

Brendon Wilkinson

Brendon seems to have jumped from the micro to the macro overnight, or so it appears to me who has only half an eye on what's going on.

Known for his obsessive and ambiguous miniature dioramas that switch weirdly back and forth from the apparently real, to the apparently not, Brendon has now found a way to spread this bizarre and cock-eyed universe over some impressively large canvases.

We don't do large and obsessive detail like this in New Zealand as a rule – something about our background of knocking things off and moving on, and a history of modest studios and zero economics – but a new generation of artists shows every sign of shedding any such cultural restraints.

Calling on body-shop art, crystal-shop mysticism, alien sci-fi storyboarding and Gustav Klimt-like decadence, Brendon has cooked up a 2D monster as intriguing and seductive as his 3D hard-hat zones.

Brendon Wilkinson
Never Ever
2008, oil on canvas
2000 x 2130 mm

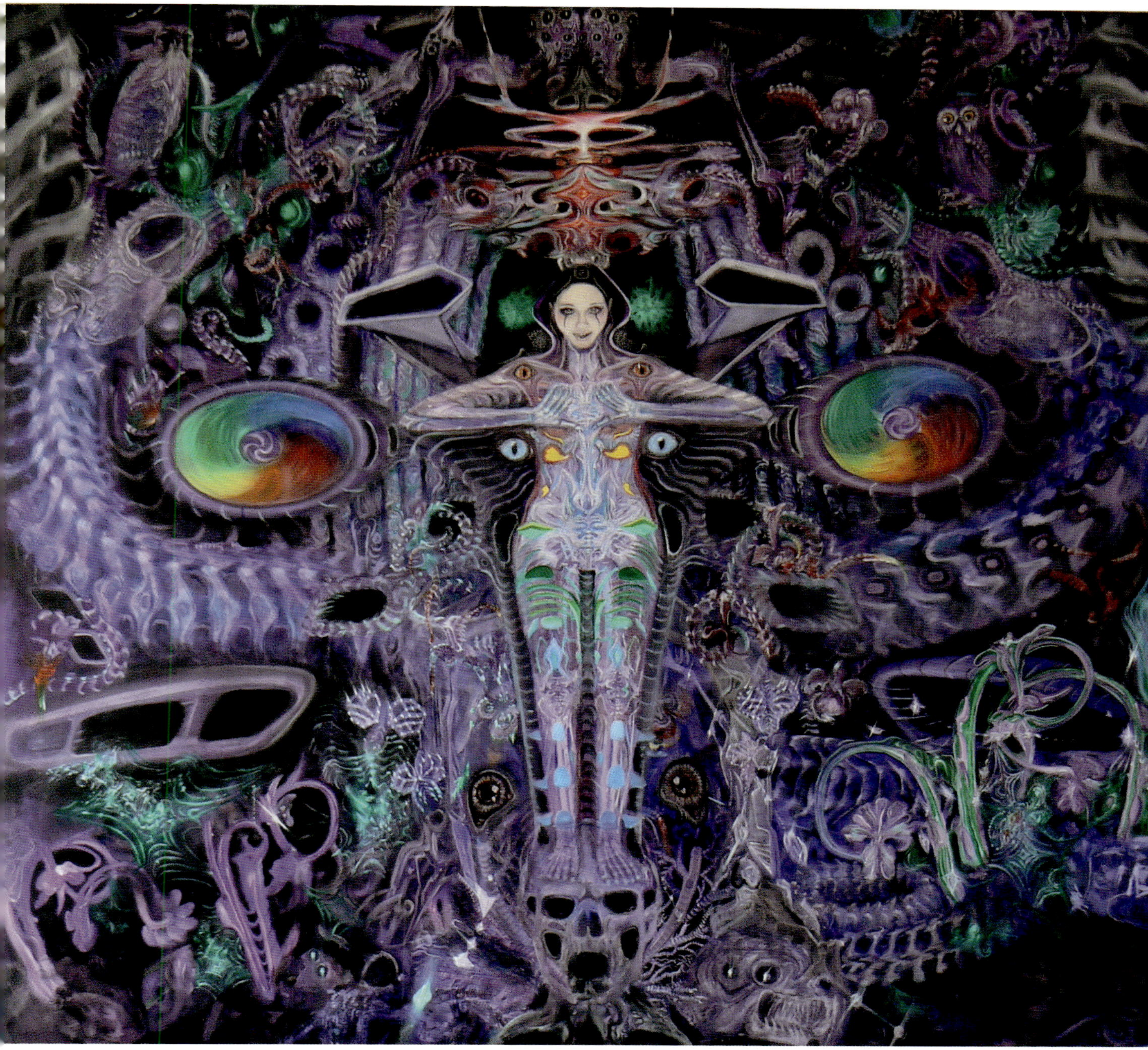

Martin Poppelwell

I've been putting this one off, the Poppelwell essay, not sure where to start with Martin. Won't start with Elam, that wouldn't work.

I read a comment from him the other day, about his new architecturally designed studio, and how the old one was so small, 'He couldn't even make his mistakes properly', which I thought summed up Martin perfectly. Cunning, contradictory, subversive, and the consummate media manipulator.

And medium manipulator: Martin has the perfect 'rightness of touch' in any discipline to which he applies himself – painting, graphics, design. He has a way of instantly sensing the system appropriate to the moment and the material. I've worked with him on a few collaborations and have always been inspired by the free and open-ended way he hits the mark.

Fast and fluid, he reinvents himself continuously within the loose parameters of his world of calculated mistakes.

Martin Poppelwell
Study for an Apricot Tree
2010, oil on canvas
1800 x 2750 mm

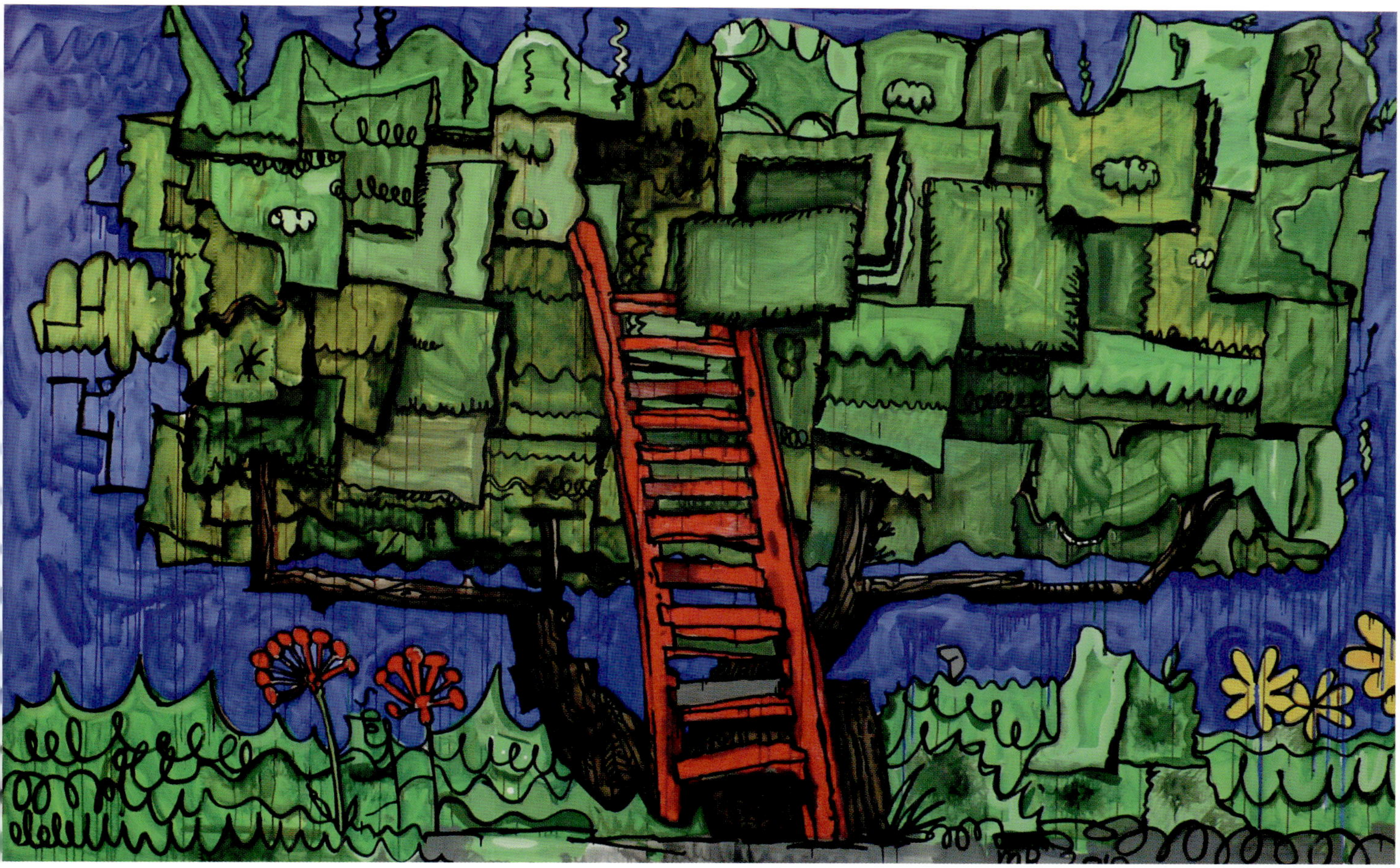

Simon Ingram

Simon was an interesting student, inhibited, I think, by a very real fear that any effort he might make to externalise what he was struggling towards internally would never measure up to his expectations. Also, the instinctive knowledge that an internally held belief, or concept, is only ever partly formed UNTIL it is externalised can create a certain stasis in the early days of the formation of an artist's philosophy.

It's quite instructive to note that Simon's ultimate solution, to date, for making that mark, was to invent a machine to do it for him! Now, of course, such is the law of unintended consequences, it's not so much about the mark as it is about the mad Heath Robinson machinery that Simon has created to make them. But the marks have their legitimacy in as much as despite our best intentions we're really only judged by the marks we leave in our wake. And lately he actually seems to have broken through to some sort of equilibrium between the machinery and the mark.

Simon Ingram
Rosnay
2011, oil on canvas
1020 x 970 mm

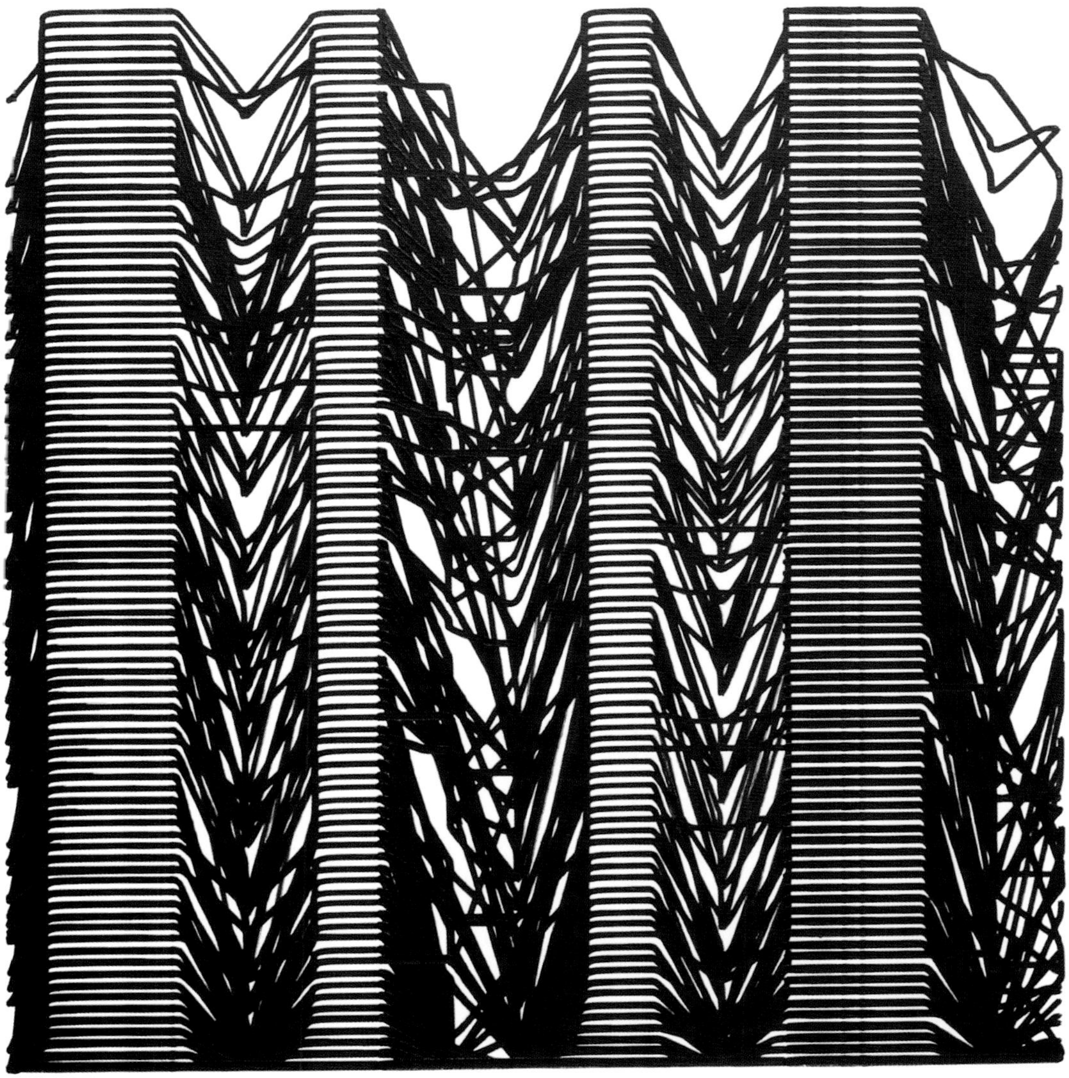

Sara Hughes

She's a dynamo, this girl! Makes me feel lazy, makes me feel I should be over there at the easel and not sitting here writing this!

Sara quite literally seemed to explode on the scene with her dynamic stencil-assisted throw-ups.

Her neo-op-art paintings looked, at first glance, as if they could be dismissed as computer-generated artefacts (which, don't get me wrong, have their place too). But that's definitely not the point that Sara was determined to make; these were PAINTINGS, and paintings they proved to be on a closer examination of the surface.

Sara's concentration on this mind-boggling trick of making the hand-made look mechanical is where, I think, the awesome fascination lies. Her drive to dig deeper, reinvent, work harder is powerfully infectious and a fabulous example of painting's refusal to lie down and die.

Sara Hughes
Oceania
2010, acrylic on linen
1000 x 800 mm

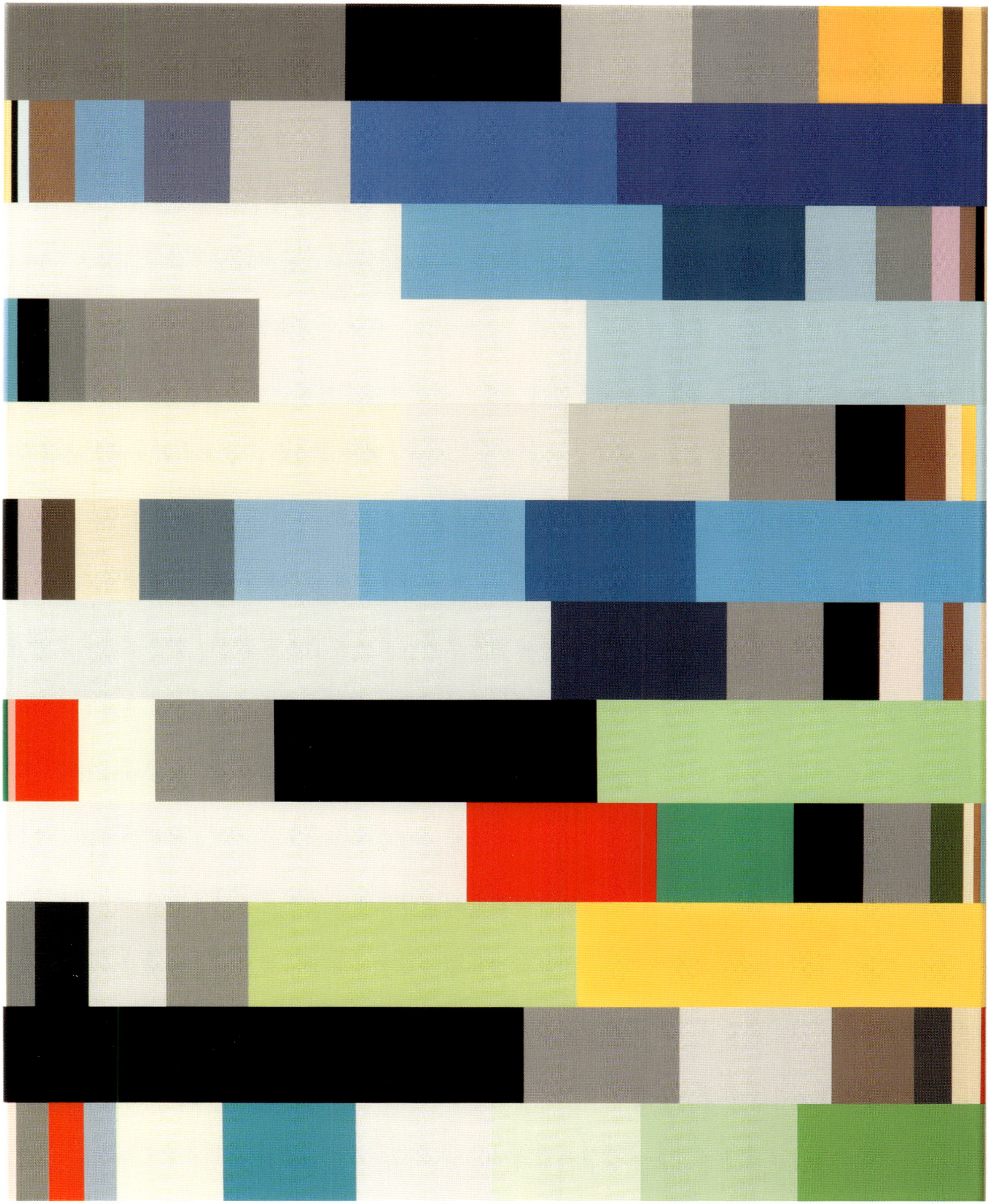

Freeman White

I wasn't going to do Freeman, but one of my contemporary pals has pulled out of the project citing conflict of interest . . . which may or may not be a polite euphemism but leaves me with a bit of a gap and I feel irresistibly drawn into the vacuum by a guilty secret that's been dogging me throughout the making of the book. Freeman represents himself on facebook with this intriguing portrait and every time I see it I wonder why I keep pushing it aside if it clings to my memory the way it does. If this book is indeed all about the image, I should be talking about this one – and talking about the curious space work like this occupies in the current 'debate'.

In fact, now that I'm warmed up, I'm going to do something else I wasn't planning on doing and that is give a group hug – to some other artists battling on in this discouraging genre: Freeman, Zarahn Southon, Sandro Kopp (and to a slightly lesser 'classical' extent, Marianne Muggeridge . . . love the portrait of the scientist Sir Paul Callaghan!).

I don't think this work is coming from that ghastly cliché, 'The Old Masters', as much as it's coming from such lateral sources as the fabulously trashy craft-meisters who rendered all those Alfred E Newman cover portraits for the 1950s *Mad* magazine. I think that just 'being here now' propels you into a pop sensibility however much you might try to Rembrandt yourself . . . IF you've got your eye on the ball and aren't just coming at it from some boorish reactionary position.

Just as Henry Miller made pornography intellectually respectable back in the '60s these artists are looking for a way to make this dodgy edifice stand up, without resorting to irony or distortion, in a very slippery and unwelcome environment. It's bloody hard to do it right, and the huge number of artists out there doing it wrong attests to that – but something is going on here. And I get a kick out of keeping an eye on it.

Freeman White
Self Portrait
2009, oil on linen
410 mm round

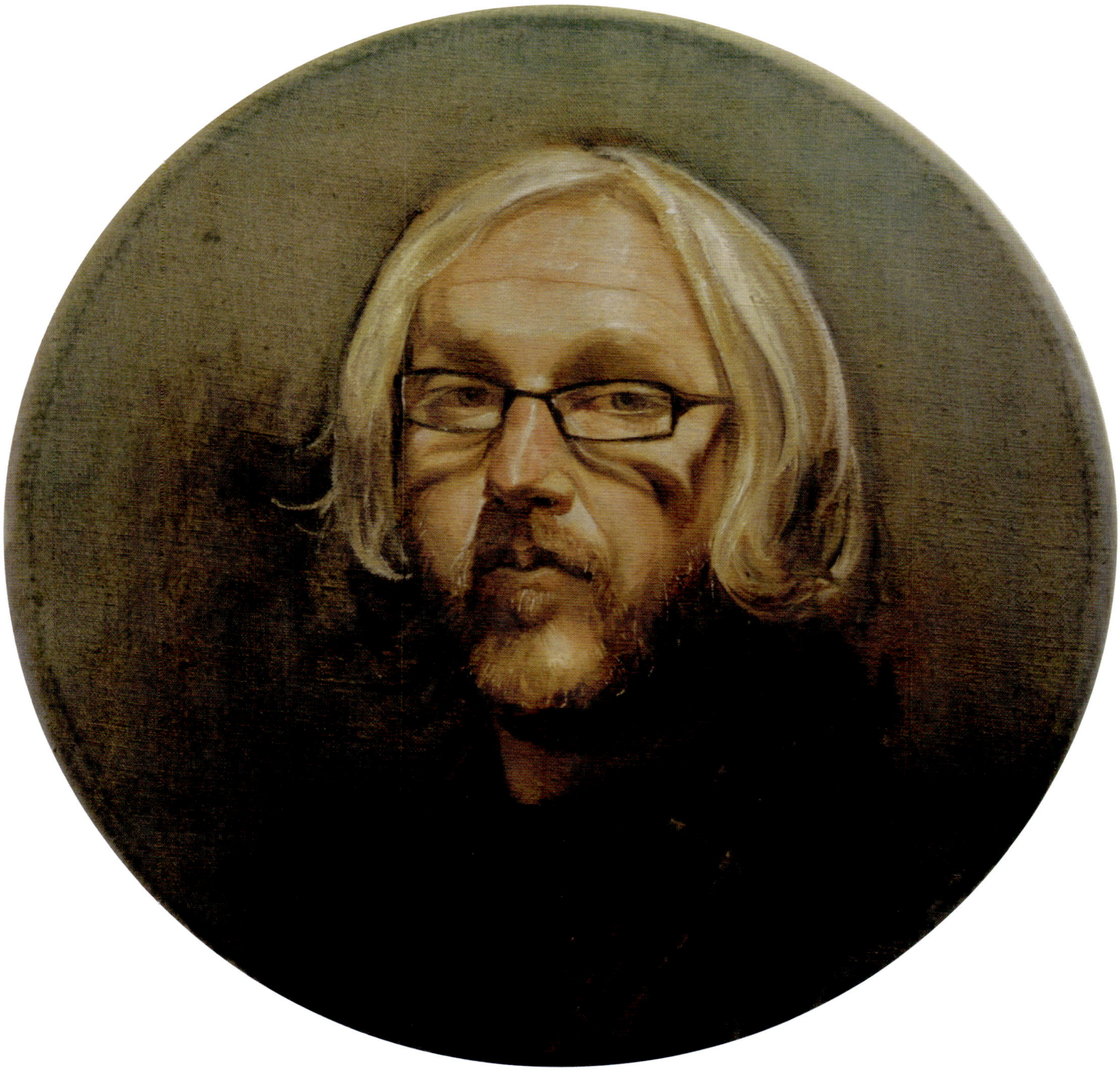

Graham Fletcher

Graham's another artist who doesn't like to sit still, isn't happy to hang back and repeat a success; he likes to push it along, develop the idea laterally.

These new works were a surprise to me; even being familiar with Graham's 'lateral leaps' didn't prepare me for this one as it seemed to come out of nowhere. When I first saw them, in reproduction, I thought he was using collage, sticking this with that, and I was amazed when I realised he was painting them.

There are plenty of other sources that attempt to explain what he's on about, the camouflaged cultural assumptions, etc. – I'm more interested in how he's doing it. I knew he could paint but rendering like this is another level of skill! If it doesn't look as slick as the commercial illustration it's exploiting, it just won't work. Apart from those promotional illustrations of apartment blocks that haven't been built yet, you just don't see this kind of work anymore. Did he sneak off and take a course in Singapore? Just joking; I know that if you know paint it doesn't take long to figure it out, and besides, we're painting the illustrated mark, not just making it.

Well done, Graham! (All these essays! I feel like a teacher writing out report cards.)

Graham Fletcher
Untitled (Lounge Room Tribalism)
2010, oil on canvas
1300 x 1620 mm

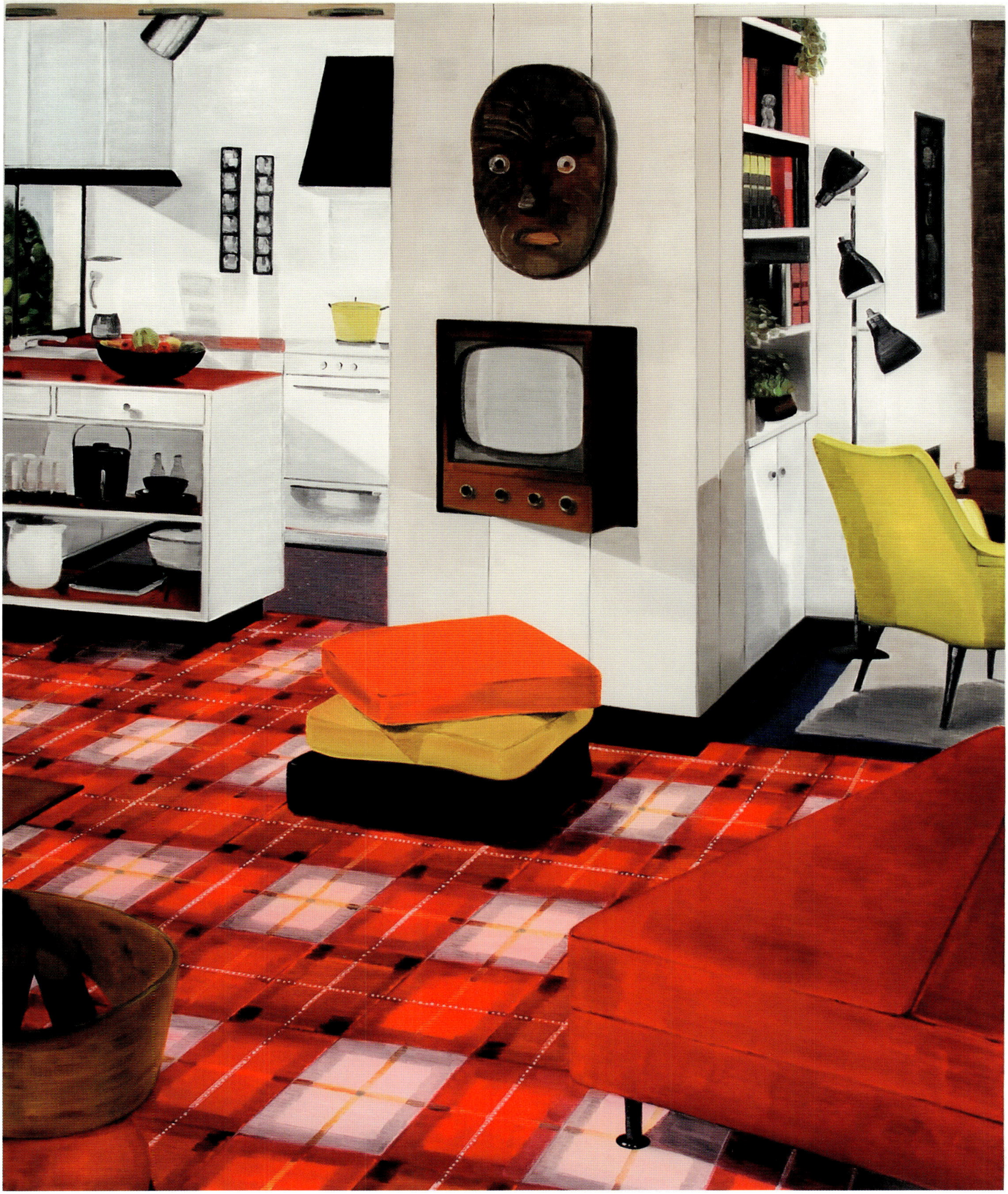

Sam Mitchell

Sam slipped and slid through Elam on a sort of private mission of social subterfuge. And I guess I'd have to admit that we, the lecturing staff, WERE becoming increasingly remote from the world these students inhabited. The connection you'd have to say was getting a tad tenuous.

Sam kept her head down (literally!), snuck through somehow, went away and then, some time later, popped up on the scene with her salty language of love and hate fully formed! To be honest I thought this Sam was a completely different person for a while there.

Anyway, she nailed it and has been keeping it rolling along in a couth and eloquent manner ever since! Nice work.

Sam Mitchell
Charles Atlas
2011, watercolour on digital archival print on Hahnemuhle photo rag 308 gsm
705 x 530 mm

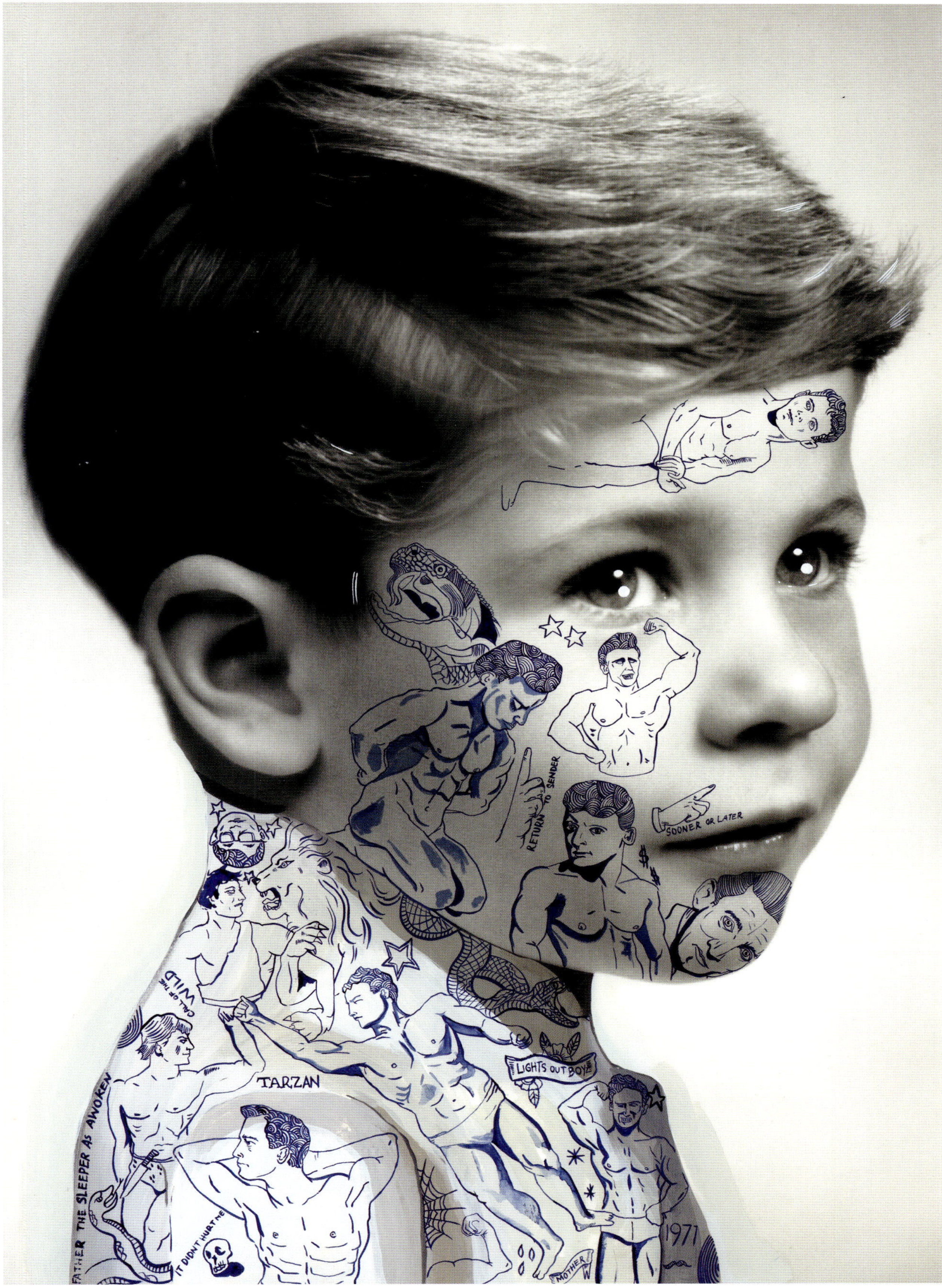
RETURN TO SENDER
SOONER OR LATER
CALL OF THE WILD
LIGHTS OUT BOY
TARZAN
FATHER THE SLEEPER AS AWOKEN
IT DIDN'T HURT ME
MOTHER
1971

Gavin Hurley

Gavin turned up at Elam about the same time as Sam Mitchell, pretty much at the same time as my enthusiasm for the new 'restructured' art school environment was starting to wane. But I'm glad I was there to see these youngsters struggle through the system.

Gavin was a quiet surprise . . . didn't say a lot but was obviously serious about figuring it all out, and not afraid to dig in and soak up the current influences and trends and paint his way through them. I remember him once painting up a 'portrait' of all his shoes in the 'butterfly collection' layout popular at the time and thinking, Hello, this boy's got it!

I can't remember when his 'house style' came into focus but I wasn't too surprised when it did, he was always going to be a class act.

Gavin Hurley
Coming and Going series
2011, paper collage
380 x 280 mm

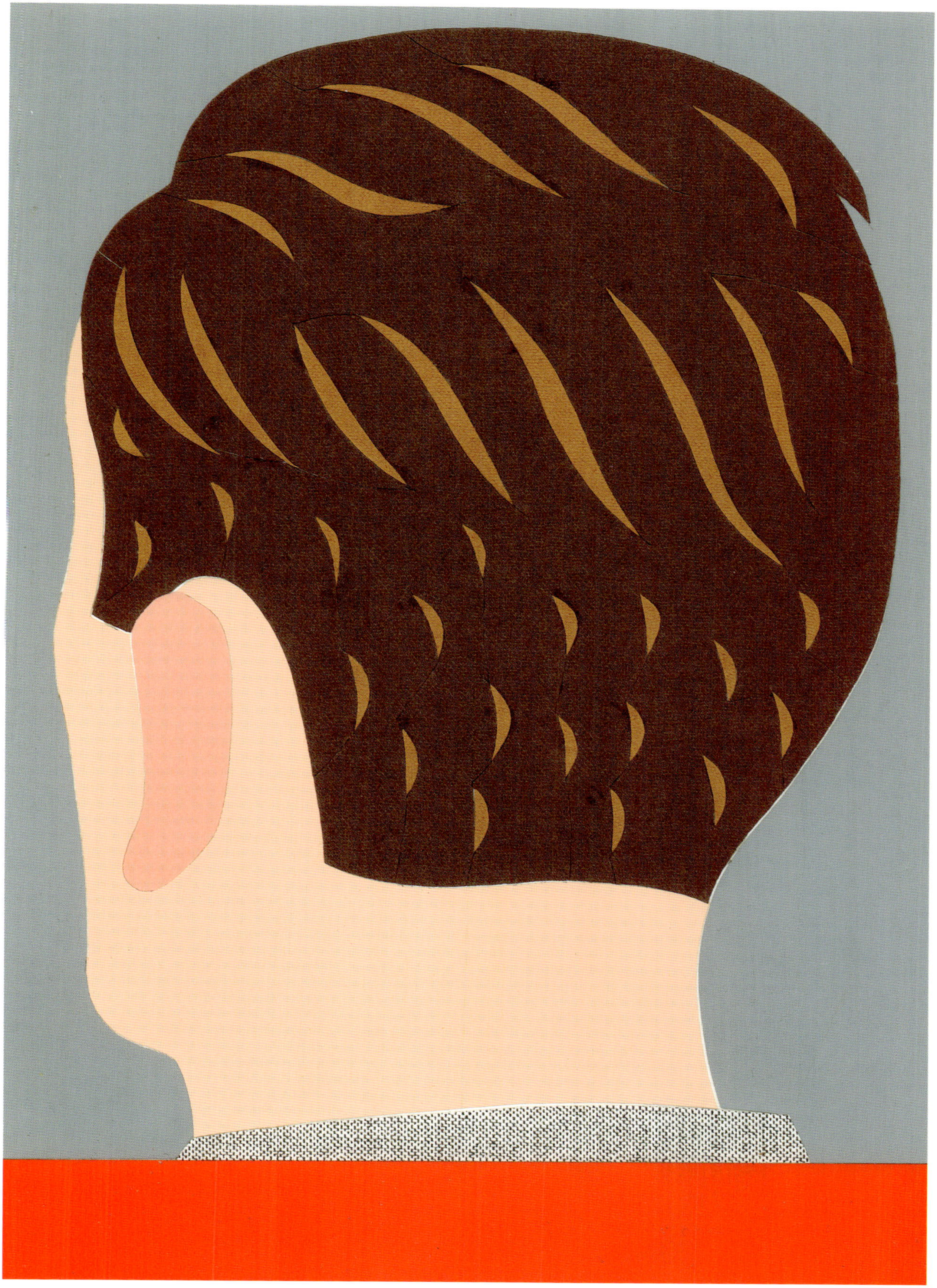

Emily Wolfe

I remember thinking the first time I saw these gauzy canvases, Oh, perfect outcome, she got there!

As a student, Emily displayed a very single-minded determination to paint the ephemeral and to render romantic loss on some level (I can define it now, but it was a bit hard to pin down at the time), and struggled with the fact that it was obviously going to take considerable technical skill and a unique personal vision to do so. Both of these things are very difficult and frustrating to arrive at in as much as they never seem to get here quick enough, despite all the well-meaning advice on offer.

But, anyway, as I said, she got there, found an eloquent and simple metaphor to express all this. And, more importantly, having confidently embraced all that, she has evolved continually fresh and interesting ways of extending and developing this fragile viewpoint.

Emily Wolfe
The Lovers
2010, oil on canvas
305 x 355 mm

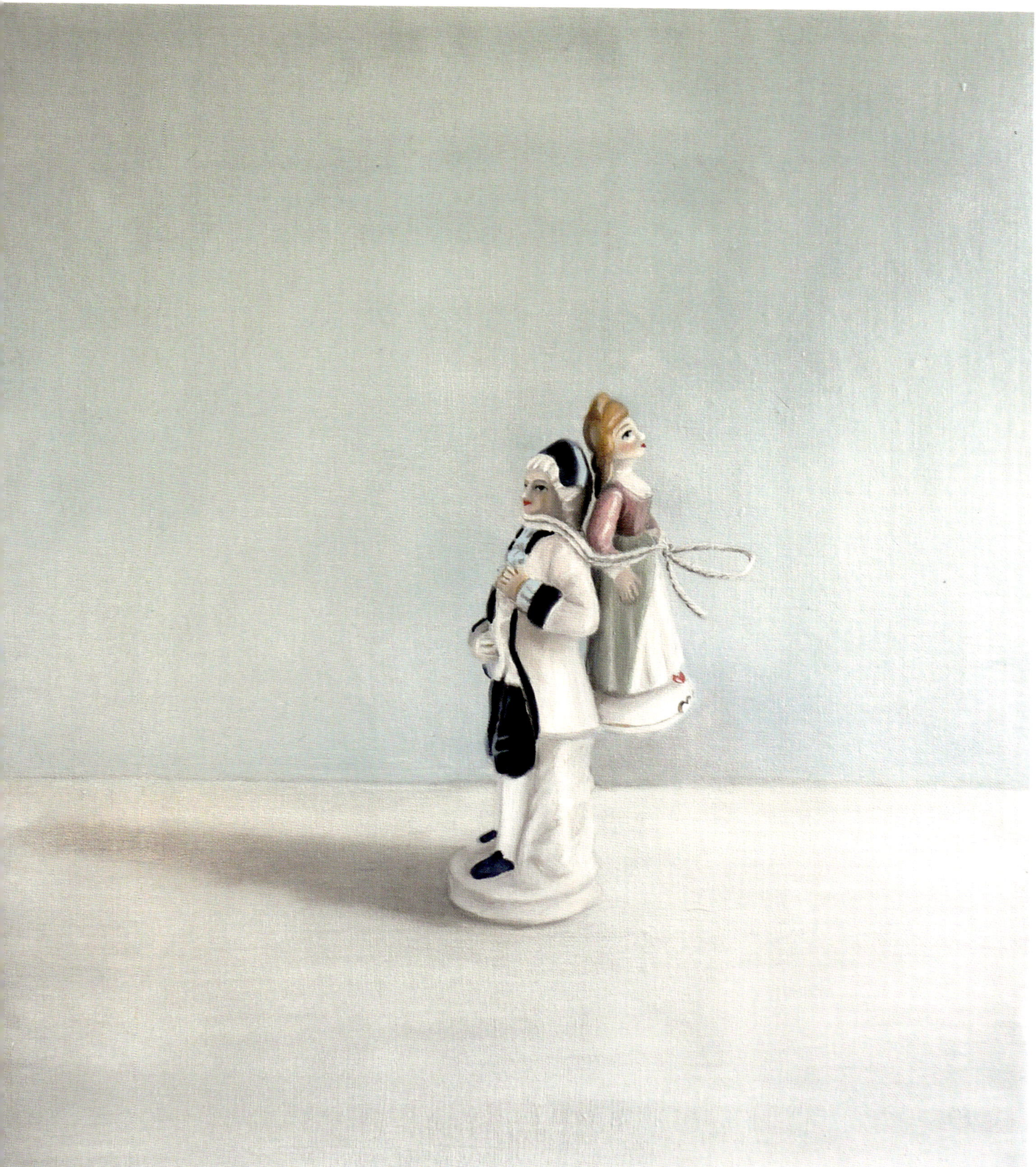

Ruth Cleland

I only met Ruth recently . . . judged her work for the Wallace Award and was taken immediately by it. Ruth takes photorealism to a whole new level, scrunching everything down so that the transcribable limit (the relationship of the tools doing the transcribing to the thing being transcribed) becomes seriously challenged. You see things being done with a pencil, for example, that normal expectations tell you shouldn't be possible.

What saves Ruth's work from becoming a sort of elevated version of the Lord's Prayer on a grain of rice is the quite obvious knowingness of the compositions, the purity of the strong abstract armature that holds them together. It's like looking through something as solid but transparent as a diamond into a meditative space that you know won't let you down.

Ruth Cleland
Level 2
2007–2008, acrylic on linen
560 x 835 mm

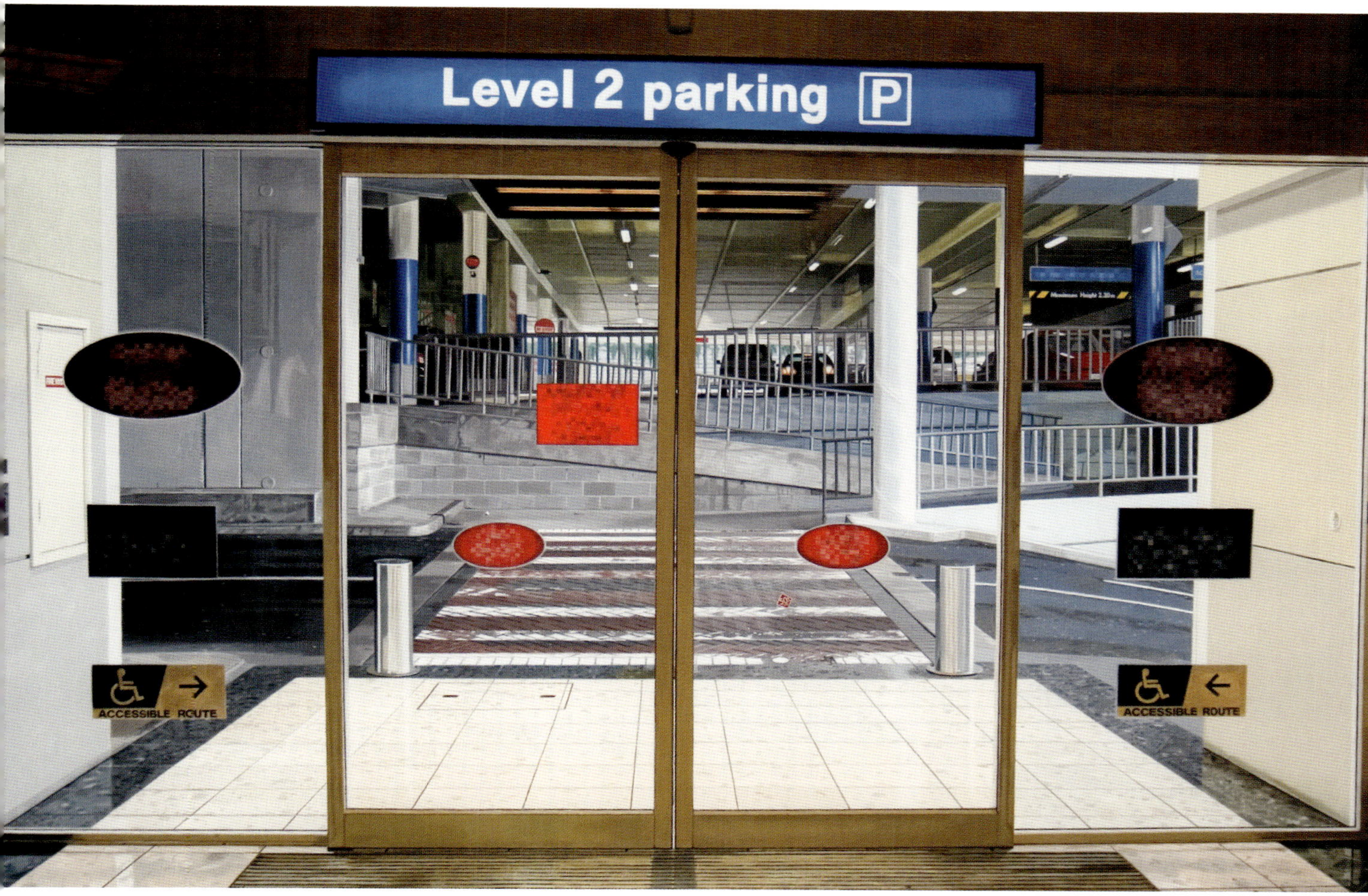
Level 2 parking P
ACCESSIBLE ROUTE
ACCESSIBLE ROUTE

Tim Thatcher

Another newcomer, especially to me, and I have to say it took me a while to warm to Tim's work. For a time there, I thought his odd system of painting things that look like something, but aren't, was more the result of incompetent drawing than a deliberate strategy. (Well, not really, but the thought does arise.) I should have known better really, or why was Janne Land exhibiting them? Coming upon them out of the blue didn't help of course.

Now that I've learnt to read them they make perfect contemporary sense, the clever give and take: 'I give you a meaningful narrative, without meaning.' It's a creative way of painting about the world without pretending that you have any of the answers. The best answer a painter can offer is a good painting, an honest painting.

Tim Thatcher
A Centre
2009, oil on canvas
1520 x 1010 mm

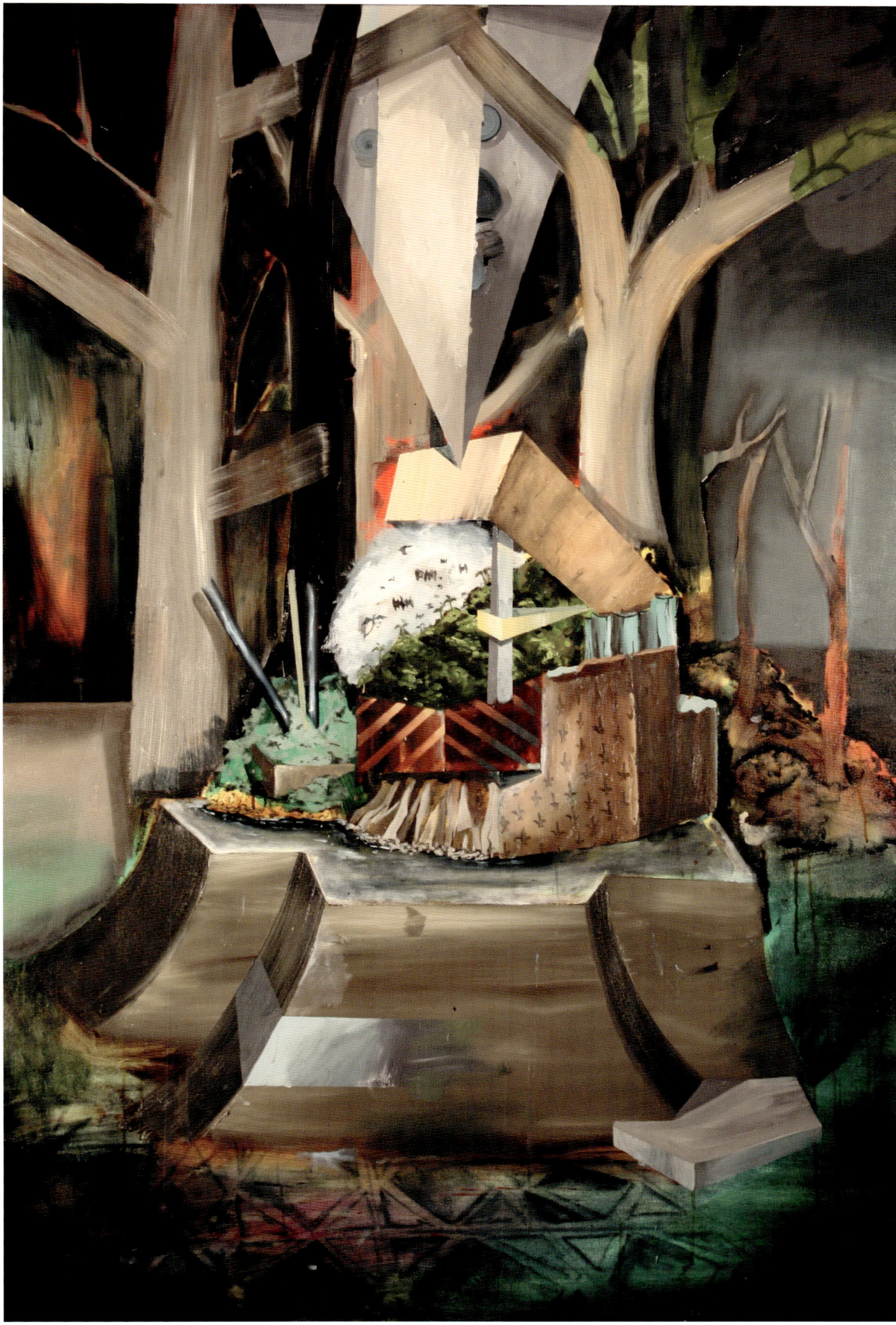

Matt Summers

Here's more newness, arriving from where you'd least expect it. Bob Dylan said, 'Who said you can't go back, of course you can!'

But what happens when you DO go back? You can pretty much rely on things never being the same, too many things in the way, too many cultural signifiers having dropped away in the intervening years.

I don't even know if Matt has been looking at Stuart Davis and similar artists from that era but I'd be very surprised if he hasn't, the fairground colours, the choppy impasto, the similar clustering of rhyming shapes throughout the composition.

Fascinating, to me, to see these strange vehicles drive up from out of nowhere and park in front of me. These influences would be so ancient to a 23-year-old, which is probably the entire point, like me looking at Albert Marquet at art school . . . over a 60-year gap . . . safe enough for the heat to have died down . . . and Matt looking at American abstraction of the '40s, a 60-year gap! Interesting . . . and utterly meaningless, I'm sure. Bloody good painting though!

Matt Summers
The Lauterbrunnen Valley, Switzerland
2006, oil on plywood (board)
235 x 210 mm

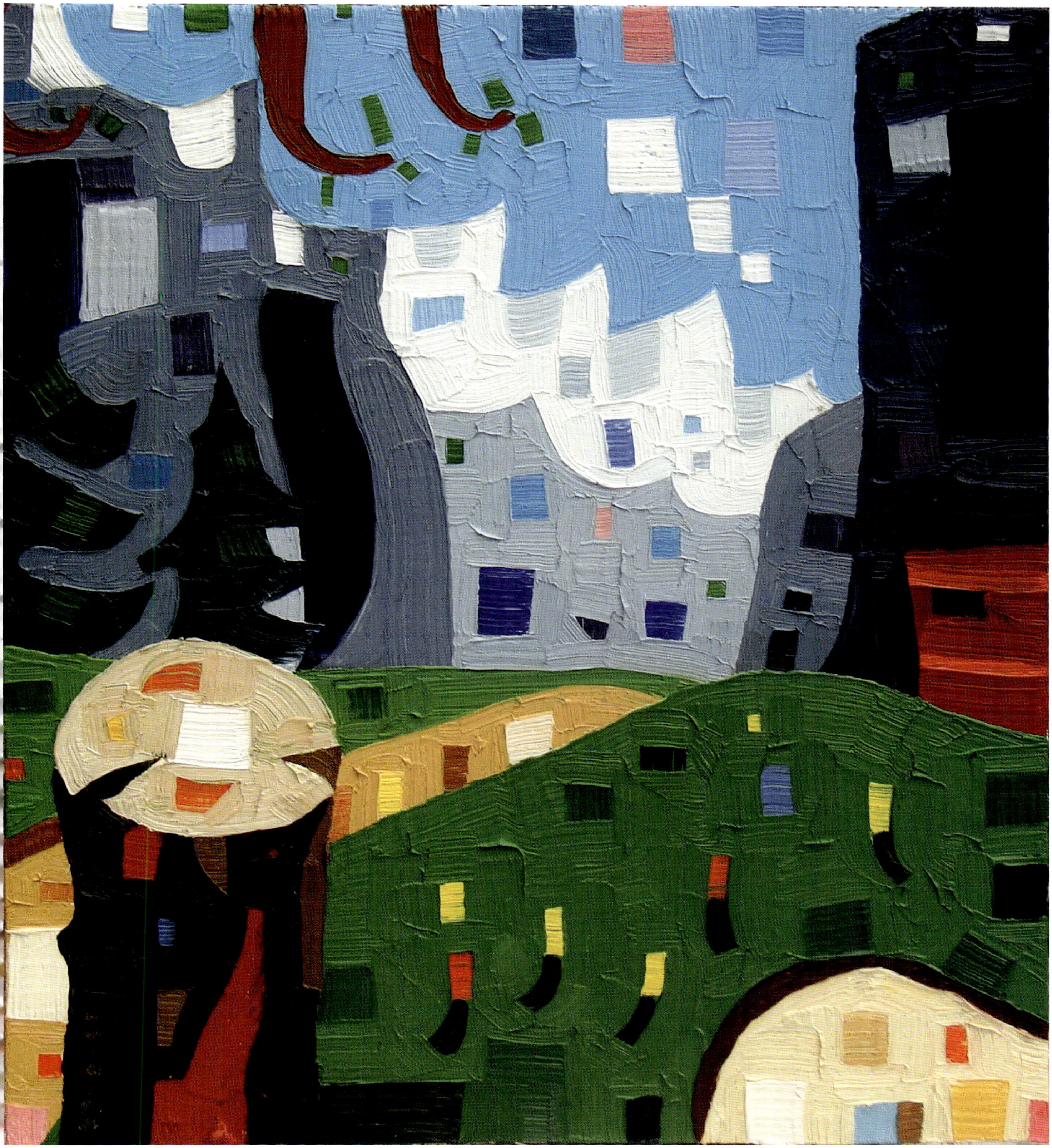

André Hemer

We're moving into terra incognita here for me. I'm familiar with André's work, and have been for some time through judging various art competitions and so on, but know very little about him. I could of course, read him up, but this book isn't about that, it's all about the image.

I've included André because I've been intrigued by his paintings from the first and find myself mentally trying to unpick the construction of them. It looks as if he starts with a finished painting, and then peels it back until it looks like he's just getting going . . . till he gets down to that interesting less self-conscious stage where he can throw it around knowing that any mistakes he's likely to make can be 'corrected' further down the track.

Painters are always looking for that magic space where we can ambush ourselves into making that spontaneous mark, where we can make room for the painting to tell us what it wants to do, and André seems to have found a very original way of doing just that.

Whatever the actual system he's deploying, the finished result is interesting to me precisely because of these conundrums; we arrive at a place where normal expectations of 'finish' get subverted.

André Hemer
The Triumph of Painting (when it's hotting up in Deutschland it's eis-eis, baby)
2007, acrylic on canvas
1680 × 1680 mm

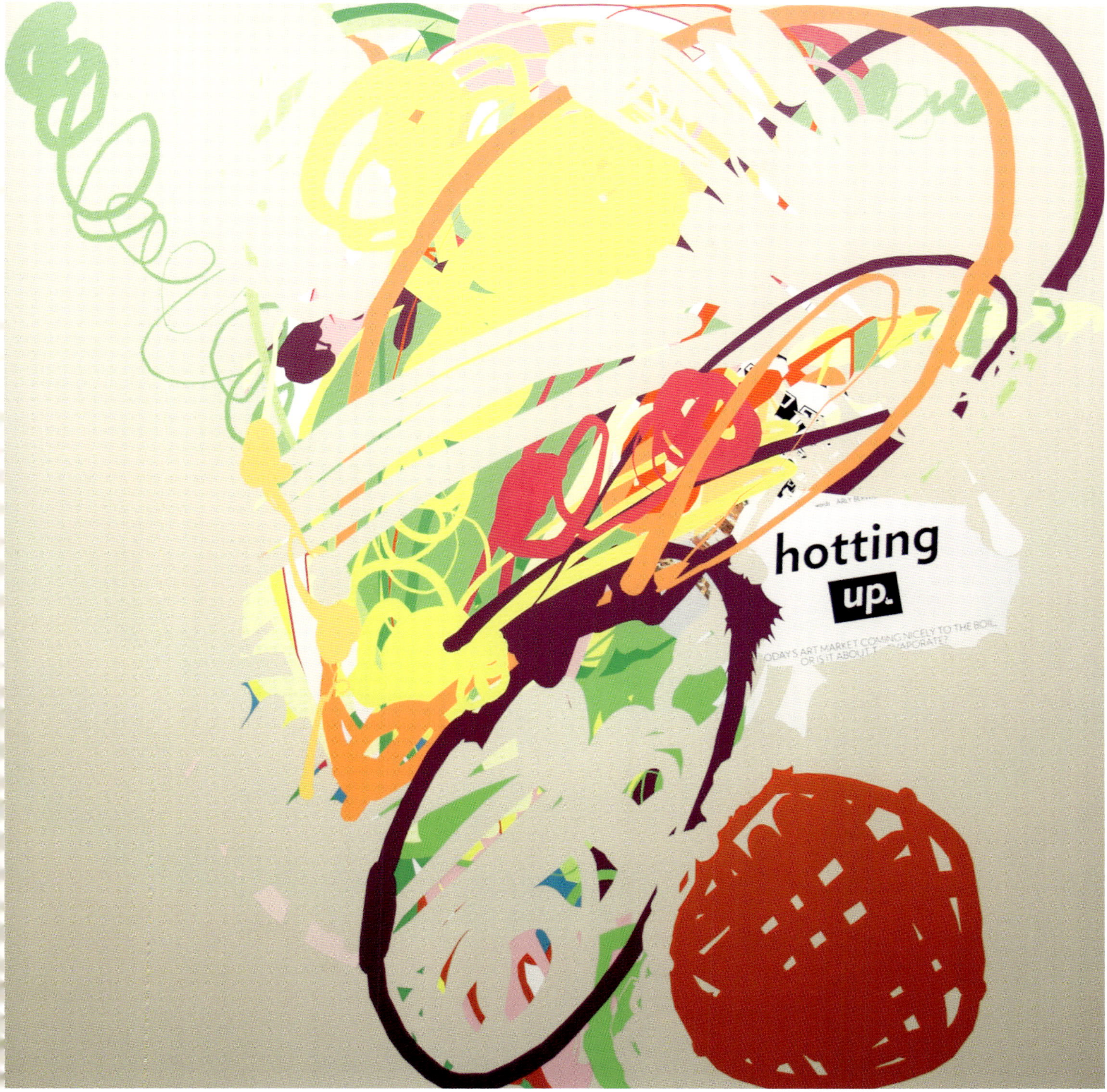
hotting
up.
ODAYS ART MARKET COMING NICELY TO THE BOIL

Kushana Bush

Such is the sophistication of the rendering and the undeniably exotic 'otherness' in Kushana's work that I have to admit I thought it was coming from somewhere else (God knows where) when I first saw it, which tells you something about how used we get to a certain level of production and management here in New Zealand. (And I don't think I speak entirely for myself here.)

It's a real delight to be surprised like this, to find something that instantly impresses with the depth of its technical prowess but stops you in your tracks with the absolutely alien nature of its content.

The intensity of the implied narrative and the endless invention in the execution of that narrative within the confines of a strongly bounded convention carries you along on a trip you find yourself happy to be part of despite not having any idea where you're going.

Kushana Bush
Calm Tight Bevy
2010, gouache
and pencil on paper
770 x 570 mm

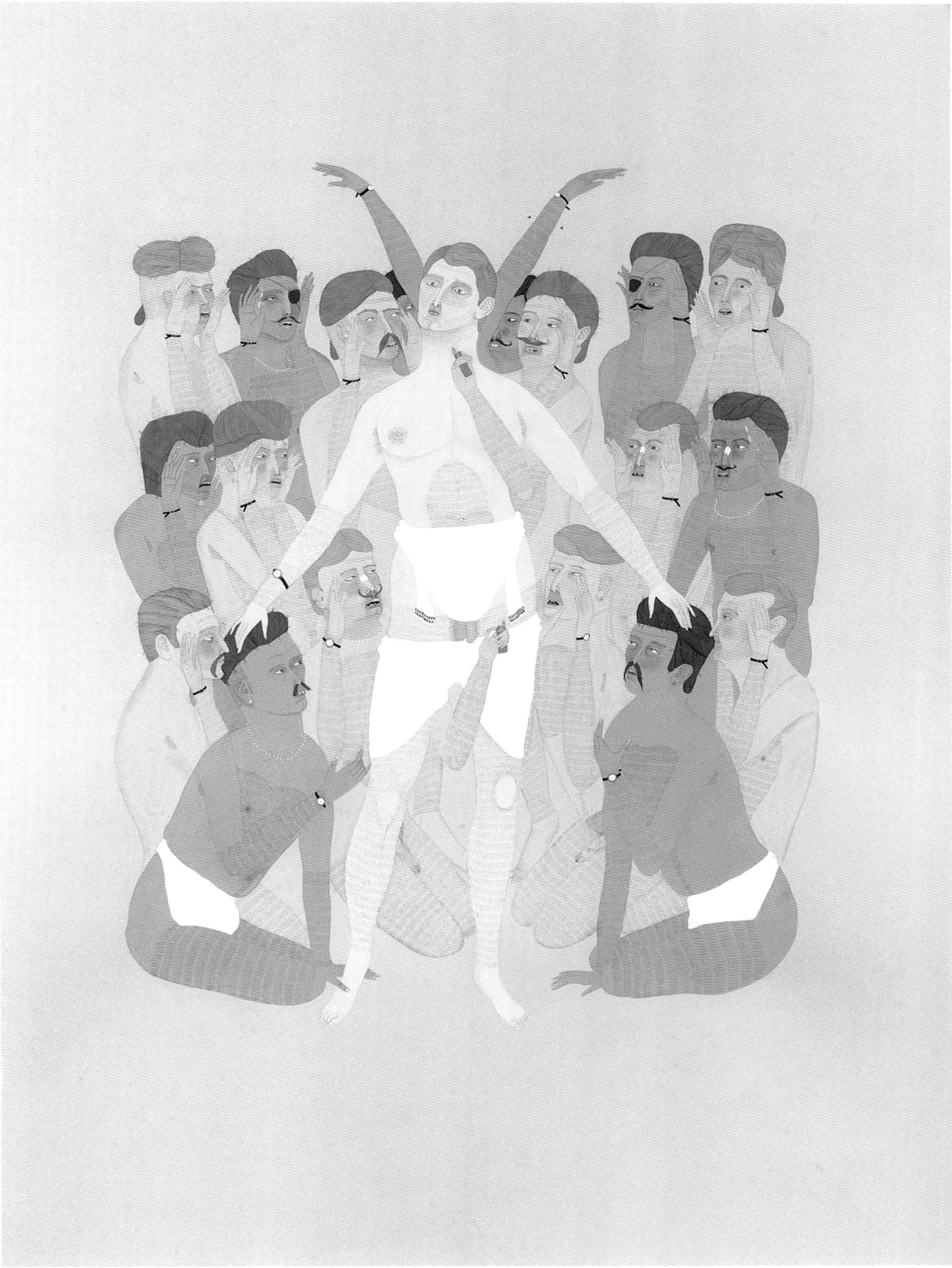

Seung Yul Oh

This is what I mean about those contemporary cross-genre mash-ups.

Here, the Asian/pop/abject/cute gets woven into a classic puddle-and-drip abstract expressionist framework. Though quite a popular mode right now it's difficult to do properly and a lot of it hardly transcends the trash that inspires it – but Seung seems to be getting it right.

Hard to pinpoint where it does transcend but we've been arguing that one since Duchamp exhibited his famous toilet. As usual it seems to come down to talent, intensity and knowledge, lots of knowledge. There's no short-cut to poetry.

Seung Yul Oh
Brambly Brim
2006, acrylic on board

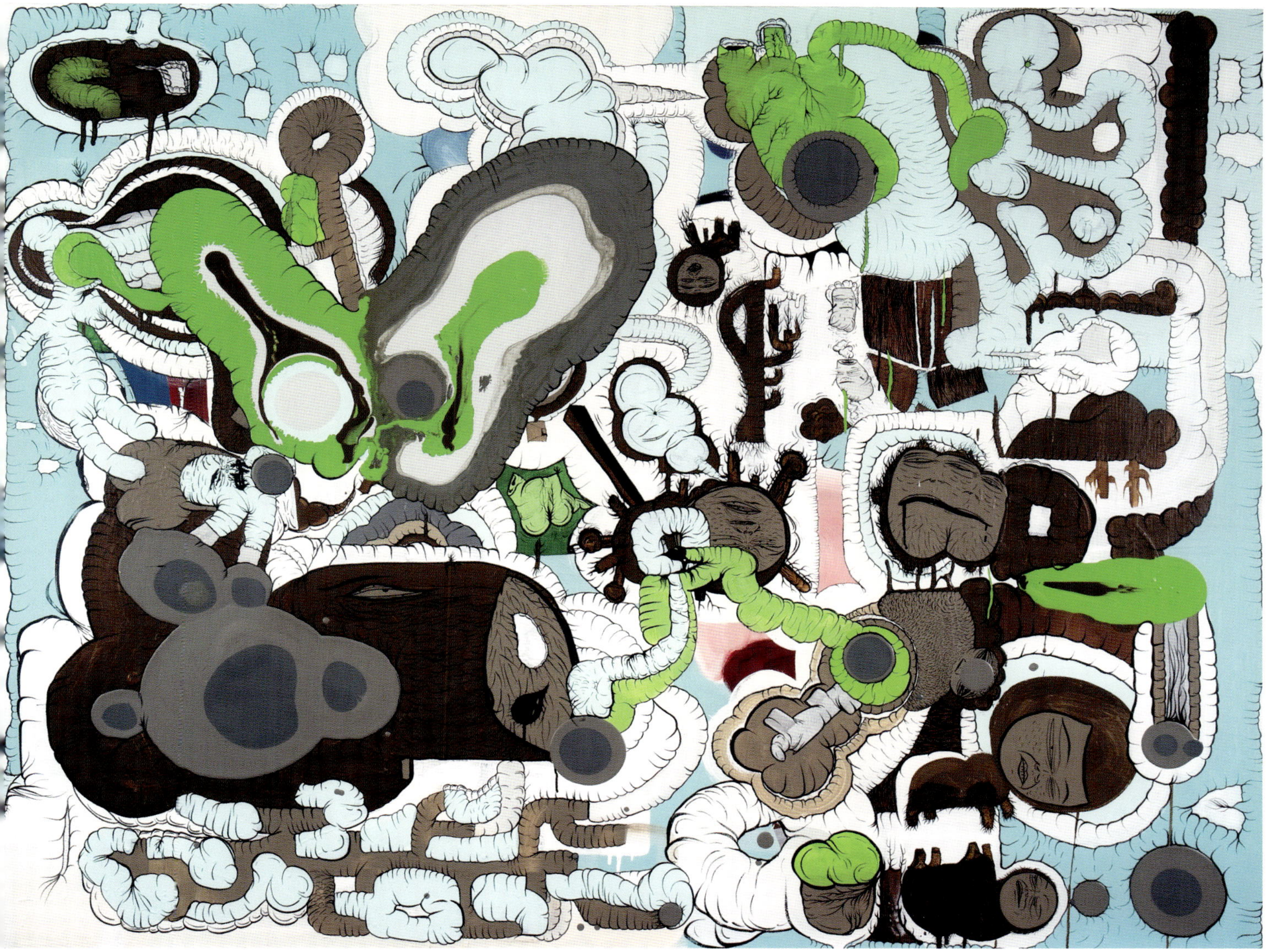

Otis Frizzell

Otis is a classic combination of the academically neutral autodidact and the democratically engaged realist, charging in with a powerfully informed worldview and a boundless generosity of spirit.

After a lifetime of having me in his ear, Otis has magnificently managed to disregard me almost entirely and trust his own instincts. He doesn't operate as an observer outside of popular culture, so much as illustrate it from within. And he does this with terrific verve and technical skill.

Hero Tiki is the prototype for a 'one-off' multiple, where, with the use of spraycans and stencils, he can produce a limited edition with each reproduction having its own hand-made imprimatur.

Otis Frizzell
Hero Tiki
2006, enamel spray paint stencil on canvas
450 x 450 mm

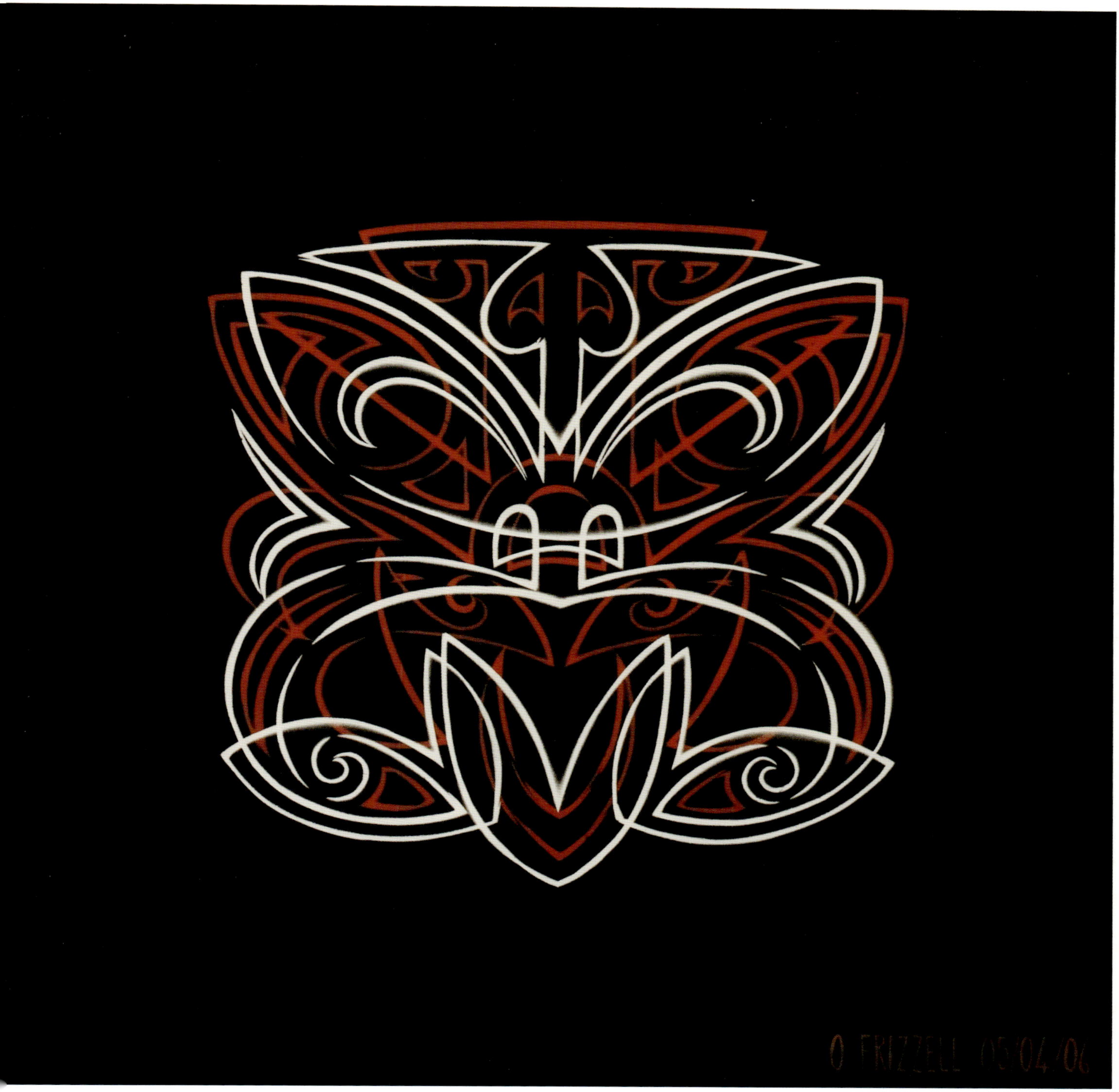
O FRIZZELL 05/04/06

Simon Esling

I include Simon not just because I think he deserves to be here but because he nicely rounds out a certain collective aesthetic I hope comes through from the young contemporaries that I've chosen from current practice.

A whole new reference library seems to have been thrown open for legitimate research. This subtle creep of new material manifests itself in surprisingly diverse forms but it is definitely expressing a common zeitgeist.

It's quite a trick to take these 'shared' elements and assemble them in a fresh and original way, but Simon has definitely done that . . . floating in space with his tanks and his tendons. What's been released for exploitation is all the material that used to reside on the graphic novel, sci-fi nerd side of the great fine-art/graphic-art divide.

No one even anguishes over it anymore; poor old Saul Steinberg, for example, back in the 1970s, was 'allowed' to brush up close to the fine-art fraternity but only in the faintly patronising way typical of the time. I don't think young artists like Simon even see their work as a revolution of form, it's just what they do!

Simon Esling
Cascade
2011, watercolour, ink and Indian ink on 300 gsm cold press paper
760 x 570 mm

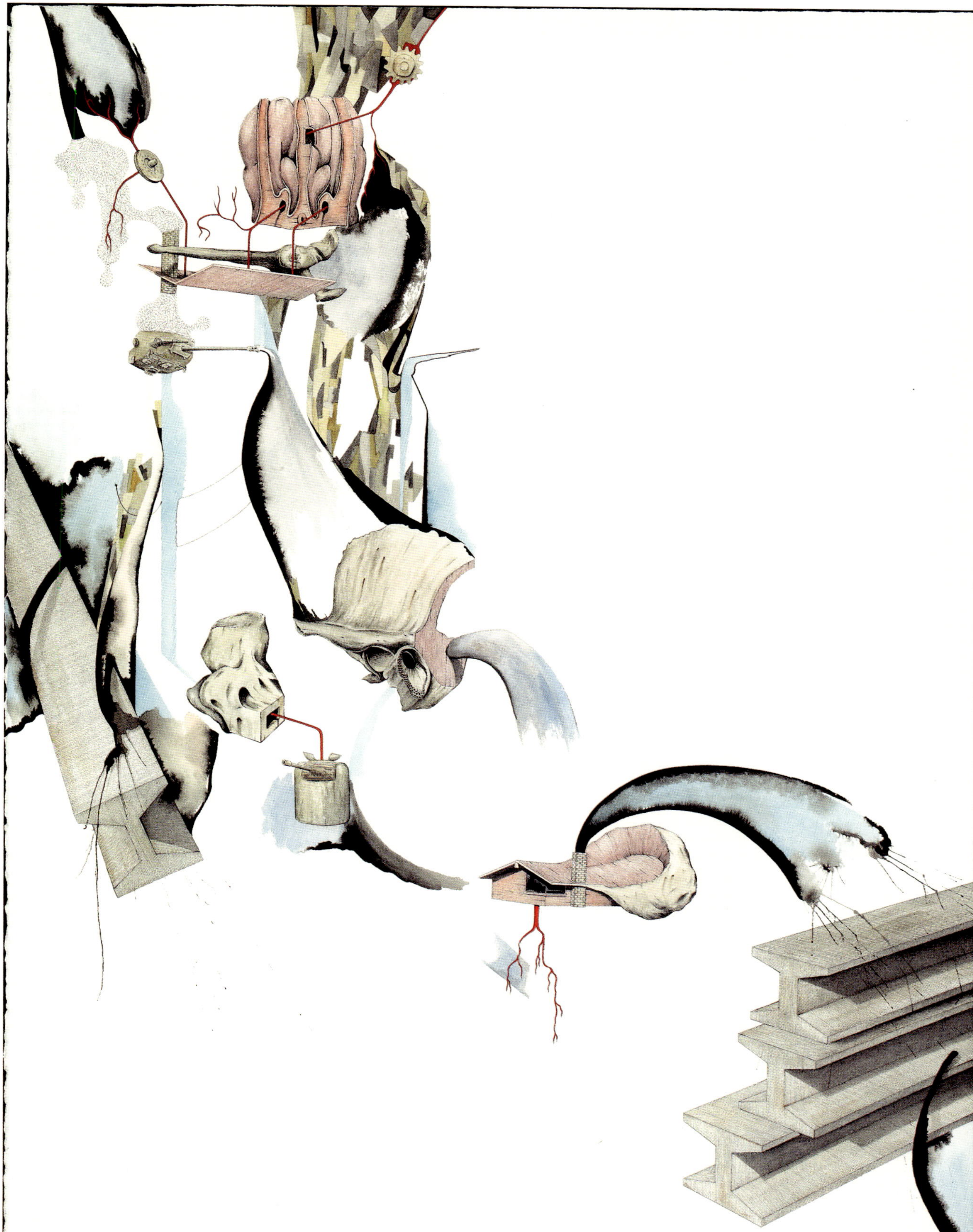

Dave Beazley

I'm not 100 per cent sure about this . . . dangerous territory . . . is all this Sponge Bobbery real or is it a transitory fad? I'm travelling out to the limits of my tolerance levels with this one. I can recognise what's going on, and recognise that Dave's pretty damn good at it, but not sure what the good is.

There's obviously something going on or I wouldn't be talking about it, even if I only see it as an opportunity to talk about possible futures, because as I said in the intro this business never stops. (Reminds me of the little old lady who said, 'I've got nothing against progress, I just think it went on a bit.') The shock of the new is a very real thing and we can all get caught out no matter the breadth of our understanding and experience.

But it's worth pointing out here that despite the superficial appearance of relentless, accelerating change, at one level nothing changes. The Western aesthetic is so profoundly inculcated in our sense of values (and not just Western, actually, it's basically about how humans ergonomically engage with their world) that no matter how much appearances might change – the look, content, style, or whatever you want to call it – at its root it's always the same thing.

You could just about transpose the negative and positive spaces, the structure, in this painting with, say, a Max Ernst or Claude Lorrain and it would still say the same thing formally. (Or what they used to call 'plastically'.)

It's always the same question, and it's always the same answer.

Dave Beazley
When you asked to join a war about nothing you may as well have joined a circus
2007, oil on board
900 x 1200 mm

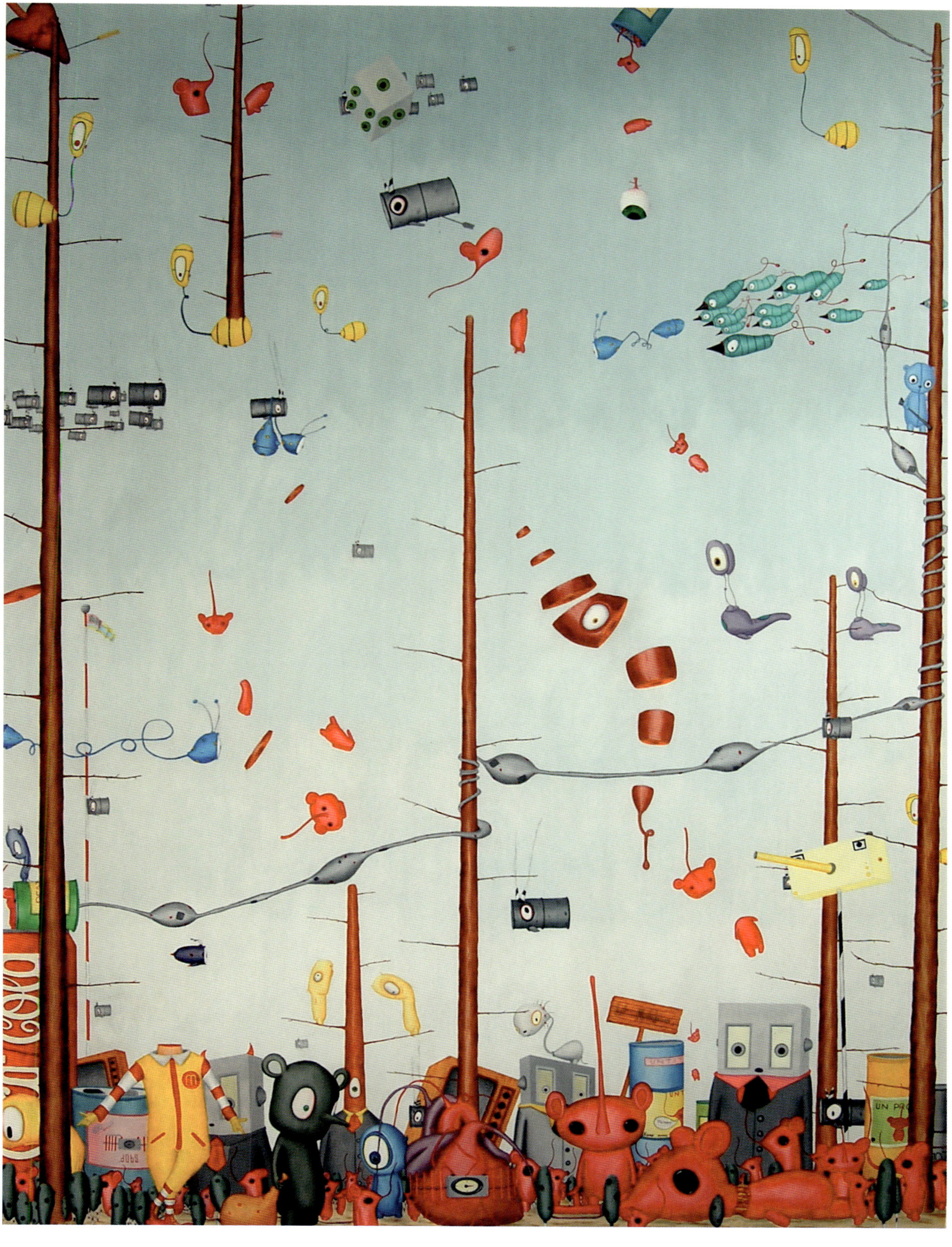

Krystie Wade

Krystie is an interesting example of how subtle and fascinating this thing called 'newness', which I keep banging on about, actually is. She crept up on me; I first saw her work in an intake of paintings for the Wallace Award (now there's something that gives you an interesting, ongoing overview!) and found myself wondering how something so obvious should be so captivating.

On one level all she does is move paint around on canvas . . . shapes, colours, and so on, but what happens, or what I think happens, is a tiny but significant shift in the weights and measures. Sharp eyes from every generation arrive at their own way of measuring the world, and that becomes a standard which as a rule is adopted and perpetuated by subsequent followers. After a spell a new set of sharp eyes finds these rules inadequate for describing the world as they're seeing it, and readjusts all the measurements. Commonly called a 'paradigm shift'. Moving on by getting it wrong, again.

Everything in Krystie's compositions illustrates this, the odd junctions of mass and line . . . where things start and where things stop . . . The on-edge tonal relationships. Things break off where they're not 'meant' to, colour misbehaves.

The first trick for the artist is to intuit all this and the second one is knowing how to exploit it . . . taking the familiar and refreshing it.

Krystie Wade
Shadows Evolved
2007, oil on hardboard
1200 x 1200 mm

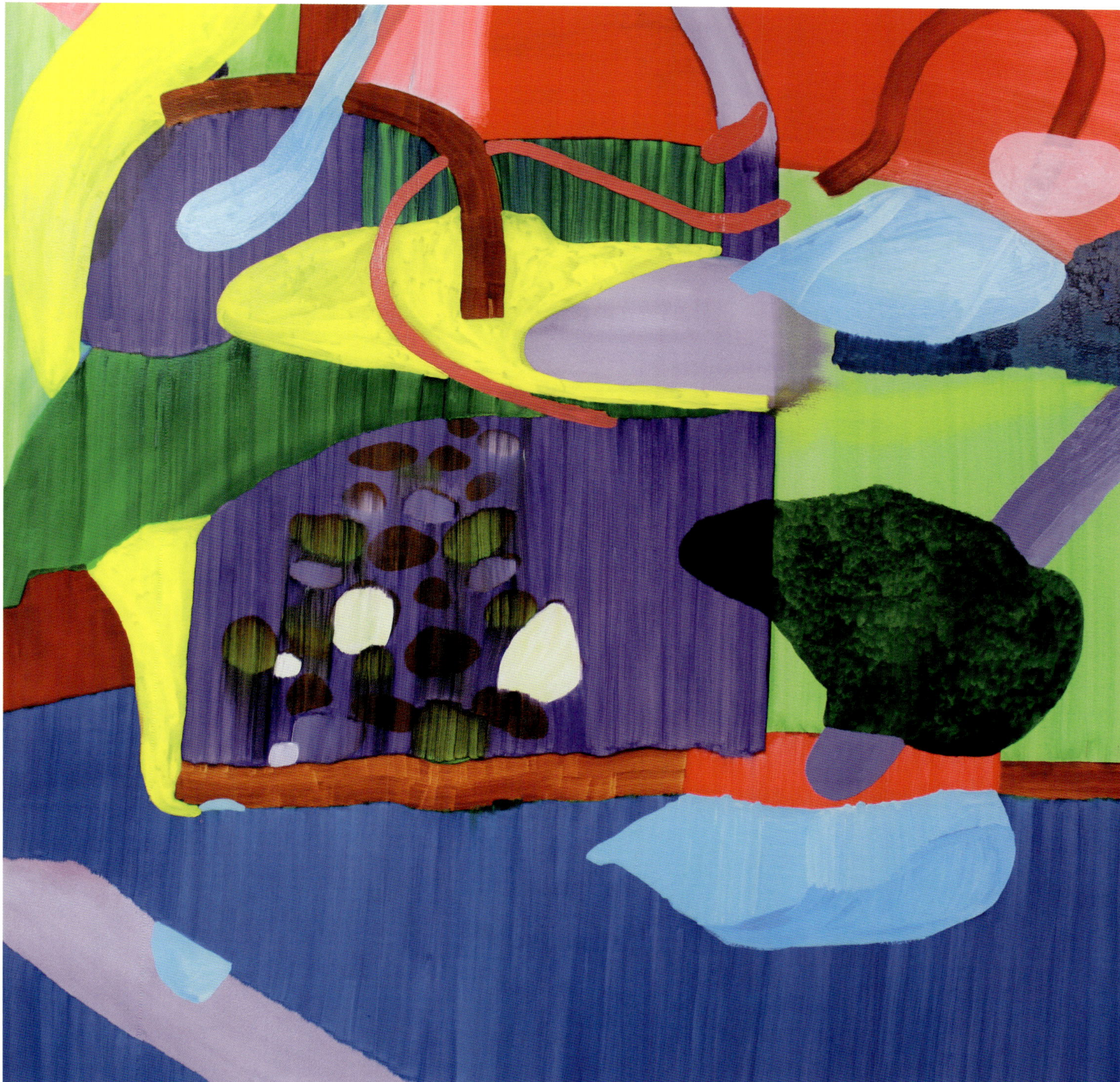

Grant Whibley

I can clearly recall Grant's first day at Elam; he was an older student, been out in the world, and he turned up in a heavy, studded and strappy, black leather motorcycle jacket. Looked like he'd wandered in off the street by accident. Can't remember the art student dress code at the time (grunge, I suppose) but Grant looked a bit – I don't know – 'shiny'.

It shouldn't matter, and it didn't in the end, but you're always on the lookout for the signals, for the signs, hints of things to come. And what interesting things did come! Eventually. He joined in, stopped polishing his jacket or whatever the hell happened and acquitted himself pretty well. But I never saw this coming, the bird thing.

Who would have thought there'd be so much conceptual mileage left in bird painting?! Well, possibly it's limitless, but Grant has certainly found an interesting angle with these portraits. More than portraits of course. They look like Wanted posters, or, more significantly, the reverse, the accusatory stare: 'Are you looking at me?'

The kiwi stare or 'look' reproduced here is one of the weirdest. A pale survivor resigned to the odds – or defying them – it's hard to know but you definitely feel you're being put on the spot for something!

These limpid, strangely liquid paintings are worth checking out . . . confident ghosts of our very recent past peering out of the museum gloom, isolated in their luminous auras. Shiny even!

Grant Whibley
Look
2003, oil on linen
1500 x 1500 mm

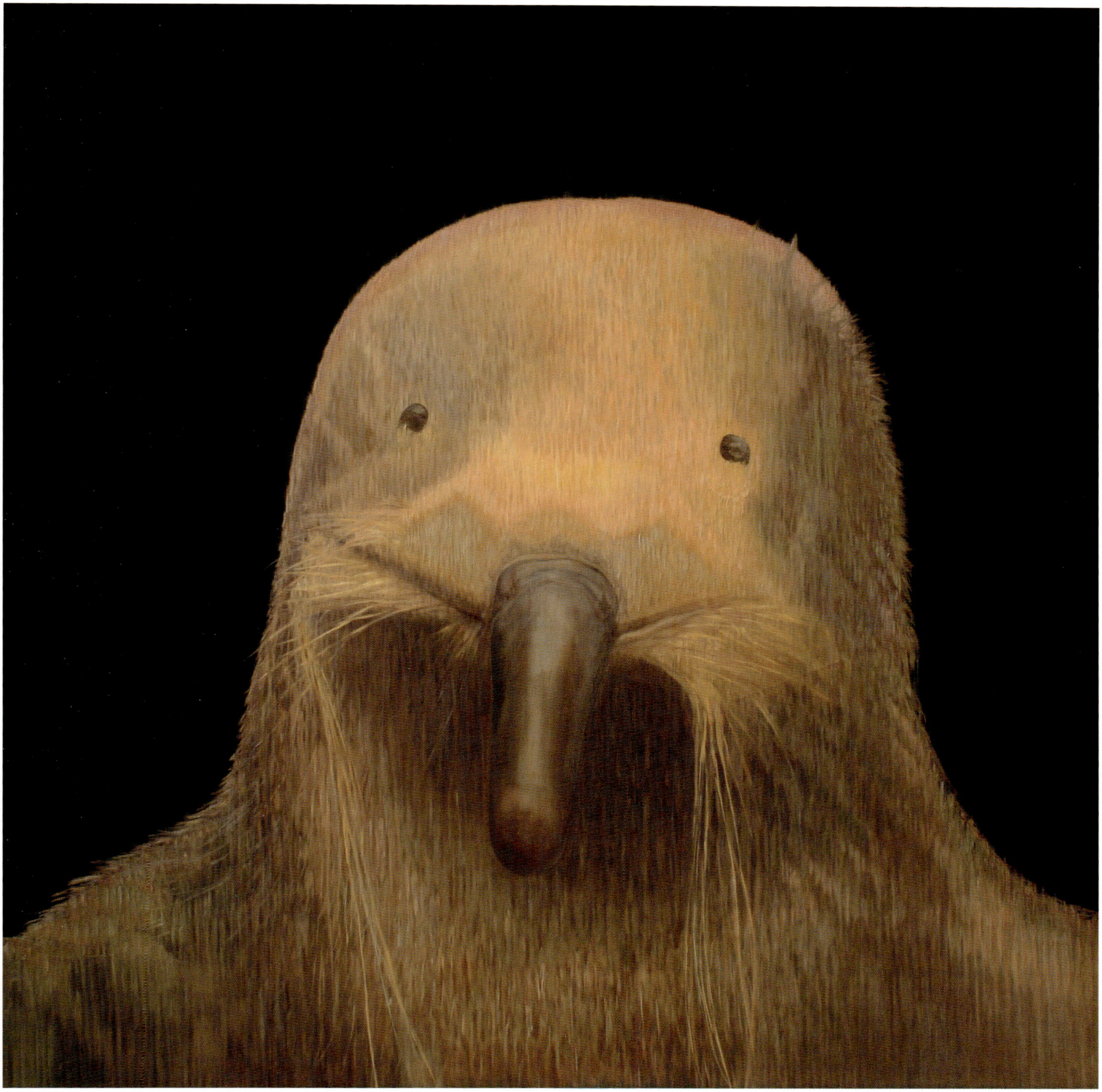

Leo Bensemann

I've dropped this painting in here because it's a brand-new favourite. The image arrived on my desk in the form of a flyer from the Christchurch Art Gallery as I was writing this book. I can't wait to see the original! What was Leo thinking?! What a shocker; the lad looks like Straw Peter. (A poem I'm sure Leo would have been familiar with.)

I was wavering about putting Leo in the book and have never been convinced by his lurid palette and his rather, er, florid drawing style (which looks like a writer's hyperactive idea of how a painting should be), but everything I didn't like makes sense in this fabulous explosion!

I know nothing about the background of this painting, and very little about Leo himself, but like all images that do the business this will compel me to dig deeper.

Note: Since I wrote this Peter Simpson's book on Bensemann has come out and now I'm a total convert.

Leo Bensemann
St Olaf
c.1937, oil on canvas
on board

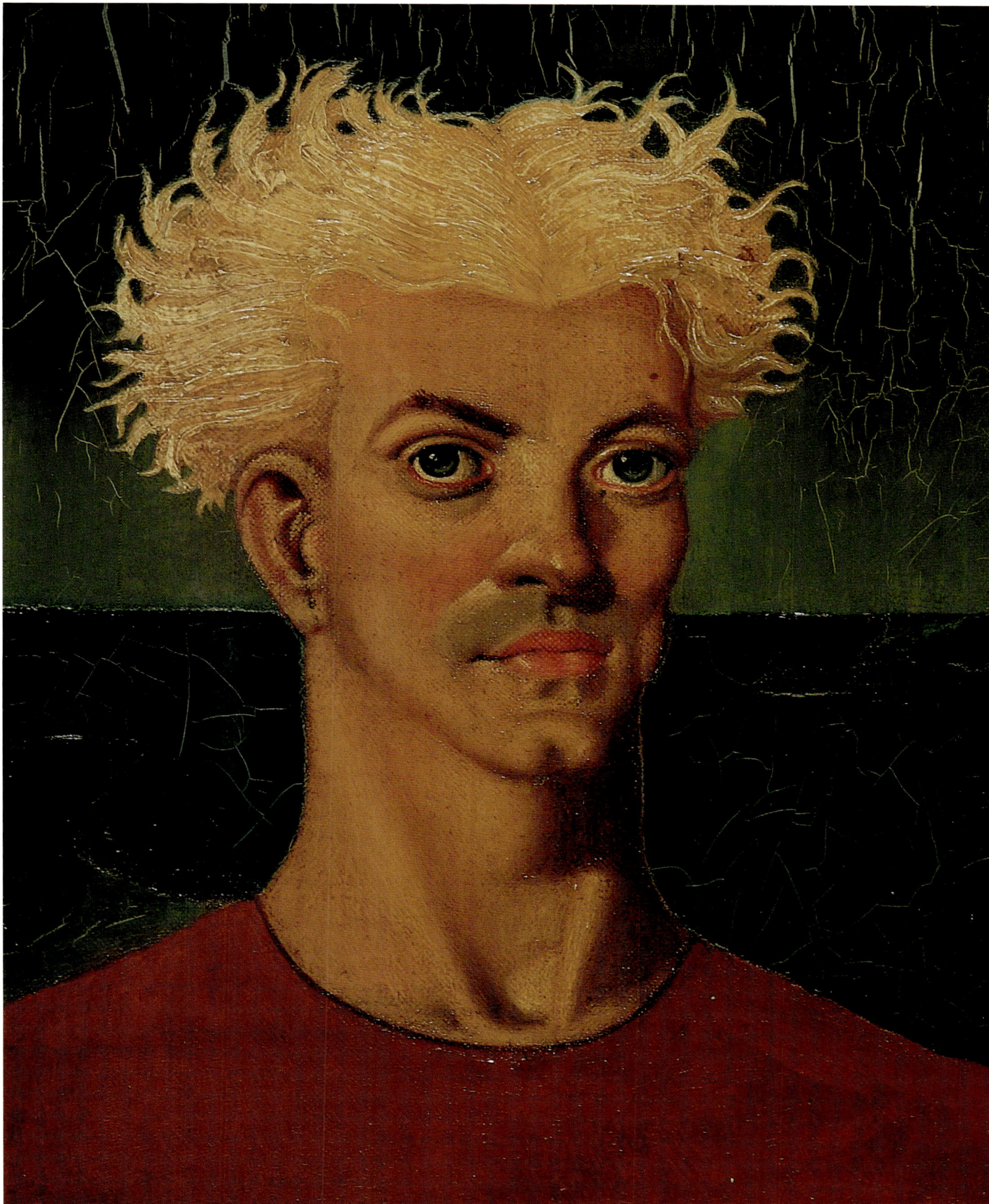

Acknowledgements

When Jenny Hellen at Random House rang me up with the idea for this project she said, 'This one will be a lot more straightforward than the last one, Dick,' referring to *Dick Frizzell The Painter*, a mind-boggling research and assembly job that nearly killed me. And to some extent she was right, but my, oh my, what an adventure it's been. Writing it was okay – the intro and all my 'school reports' – but pulling all the images together has been somewhat less than 'straightforward'.

While I didn't have to burrow through the official channels, do all the bureaucratic legwork (Jenny's team did that), I still had to track down and nominate all the works I wanted for the book – and I have a lot of people to thank for helping me do that.

First, I must thank everyone at all the public institutions who responded so positively to our requests, providing what we wanted and more. We made some wonderful discoveries. The auction houses who let me plunder their files, Peter Webb, Art + Object.

All the art dealers who let me sit at their elbow while they trawled through their files for the perfect image, working through my wishlists for me, trying to find the work closest to the one I'd painted in my head. John Gow, Gary Langsford, Anna Jackson and the team at Gow Langsford Gallery; Melanie Rogers; Hamish McKay; Ivan Anthony; Michael Lett; Andrew Jensen; James Wallace; Bridget McIntosh; Jane Sanders; Jenny Neligan; Marcia Page and James Blackie; Dick Bett; Bill Milbank; and Steve Higginson and the lively lads at Paul Nache.

The 'Dick Frizzell' team at Random House: Jenny Hellen for putting me up to this in the first place – thank you, Jenny, it's been quite an 'illuminatin' experience', as my father used to say. Leonie Freeman and Kimberley Davis who did a brilliant job of collating, connecting and constructing. I knew what I wanted, and you made it happen. The patient editor, Rebecca Lal, who grappled with all my dots and dashes, and my general illiteracy.

And all my artist friends who entered so wholeheartedly into the project – often without any knowledge of what I'd written about them – which was impressive. In fact I was quite overwhelmed with the response from everybody involved; I waited and waited nervously for someone to tell me to get lost, but it never happened! Everyone's been so damned helpful!

Patrick Reynolds for running round town, bursting into people's houses and dealers' stock-rooms with his camera.

Jude, for putting me right on the image suitable for my page. So obvious I couldn't see it.

And last; I'd like to thank my clever daughter-in-law Sarah Frizzell, who pointed me in the direction of the book *Wisdom* by Andrew Zuckerman when I told her I was thinking of exercising my old '70s Helvetica muscles on the design for this one. Perfect pointing, Sarah! I love the look of this book! It's all about the image. Bella figura.

Artist Biographies

Rita Angus (1908–1970) was born in Hastings and grew up in Hawke's Bay and the Manawatu. She attended Canterbury College School of Art between 1927 and 1930, and was exhibiting in Christchurch from the early 1930s. She produced a considerable body of work in the 1930s and 1940s, including the well-known *Cass* (1936), and later her 'goddess' paintings, which reflected her strong pacifist views. In 1958, with the help of a fellowship, Angus travelled to Europe and spent a year based in London. She produced some of her finest landscapes after her return to New Zealand and in the late 1960s.

Dave Beazley was born in 1982, in Auckland, where he currently lives. He gained a Diploma in Cabinetmaking from Whangarei Polytechnic in 2000, and worked as a cabinetmaker for two years. After teaching himself to paint in oils, he enrolled in the Bachelor of Design (Painting) course at Unitec in Auckland, graduating in 2006. Beazley's paintings feature eccentric subjects and characters, some of which he transforms into life-size soft sculptures, combining his painting, sculpture and computer skills.

Leo Bensemann (1912–1986) was highly skilled not only as a painter, but as an illustrator, engraver and designer. He had a long association with the Caxton Press, as both illustrator and publisher. Bensemann was born in Takaka, of German and Irish ancestry, moved with his family to Nelson, then in 1931 he settled in Christchurch. Although he briefly attended night classes at the Canterbury College School of Art, he was largely self-taught. He exhibited with The Group from 1938, and designed and printed its annual catalogues. Bensemann's output included highly individual line drawings, portraits and landscapes.

Don Binney was born in Auckland in 1940. He studied with John Weeks and RB Sibson, and from 1958–61 attended Elam School of Fine Arts. He held his first solo exhibition in 1963, and in 1967 was awarded a Queen Elizabeth II Arts Council Travel Fellowship, travelling and working in Europe, North and South America, and Mexico for an extended period. In 1974 he began tutoring at Elam, retiring in 1998 as head of painting. Binney works in a wide range of media, often depicting the west coast of Auckland and Northland, and is particularly known for his depictions of sea, sky and native birds.

Joanna Braithwaite has lived in New Zealand and Australia for most of her life, although she was born, in 1962, in Halifax, England. She arrived in New Zealand in 1965, and later studied at the University of Canterbury School of Fine Arts, graduating BFA in 1984. After living for several years in Melbourne and Christchurch, she moved to Sydney in 1999, studying for an MFA at the city's College of Fine Arts. Her work has a slightly surreal bent, and often features the relationships between animals and humans.

Frank Brangwyn (1867–1956) was one of England's most versatile artists, whose output included oil paintings and watercolours, etchings, murals, stained glass, mosaics and pottery, as well as works of architecture and interiors. He was born in Bruges, Belgium, in 1867, into an Anglo-Welsh family, and lived most of his life in England. He travelled widely, and undertook major commissions to produce murals in the US and Canada in addition to the UK. He died in 1956.

Mark Braunias was the inaugural winner of the James Wallace Art Award in 1992. He was born in Tauranga in 1955, and studied at the Canterbury University School of Fine Arts, graduating with a BFA in 1987. He was artist in residence at the Dunedin Public Art Gallery in 2002, Southland Museum and Art Gallery in 2005, and the Sarjeant Gallery, Whanganui, in 2007. In 2010 Braunias was awarded a Fulbright/Wallace scholarship to take up a residency at the Headlands Center for the Arts in San Francisco. He currently lives and works in Auckland and Kawhia.

Kushana Bush uses the media of gouache, watercolour and pencil to explore aspects of the human experience such as anxiety, death and sexuality in delicate works that often take the viewer by surprise. Bush was born in 1983 in Dunedin, where she currently lives, and graduated BFA from Otago Polytechnic in 2004. She has spent time at the Changdong Art Studio in Seoul, and in 2009 she won the Art & Australia Contemporary Art Award. Bush was also the 2011 Frances Hodgkins Fellow at the University of Otago.

Gavin Chilcott works in a range of media, producing watercolour and oil paintings, ceramics, sculpture and installations, as well as collaborating in the design of furniture and rugs. Born in Auckland in 1950, Chilcott began his studies at Auckland Technical Institute in 1967, then attended Elam School of Fine Arts from 1968–70, graduating with a Diploma in Fine Arts. His first exhibition was held at the Barry Lett Gallery in Auckland in 1976, and since that time he has exhibited regularly throughout New Zealand and internationally. He currently lives in Auckland.

Philip Clairmont (1949–1984) was one of New Zealand's most gifted expressionist painters. He was born in Nelson, and from 1967–70 studied at the University of Canterbury School of Fine Arts, where his tutors included Rudi Gopas, although it has been said that he needed only encouragement, not tuition. His work is powerful, sometimes disturbing, and full of vibrant colour, often hallucinogenic in style. His subjects range from domestic interiors, which often have anthropomorphic elements, to portraits, self-portraits, nudes and crucifixions.

Russell Clark (1905–1966) was born in Christchurch and studied at the Canterbury College School of Fine Arts from 1922 to 1927. He later became known for his work as an illustrator, particularly with the *School Journal* and the *New Zealand Listener*, but he was also an accomplished painter, muralist and sculptor. During the Second World War he was an official war artist, and from 1947 until his death he taught at the University of Canterbury School of Art.

Ruth Cleland works in a photo-realist style, often pairing images of different locations in meticulously created works that may combine painting, drawing and printmaking. Cleland was born in Hamilton in 1976, and studied at the Otago School of Art, Dunedin, graduating with a Bachelor of Fine Arts in 1998 and a Masters in 2002. She also worked at the school from 2003–2005 as a lecturer in printmaking. In 2009 she undertook a three-month artist's residency at the Vermont Studio Center in the US. She currently lives and works in Auckland.

John Coley was born in 1935, in Palmerston North, and it was here that he received his first training as an artist. Later he studied at the University of Canterbury School of Fine Arts, where one of his tutors was Rudi Gopas. He was also a founding member of the 20/20 Vision group of artists. Coley has had a long career as an artist, teacher, commentator and administrator. Between 1981 and 1995 he was director of the Robert McDougall Art Gallery, the forerunner of the Christchurch Art Gallery. He now lives in Auckland.

Shane Cotton (Nga Puhi, Ngati Rangi, Ngati Hine) studied at the University of Canterbury School of Fine Arts, graduating in painting in 1988. In 1998 he was awarded the Frances Hodgkins Fellowship at the University of Otago, and the same year won the Seppelt Contemporary Art Award, administered by the Sydney Museum of Contemporary Art. His work frequently addresses issues of cultural identity, colonialism and Maori spirituality. Best known as a painter, he has also produced several series of lithographs, and has taught at Massey University. Cotton was born in Upper Hutt in 1964, and currently lives in Palmerston North.

Matthew Couper studied at the Quay School of the Arts, Whanganui, graduating in 1998 with a Bachelor of Fine Arts. Since then he has travelled widely, and his work was strongly influenced by his first-hand discovery of art in Europe, particularly Italy, and the US, and later the folk art traditions of Mexico. He works in a range of media, including painting, drawing, etching and model-making, and his style changes frequently as he investigates new ideas. Couper was born in Hastings in 1976, and currently lives in Los Angeles.

Julian Dashper (1960–2009) was born in Auckland in 1960, and studied at Elam School of Fine Arts, graduating in 1982. Throughout his career he exhibited widely in New Zealand, Australia and Europe, and his work is held in major collections including the Museum of Contemporary Art, Sydney; the Ludwig Forum für Internationale Kunst in Aachen, Germany, and the Stedelijk Museum in Amsterdam. In

2005 a retrospective of his work was mounted at the Sioux City Art Center in Iowa, USA. Julian Dashper died in Auckland in 2009.

Tony de Lautour has lived in Christchurch for most of his life, although he was born in Melbourne, in 1965. He studied at the University of Canterbury School of Fine Arts, and in 1988 graduated with a Bachelor of Fine Arts majoring in sculpture. He held his first solo exhibition in 1994, and a year later won the Visa Gold Art Award. De Lautour is best known as a painter, and his work is held in major collections including Te Papa Tongarewa, Christchurch Art Gallery, Auckland Art Gallery, and the National Gallery of Australia.

Austen Deans, who is a descendant of Christchurch's pioneering Deans family, has had a long career as a landscape artist. He was born in 1915 and studied at the University of Canterbury School of Art, graduating in 1938. During the Second World War he was an assistant to war artist Peter McIntyre, and before returning to New Zealand he studied at the Sir John Cass College in London. He is best known for his Canterbury landscapes, but he also produced a series of paintings and photographs of Antarctica after travelling there in 1981. Deans has lived for many years at Peel Forest, South Canterbury.

Bryan Dew was born in Hastings in 1940. He studied at Elam School of Fine Arts, and early in his career developed a reputation for his satirical paintings. In 1963 he moved to London to study at the Royal College of Art Design School, later travelling to the US to study design at Indiana University. In 1967 he moved to New York City to work as a graphic designer, and it was only in the late 1980s that he took up painting again. Bryan Dew died in New York in 2006.

Robert Ellis was born in Northampton, England, in 1929, and now lives in Auckland. He studied at Northampton School of Art and the Royal College of Art in London before coming to New Zealand in 1957 to take up a lectureship at Elam School of Fine Arts, where he remained until 1994. Primarily known as a painter, Ellis has also worked in etching, tapestry, lithography, medallic casting, photography and video.

Simon Esling works as a graphic artist, producing works on paper in a highly individual, often somewhat surreal style. He usually works in ink and watercolour, and his subjects range from fragments of landscape to weapons, figures and unidentifiable forms. Esling was born in 1973 in Auckland, where he currently lives, and he has a BA (Hons) and an MFA (Hons) from the University of Auckland.

Jacqueline Fahey was born in Timaru in 1929. She studied at Canterbury College School of Art, graduating with a Bachelor of Fine Arts in 1950, but it was not until the late 1960s that her career as a painter began to develop. She is best known for paintings that show domestic and feminist concerns, and in 2007 her work was included in the exhibition 100 Feminist Painters, held at the Los Angeles Museum of Contemporary Art. In later years her paintings have also included urban scenes and more political themes. Fahey has lived for many years in Auckland.

Graham Fletcher is a New Zealand-born Samoan artist who is based in Auckland. He was born in 1969, and has been a practising artist since 1997. Fletcher studied at Elam, graduating with an MFA in 2004, and more recently has been working toward a Doctorate of Fine Arts. His work has been described as exploring cultural issues in a post-colonial context, although his style changes frequently, and he has produced multi-layered collages and sculptural works in addition to paintings.

Tony Fomison (1939–1990) originally trained as a sculptor, although he is known primarily for his painting. A contemporary of Allen Maddox and Philip Clairmont, he studied at the Canterbury School of Fine Arts from 1956–60, and also worked as an archaeological assistant at Canterbury Museum, which introduced him to the Maori rock art of the South Island. Extended travel in Europe enabled him to study the old masters, which had a major influence on his career, while his later work particularly reflected his strong interest in Samoan culture. From the 1970s he mainly lived in Auckland.

Otis Frizzell (born 1971) has been a graffiti artist for over 20 years, and his work appears on the walls of offices such as Saatchi & Saatchi, on record sleeves and television promotions, on tee-shirts and packaging. He has been described as an artistic innovator, style leader, hip hop performer, radio and TV personality, tattooist and graphic designer. A painter, printmaker and illustrator, he is currently collaborating with Mike Weston as Weston Frizzell, producing limited edition stencilled and hand-painted works that are both light-hearted and challenging.

Max Gimblett has mainly lived in New York since 1972, although he was born in Auckland, in 1935. In the 1960s he studied drawing at the Ontario College of Art, Toronto, and painting at the San Francisco Art Institute. He is influenced by both Eastern and Western spiritual beliefs and psychology, and from 1983–2007 he studied at the CG Jung Foundation in New York. These interests are reflected in his use of shaped canvases, with their range of associations and symbolism, and varied combinations of materials, including gold, silver, copper and bronze.

Charles Goldie (1870–1947) was born in Auckland, where as a young man he studied art part-time under Louis John Steele. In 1893, at the age of 22, he moved to Paris to begin studies at the Académie Julian, receiving a thorough, but conservative, training in traditional painting and drawing. After returning to Auckland in 1898 he established a career as a painter of portraits and historical allegories. Later he turned to the portraits of elderly Maori for which he is known today, recording in almost photographic detail what he saw as 'the noble relics of a noble race'.

Rudi Gopas (1913–1983) came to New Zealand after the Second World War, settling first in Dunedin then in Christchurch, where he taught at the Canterbury University School of Fine Arts for almost 20 years from 1959. Gopas was born in Lithuania and studied at the Kannas Art School from 1933–38. Earlier in his career his style reflected a form of expressionist realism, although it became more abstract in the 1960s. His work is characterised by his strong use of colour and the intensity of his brushwork.

Edward Halliday (1902–1984) was a British artist who main-tained a high reputation as a portrait painter from 1930 to 1960. He also produced murals and was a commentator on art and design. His 1955 portrait of Sir Edmund Hillary was commissioned for the city of Auckland by Sir Ernest and Lady Davies, and at the time was regarded as one of his finest works. Halliday was born in Liverpool in 1902 and died in 1984.

Bill Hammond was born in Christchurch in 1947, and today lives and works in Lyttelton. Although he studied at Ilam School of Fine Arts from 1966–68, he did not begin exhibiting his paintings until 1980. Previously he had worked as a toy-maker. Hammond began to create his paintings of creatures that are half-human, half-bird, the works for which he is best-known, after a trip to the Auckland Islands in 1991. His painting *Waiting for Buller* was the winner of the Paramount Award in the 1994 Wallace Art Awards.

Pat Hanly (1932–2004) grew up in Palmerston North and studied at the Canterbury College School of Art before travelling to Europe in 1957. His studies there included attending night classes at the Chelsea School of Art, and he also exhibited in London, Liverpool and Edinburgh. After returning to New Zealand in 1962 he developed a strong reputation as a painter and printmaker, and his work has been exhibited widely both in New Zealand and internationally. Hanly's work is known for its brilliant use of colour and its vitality, often combined with a serious message.

Jeffrey Harris has been painting since 1970, and was the Frances Hodgkins Fellow at the University of Otago in 1977. He also represented New Zealand at the Carnegie Institute Biennale in Pittsburgh, Pennsylvania, in 1982, and in 2003 won the Paramount Prize in the James Wallace Art Awards. A self-taught artist, in the early part of his career Harris created works that were expressionist in style, becoming more abstract following a move to Melbourne in 1986. Since his return to New Zealand in 2000 his work has again become more figurative. Born in Akaroa in 1949, Harris now lives and works in Dunedin.

Michael Harrison was born on Auckland's North Shore in 1961. He began his art studies at Auckland Technical Institute in 1980–81, then attended Elam School of Fine Arts, completing a BFA in 1985, and later following this with a Master's degree (1997). He also tutored part-time at Elam from 1995–98 before becoming a full-time artist. His paintings are usually small in scale, often featuring people and animals in ways that have been described as inventive, witty and ambiguous. He exhibits widely in New Zealand and Australia, and his work is held in major collections including Te Papa Tongarewa.

Paul Hartigan was born in 1953 in Timaru, and moved to Auckland in 1968. After studying at Elam School of Fine Arts in the early 1970s he trained in commercial screenprinting in Melbourne. Returning to Auckland in 1974, he established 'Snake Studios', a hand-print studio inspired by Andy Warhol's Factory. Since the 1980s Hartigan has used neon tubing to create abstract works of art which in later years have become more complex and sculptural in form. His work is held in many of New Zealand's major public collections, and large installations are on permanent display at the University of Auckland and the Govett-Brewster Art Gallery in New Plymouth.

Patrick Hayman (1915–1988) was born in London, although his parents had met in Dunedin. In 1936, with the threat of war in Europe and the rise of fascism, Hayman, who was Jewish, moved to Dunedin. He began to paint two years later, attending the Dunedin School of Art for a period before returning to England in 1947. Hayman has been described as one of the most original British artists of the second half of the 20th century, and he was regarded equally highly as a poet. He founded the magazine *The Painter and Sculptor*, and edited it for a number of years.

Chris Heaphy, who is of Ngai Tahu and European descent, was born in Palmerston North in 1965.

He attended the Ilam School of Fine Arts in Christchurch, graduating in 1991 with a BFA in painting, and has an MFA from the RMIT University in Melbourne. He has undertaken residencies in Paris and Champagne, as well as Melbourne, and has exhibited extensively throughout Australasia and Europe. Today Heaphy lives and works in Auckland.

Des Helmore was born in 1940 in Takapau, Hawke's Bay. He studied at Ilam School of Fine Arts, Christchurch, graduating with a Diploma in Fine Arts (Hons) in 1962. In 1966 he moved to London, where he worked as a geographical illustrator at the University College of London, before returning to New Zealand in 1969. He is a highly respected entomological illustrator. His artwork has gained a strong following for its unique observational style, and is held in a number of public and private collections. Since 1975 Helmore has lived in Auckland.

André Hemer was born in Queenstown in 1981, and gained an MFA with distinction from the University of Canterbury School of Fine Arts in 2005. He is the founder of Paintlust, which he describes as a roaming international project space run by a collective of painters, and his work has been exhibited widely in New Zealand, Australia, Korea, Taiwan, Germany and the UK. In 2011 Hemer was based in Sydney, where he was working on a PhD in painting at the University of Sydney.

Michael Hight is a self-taught artist who began painting at the age of 14. He was born in Stratford, Taranaki, in 1961, and spent time in Kawerau and Rotorua. After studying for a Bachelor of Social Science at Victoria University of Wellington he spent time travelling from 1984–87, and lived and painted in London. His interest in beehives, which he uses as a metaphor in many of his realist paintings, dates from the mid-1990s. Hight has worked full-time as an artist since 2001, and now lives and works in Auckland.

Arthur Hipwell (1894–1964) was born in England, but studied at the Elam School of Art, Auckland, and later at Canterbury College School of Art. He settled in Auckland, working as a painter and printmaker, and for a time was art master at King's College, Otahuhu. Hipwell exhibited in the 1940 Centennial Exhibition, and in 1957 won first prize in the Kelliher Art Competition with *Mt Taratara*.

Frances Hodgkins (1869–1947) was born in Dunedin in 1869 and received her first art lessons from her father, an amateur watercolourist. In 1893 she studied with Girolamo Nerli in Dunedin, and from 1895–96 attended the Dunedin School of Art. In 1901 she travelled to Europe to study and work, and from 1903 she was exhibiting at the Royal Academy in London. Although she returned to New Zealand several times, and exhibited her work here, Hodgkins' life and career became firmly established in Europe, where she was a prominent member of the avant garde during the 1930s and 1940s. She died in Dorset, Engand, in 1947.

John Holmwood (1910–1987) was born in Wellington, and at an early age took drawing lessons with H Linley Richardson. At the age of 14 he began work as a commercial artist in the New Zealand Railways Advertising Studios, but he continued to attend evening classes at Wellington Technical College (where he later taught part-time). In the 1940s he moved to Auckland, where he was able to concentrate more on his own painting, and in the 1950s his work was often included in the Auckland City Art Gallery's exhibitions of contemporary New Zealand painting. His paintings were wide-ranging in style and subject, often witty, and full of colour.

Ralph Hotere (Te Aupouri) was born near Mitimiti, Northland, in 1931. He attended Auckland Teachers' College, then in 1952 moved to Dunedin to specialise in art. After working as an art advisor for the Education Department he received a New Zealand Art Societies Fellowship which enabled him to study at the Central School of Art in London in 1961. He returned to New Zealand in 1965, and has since worked full-time as a painter, sculptor, printmaker and collaborative artist, perhaps most notably in the neon works created with Bill Culbert. Hotere lives and works near Port Chalmers, Otago.

Sara Hughes is a painter and installation artist. Born in Vancouver in 1971, Hughes now lives in Auckland, and has a BFA and an MFA from the Elam School of Fine Arts. In 2005 she won both the Wallace Art Award and the Norsewear Art Award, and in 2008 she was the first New Zealand recipient of the RIPE: Art and Australia/ANZ Private Bank Contemporary Art Award. She was the Frances Hodgkins Fellow at the University of Otago in 2003, attended the International Studio and Curatorial Program in New York in 2007, and was awarded the Creative New Zealand Visual Artists Residency at the Künstlerhaus Bethanien, Berlin in 2008/09.

Gavin Hurley, who was born in Auckland in 1973, graduated from Elam School of Fine Arts in 1998 with a Bachelor of Fine Arts in painting. He has become known particularly for his witty and meticulously constructed portraits of historical figures. His work has been exhibited widely, both nationally and internationally, including in the 2011 About Face: Aspects of Portraiture at the Papakura Art Gallery, Papakura. Hurley has also collaborated with other artists such as Martin Poppelwell and Sam Mitchell.

Michael Illingworth (1932–1988) was born in Yorkshire and moved to New Zealand in 1951. He studied painting in Europe between 1957 and 1960 before returning to New Zealand and settling in Puhoi, north of Auckland. In 1965 he became the first Frances Hodgkins Fellow at the University of Otago. Many of his paintings feature highly stylised figures that look directly out at the viewer in a detached and apparently bleak manner, but he is also remembered for his landscapes and still-lifes, and his strong use of colour.

Simon Ingram is a senior lecturer at Elam School of Fine Arts as well as a practising artist with a particular interest in the connections between art and contemporary technology. He was born in Wellington in 1971, and has studied at Elam (BA Fine Art 1992 and DocFA 2006), the Sydney College of Art (postgraduate diploma 1995 and Master of Visual Arts 1999) and Sydney TAFE (Certificate in Information Technology). His work is exhibited nationally and internationally, and held in major New Zealand public and private collections.

John Kinder (1819–1903) was a London-born clergyman who came to New Zealand in 1855 to take up the position of headmaster of Auckland's Church of England Grammar School. He had painted in watercolours from an early age, and during the 1860s he also developed an interest in photography. He remained in New Zealand for the rest of his life, and during his extensive travels through the country he painted and photographed all aspects of the landscape and society. He produced nearly a thousand paintings, drawings, and photographs, although his work was rarely exhibited during his lifetime.

Tom Kreisler (1938–2007) was born in Buenos Aires in 1938, and came to New Zealand in 1952.

In the mid-1960s he studied at the Ilam School of Fine Arts, where his tutors included Rudi Gopas and Bill Sutton. He moved to New Plymouth in 1968, and was closely associated with the Govett-Brewster Gallery. After spending time in Mexico in the late 1970s he produced a significant body of work that focused on a range of cultural, political and social issues. Kreisler died in New Plymouth in 2002, but he is remembered as an influential painter, poet and teacher.

Tony Lane has been a working artist for over 40 years, since graduating from Elam School of Fine Arts in 1970. He was born in Katikati in 1949, and currently lives in Auckland. Lane's work has a strong connection to Western art traditions, and he maintains a fascination with early Italian, Dutch and Spanish painters. His work is sophisticated and intelligent, often depicting everyday objects, and frequently incorporating materials such as gold and silver leaf to create a luminous surface. A survey exhibition of his work was held at the City Gallery Wellington in 2006–07, and his paintings are held in major collections throughout New Zealand.

Eric Lee-Johnson (1908–1993) was an artist, illustrator, designer and photographer. He was born in Suva, moving to New Zealand with his family when he was four. He attended Elam School of Fine Arts from 1923–26, after which he began work as a commercial artist with Wilson and Horton. In 1930 he moved to London, working in an advertising agency and attending evening classes at the Central School of Arts and Crafts. He returned to New Zealand in 1938, and after a period of illness moved to Piha where he became a full-time artist.

Saskia Leek was born in 1970 in Christchurch, and has a Bachelor of Fine Arts from the University of Canterbury School of Fine Arts. In 2005 she was artist in residence at the Govett Brewster Art Gallery in New Plymouth. She completed a Master's at Elam School of Fine Arts in Auckland in 2005, also winning the painting prize scholarship. In 2010 she was a finalist for the Walters Prize. Leek's work has been shown in solo exhibitions in Sydney and San Francisco, and is held in all major New Zealand public collections. She currently lives and works in Auckland.

Richard Lewer was born in Hamilton in 1970 and studied at Elam School of Fine Arts before completing a Master of Visual Arts at the Victoria College of Arts, University of Melbourne. In 2008 he won the Paramount Award at the Wallace Art Awards, and he was also a finalist in Australia's Basil Sellers Art Prize, for art that incorporates sport in the widest sense, in both 2008 and 2010. Lewer's work focuses on the ambivalent, the unsolved and the newsworthy, which he explores using a wide range of techniques and materials. He is currently based in Melbourne.

Doris Lusk (1916–90) was born in Dunedin, and studied at the Dunedin School of Art from 1933 to 1938. After leaving art school she worked as a commercial ticket writer and taught art part-time at two Dunedin schools before moving to Christchurch in 1941. She was a member of The Group artists, and became a leading exponent of the New Zealand regionalist landscape school. Lusk also painted portraits, and was an accomplished potter. In 1968 she was appointed lecturer at the Canterbury School of Fine Arts, remaining there until her retirement in 1981.

Douglas MacDiarmid was born in New Zealand in 1922, although he has lived in Paris since the late 1940s. He studied at the University of

Canterbury and was for a time a member of Christchurch's Group artists. His work has been exhibited in Paris, Athens, Casablanca and London, as well as in New Zealand, and is held in all major public collections in this country. Although his early work was influenced by expressionism and he is known for his sense of colour, he has remained independent of current movements in art.

Allen Maddox (1948–2000) was born in Liverpool in 1948. His family moved to New Zealand in 1963, settling in Napier. Maddox attended Ilam School of Fine Arts briefly, from 1967 to 1968. He was a finalist in the Benson and Hedges Art Award in 1976 and 1978, and had his first solo exhibition in 1977. His work was shown in a number of solo and group exhibitions throughout his career, including a solo show at Wellington City Gallery in 2000, the year in which he died. Maddox is today regarded as one of New Zealand's finest abstract expressionists.

Karl Maughan is well known for his hyper-real paintings of gardens and native flora, although in later years his works have taken a longer view, focusing more on the landscape. Maughan was born in Wellington in 1964, and studied at Elam School of Fine Arts, graduating MFA in 1987. He moved to London in the 1990s, and in 1997 was a finalist in the John Moore Painting Award, regarded as one of the two premier art awards in Britain. Maughan returned to New Zealand in 2005, and he now lives in Auckland.

Liz Maw was born in Wellington in 1966. She studied for a Diploma of Visual Arts at the Eastern Institute of Technology in Hawke's Bay, and later attended Elam School of Fine Arts, graduating in 2002. Her work has been shown in a number of major exhibitions, including Telecom Prospect 2004: New Art New Zealand, at the City Gallery Wellington, and Mystic Truths (2007) at the Auckland Art Gallery. In 2008 she published *My Beloved Hackneyed*, which features both her paintings and her poetry. Liz Maw currently lives in Auckland.

Colin McCahon was born in Timaru in 1919. He was largely self-taught as an artist, although he studied with Russell Clark in Christchurch from 1933–35 and at the Dunedin Technical College from 1937–39. McCahon lived for a time between Dunedin and the Nelson-Motueka area, moving to Christchurch in 1948, and to Auckland in 1953. He joined the staff of the Auckland City Art Gallery, and later tutored in painting at Elam School of Fine Arts. In 1958 McCahon toured the US, visiting as many art museums as he could, and later that year he produced his *Northland Panels*. It was not until 1971 that he began to paint full-time, however. McCahon remained in Auckland, living in Titirangi, until his death in 1987.

Peter McIntyre (1910–1995) grew up in Dunedin but received most of his training at the Slade School of Fine Art in London, where he studied from 1931 to 1934. He remained in England through the 1930s, working as a freelance commercial artist while also exhibiting modernist contemporary paintings. In 1941 he was appointed New Zealand's official war artist, and it was during the war that McIntyre moved away from the avant garde. McIntyre returned to New Zealand in 1946 and developed a highly successful career, although his later work attracted derision from many in the art establishment who regarded it as outdated and conservative in style.

Raymond McIntyre (1879–1933) was born in

Christchurch and from the age of 15 attended evening classes at the Canterbury School of Fine Arts. He also studied with Petrus van der Velden before moving in 1909 to London, where his teachers included Walter Sickert and William Nicholson. McIntyre painted portraits, interior scenes and landscapes, although today he is best known for his portraits. He was also a writer, printmaker, photographer and theatre and music critic, and between 1923 and 1931 he contributed art reviews to the London journal *Architectural Review*.

Andrew McLeod was born in Rotorua in 1976 and grew up in Auckland, where he currently lives. He studied at Elam School of Art, graduating BFA in 1998. McLeod works in a range of media, as a painter, digital artist and printmaker. He has exhibited nationally and internationally, including taking part in How to Live Together, the 27th Bienal de Sao Paulo, Brazil, in 2006. In 2004 he won the National Drawing Award, and in 2006 was runner-up in the Wallace Art Awards.

Richard McWhannell studied at the University of Canterbury School of Fine Arts, graduating with a Diploma in Fine Arts in 1972. He has exhibited regularly since 1974. McWhannell was born in Akaroa in 1952, moving to Auckland, where he is currently based, in 1978. During the 1980s he travelled in Europe, exploring the region's art history and studying the work of the old masters. He works mainly in oil and watercolour, producing figurative works, portraits and landscapes, although he has also undertaken bronze-casting, carving in wood and stone, watercolour paintings and printmaking.

Judy Millar's work is widely recognised internationally, and she has studied and worked in Italy, France and Germany as well as New

Zealand. She was born in Auckland in 1957, and currently lives in Auckland and Berlin. She has a BFA and an MFA from Elam School of Fine Arts, and in 1991 she received an Italian government scholarship to undertake postgraduate study in Turin. She won the Paramount Award in the Wallace Awards in 2002, and in 2009 she represented New Zealand at the Venice Biennale with her work *Giraffe Bottle Gun*.

Sam Mitchell was born in Colorado Springs in the US, and moved to New Zealand with her family as a young girl. She studied at Elam School of Fine Arts, completing a BFA in 1998 and an MFA in 2000. In 2010 she won the Paramount Prize in the Wallace Art Awards, leading to a six-month residency at the International Studio and Curatorial Program in New York. Her work reflects her fascination with the techniques of cartooning and tattooing, which she often combines to create incongruous and thought-provoking images.

Milan Mrkusich, who is of Dalmatian descent, was born in Dargaville in 1925. When he was two his family moved to Auckland, where he still lives. He is mainly self-taught as an artist, although he studied commercial art in the 1940s. In 1949 he was one of the founders of Brenner Associates, an architectural design company, working there throughout the 1950s as a colour consultant and exhibition designer, while painting in his spare time. Mrkusich was one of New Zealand's earliest abstract artists, and is known for the subtlety of his surfaces and his continual exploration of colour.

Archibald Nicoll (1886–1953) was one of New Zealand's leading portrait and landscape painters of the 1920s and 1930s. Born in Lincoln, Canterbury, he studied at the Canterbury School of Art under Sydney Lough Thompson. After a short period teaching at Elam School of Fine Arts in Auckland he travelled to Europe in 1910, studying at the Westminster School of Art,

Edinburgh College of Art and later the Scottish Academy School of Art. He later returned to New Zealand, and between 1920 and 1928 was director of the Canterbury College School of Art.

Seung Yul Oh was born in Seoul, Korea, in 1981, and moved to New Zealand as a teenager. He studied at Elam, gaining a BFA and an MFA (2005). In 2004 he won the Waikato National Art Award, and since then his work has become increasingly exhibited. Oh is a painter and a sculptor, and he has used such widely varying materials as wood, concrete, found objects, extruded foam, popcorn and balloons. He also incorporates sound and video in his work at times. In 2010 Oh was awarded the Harriet Friedlander Residency, which enabled him to live and work in New York.

Reuben Paterson (Ngati Rangitihi and Tuhoe) lives and works in Auckland, where he was born in 1973. He studied at Elam School of Fine Arts, graduating in 1997. After being awarded the Moët and Chandon Fellowship to France, he remained in Europe for a further two years, travelling widely and living in England. He has also lived and worked in Greece. Paterson has represented New Zealand at a number of events, including the 8th Festival of Pacific Arts Biennale d'Art Contemporain (2000), the Prague International Biennale of Contemporary Art (2005) and the 17th Biennale of Sydney (2010).

Johanna Pegler is known particularly for her idiosyncratic landscapes. She graduated from Elam School of Fine Arts in 1987, and after a period travelling and working in the South Island in the early nineties she settled in Waikawau Bay, at the tip of the Coromandel Peninsula. In 2004 she moved to Whanganui, initially as artist in residence at Tylee Cottage, and in 2009 was artist in residence at Awhitu Regional Park, on the shores of the Manukau Harbour. Pegler was born in Auckland in 1965.

Christopher Perkins (1891–1968) was born in Peterborough, England. He studied in London at the Heatherley's School of Art and the Slade School of Fine Art, as well as in Italy. In 1929 he emigrated to New Zealand to teach art at Wellington Technical College, later moving to Rotorua. He advocated a distinctly New Zealand school of painting, emphasising the country's clear light and the use of local subjects, and had a strong interest in Maori art. In 1934 Perkins returned to England, where he is best known for his portraits and work as an unofficial war artist.

Juliet Peter (1915–2010) was a painter, print-maker, potter and designer. She was born in Canterbury, and studied at the Canterbury College School of Art in the 1930s. After moving to Wellington she painted and worked as an illustrator for the *School Journal* in the late 1940s, before moving to London where she studied printmaking and ceramics at Hammersmith School of Art. She returned to New Zealand in 1955, and with her husband Roy Cowan played a major part in the development of studio ceramics in this country.

Margot Philips (1902–1988) arrived in New Zealand in 1938, a refugee from Nazi Germany. She attended a number of Auckland Art Gallery summer schools with Colin McCahon in the 1950s, and was later based in Hamilton. An active member of the Waikato Society of Arts, she exhibited widely in the 1960s and 1970s. A retrospective of her work, Margot Philips: Her Own World, was held at the Waikato Art Museum in 1987.

Séraphine Pick was born in Kawakawa in 1964.

She studied at the University of Canterbury School of Fine Arts, graduating BFA in 1987, and also has a Diploma of Teaching. In 1994 she received the Olivia Spencer-Bower Foundation Art Award, and in 1995 the Rita Angus Cottage Residency in Wellington. She was also the Frances Hodgkins Fellow at the University of Otago in 1999. A survey exhibition of her work was toured in 2009. Pick now lives and works in Wellington.

Kim Pieters, who is of Dutch-English descent, was born in Rotorua in 1959. She has worked as an artist since the early 1980s, and has been exhibiting since 1989. Although best known as an abstract painter, she is also a musician and video artist. In her work Pieters uses mixed media on board and a variety of papers, including building paper and wallpaper. She currently lives and works in Dunedin.

Martin Poppelwell (born 1968) is a painter and ceramicist based in Hawke's Bay. He attended Elam School of Fine Arts in the early 1990s, and also studied under potter Ross Mitchell-Anyon in Whanganui. He works in a wide range of media, including oils and watercolours, ink, canvas, paper and clay, frequently creating layers, although line is always important. His work has been widely exhibited, and features in Collecting Contemporary at Te Papa Tongarewa from June 2011 to June 2012.

Patrick Pound is an artist and photographer best known for his abstract collages. He was born in Hamilton in 1962 and studied at Elam (BFA, 1987) before moving to Australia in 1989. He now lives and works in Melbourne. His work is held in a number of major collections including the National Gallery of Australia, Te Papa Tongarewa and the National Gallery of Victoria. In 1995 he featured in the American

Biographical Institute's book *Five Hundred Leaders of Influence*. He is currently completing a doctorate in art history at Melbourne University.

John Pule was born in 1962 in Liku, Niue, but when he was two his family moved to Auckland, where he lives and works today. Visits to Niue as an adult inspired an interest in the island's history and mythology, and his paintings often include references to hiapo, the Niuean tapa cloth, and other symbols. A self-taught artist, he is a poet and writer as well as a painter and printmaker, often combining the different forms. His work has been included in two Asia-Pacific Triennials at the Queensland Art Gallery, and in 2004 it also formed part of Paradise Now! at the Asia Society in New York.

Jude Rae began her art studies at the Julian Ashton Art School in Sydney, where she was born in 1956. She later studied art history at the University of Sydney, graduating in 1980, and took up painting again soon after. She was awarded the Australia Council Residency in Paris, and worked in London in 1989 before moving to New Zealand, where she completed a Masters at the University of Canterbury School of Fine Arts in 1993. Although she now lives in Canberra, she continues to exhibit in New Zealand, and in 2006 was Visiting Artist at the Dunedin Public Art Gallery.

John Reynolds lives and works in Auckland, where he was born in 1956. Since graduating from Elam School of Fine Arts in 1978 he has won a number of awards, including the Montana Lindauer Award in 1988 and the VisaGold Award in 1994, and he was a finalist in the Wallace Art Awards in both 2002 and 2008. In 2006 his work *Clouds* was featured at the Zones of Contact Sydney Biennale. He works in a range of forms, and has collaborated with other artists such as the painter Ralph Hotere and poet Leigh Davis.

James Robinson has worked full-time as an

artist for almost two decades. Born in 1972, he graduated BFA from Otago Polytechnic School of Art in 2001. In 2007 he won the Paramount Award at the Wallace Art Awards, and in 2009 he was a finalist in the Waikato Art Award. He has also undertaken a number of residencies, including the International Studio and Curatorial Program in New York; artist in residence at Tylee Cottage, Whanganui, and in 2009 the Takt Kunstprojektraum art residency in East Berlin. He currently lives in Port Chalmers, Dunedin.

Peter Robinson originally trained as a sculptor, but his work includes painting, drawing, installation and digital media. He was born in Ashburton in 1966, and has a Bachelor of Fine Arts from Ilam School of Fine Arts, University of Canterbury. His early work explored issues of identity and ethnicity in relation to his own Maori heritage, but in recent years he has responded to more global issues. He has held a number of international residencies, and in 2008 was awarded the Walters Art Prize. Robinson now lives and works in Berlin.

Cedric Savage was born in Christchurch in 1901, and studied at the Canterbury College School of Art during the 1920s. He initially worked as a modeller and designer, and began painting after travelling in the Pacific islands in the late 1920s and 1930s. After serving in the Second World War he settled near Takaka, but later left New Zealand to travel and paint in Europe, although he continued to exhibit in this country. Savage is best known for his landscape paintings, and in 1961 won first prize in the Kelliher Art Awards. He died in Spain in 1969.

Michael Smither is a painter, printmaker, composer, and conservationist. He was born in New Plymouth in 1939, and after a period of study at Elam School of Fine Arts in 1959–60 he returned to Taranaki to live. Many of his paintings from the 1960s feature the landscape of this region, as well as domestic life. Smither has also created a large number of screenprints and sculptures, and for a period worked mainly on musical theory and composition. In 1970 he was the Frances Hodgkins Fellow at the University of Otago. Smither currently lives and works on the Coromandel Peninsula

---

Michael Stevenson is an installation artist who has been described as an 'anthropologist of the avant garde'. He was born in Inglewood in 1964, and currently lives in Berlin. He has held a number of artists' residencies, and his work is held in major collections including the National Gallery of Australia in Canberra, and Te Papa Tongarewa. In 2003 he represented New Zealand at the 50th Venice Biennale with his work *This is the Trekka*, and in 2011 the Museum of Contemporary Art, Sydney, held a survey exhibition of his work.

Helen Stewart (1900–1983), a contemporary of Frances Hodgkins, was born in Wellington. After early studies at Wellington Technical College she spent time in Europe, studying in London and Paris, although she reportedly described her studies at the Sydney School of Art in the early 1930s as the beginning of her 'real' art training. She lived mainly in Sydney between 1930 and 1946, when she returned to Wellington. In 1949 she was one of the Group of Nine artists who exhibited at Helen Hitchings' newly opened gallery for contemporary art, and she continued to explore new ways of working until her death in 1983.

Heather Straka is one of New Zealand's most challenging and accomplished artists. Born in 1972, she completed her Bachelor of Fine Arts at Elam in 1994, followed by a Master of Fine Arts from the University of Canterbury School of Fine Arts in 2000. In 2001 she was awarded the university's Ethel Susan Jones Fine Art Travelling Scholarship, and in 2002 the Pierce Lowe Award for excellence in painting from the Royal Overseas League, London. Straka was also the Frances Hodgkins Fellow at the University of Otago in 2008.

Matt Summers was born in Liverpool in 1976. After moving to New Zealand he studied at the Quay School of the Arts in Whanganui, graduating with a Bachelor of Fine Arts in 1998. Although he is sometimes described as a landscape painter, he has said that, for him, painting is 'about exploring relationships of form and colour. The land provides a simple basis for this.' Summers is currently based in Wellington.

Bill Sutton (1917–2000) was born in Christchurch and studied at the Canterbury College School of Art, graduating in 1937. After serving in the Second World War he also studied at the Anglo-French Art Centre in London. Returning to New Zealand, he painted the Canterbury landscape and became part of The Group, who had begun exhibiting contemporary works as an alternative to the more conservative Canterbury Society of Arts. Sutton also taught at the School of Fine Arts at the University of Canterbury for 40 years.

Grahame Sydney was born in Dunedin in 1948, and his art is strongly associated with the Otago landscape. He has a BA from the University of Otago, graduating in 1969, and held his first solo exhibition at Dunedin's Moray Gallery in 1972. Sydney has been a full-time painter since 1974, and in 1978 was the Frances Hodgkins Fellow at the University of Otago. Best known as a painter, working in oils, watercolours and tempera, he has also produced etchings and lithographs, and a striking series of photographs taken in Antarctica.

Tim Thatcher studied at Unitec in Auckland, where he completed a Bachelor of Design (Hons), and Elam School of Fine Arts, graduating

Master of Fine Arts with First Class Honours in 2006. He was born in Takapuna in 1982, and has been exhibiting since 2005. Thatcher describes his way of working as 'a process of recording uncertainty and doubt', aiming to provide viewers with 'a whimsical and intriguing space onto which they can project their concerns and develop a reflective, open relationship'. He currently lives in Wellington.

Joan Trollope is not widely known, but she did exhibit in the 1960s with The Group in Christchurch and with the Hawke's Bay and East Coast Art Society. In 1964 a solo show at Ikon Fine Arts in Auckland included still-lifes, landscapes and figures in the open, and her work was praised for its honesty, unpretentiousness and harmonious use of colour.

Philip Trusttum's works are often referred to as neo-expressionist and abstract. They demonstrate his highly accomplished sense of colour, as well as a dynamic and always questioning approach. In 2003 Trusttum produced 70 paintings based on Mussorgsky's 'Pictures at an Exhibition', which were displayed on video to accompany a performance of the work by organist Martin Setchell; by the following year the series had grown to 140. Trusttum was born in 1940, in Raetihi, and studied at the University of Canterbury School of Fine Arts, graduating with a Diploma of Fine Arts in 1964. He now lives in Christchurch.

Dennis Knight Turner was born in Whanganui in 1924. He was largely self-taught, but attended evening art classes at Wellington Technical College. He first exhibited in the mid-1940s, and in 1952 was one of a group of artists who took part in an exhibition in London organised by Helen Hitchings. Turner, along with Theo Schoon and

Gordon Walters, was one of the first European artists to incorporate Maori motifs into his work. Although he has lived in London since 1964, in 1992 Turner returned to Whanganui to take up the position of artist in residence at the Sarjeant Gallery's Tylee Cottage.

Petrus van der Velden (1837–1913) was born in Rotterdam, where he worked as a lithographer before studying at the Rotterdam Academy of Art in 1868. The following year he also studied in Berlin. He came to New Zealand in 1890, establishing a studio in Christchurch where he taught and painted. Apart from a period spent in Australia between 1898 and 1904 he remained in New Zealand until his death in Auckland in 1913. Van der Velden was an accomplished landscape artist, best known today for his series of Otira Gorge paintings.

Krystie Wade was born in Auckland in 1982, and studied at Unitec under Richard Fahey, Julian Dashper, Saskia Leek and Julian Hooper, graduating in 2004 with a Bachelor of Design majoring in painting. In 2003 she represented Unitec for one semester at Bremen University in Germany, and in 2009 she undertook an artist's residency at Can Serrat Art Centre in Spain. She has been a finalist in a number of awards, including the James Wallace Art Awards and the Agendo Art Awards in Melbourne. Wade currently lives and works in Auckland.

John Walsh, who is of Te Aitanga a Hauiti and Irish descent, was born in Tolaga Bay in 1954. Although he studied at Ilam School of Fine Arts, he is mainly self-taught. His early works were realist portraits, but his style has since evolved into a highly individual narrative form, referencing both Maori mythology and contemporary events, often with a humorous touch. In 1989 he participated in the Pathfinder International Mural project in New York, and in New Zealand his public commissions include a foyer painting for the Wellington City Council executed in 2004. He is currently based in Wellington.

Gordon Walters (1919–1995) produced works of geometric abstraction in a career that lasted over 60 years. He was also one of the first European artists to incorporate Maori motifs in his work. Walters was born in Wellington in 1919, and trained at Wellington Technical College in the 1930s. He lived in Sydney in the late 1940s, and in 1950 travelled to Europe, where he studied the work of the European abstract painters. He returned to New Zealand in 1953, and in 1956 began the koru paintings for which he is so well known. He died in Christchurch in 1995.

Denys Watkins was born in Wellington in 1945, and studied at the School of Design, Wellington Polytechnic, from 1962 to 64. He attended the Central School of Art in London in 1967, and studied painting and printmaking at the Royal College of Art between 1968 and 1970. Since 1980 Watkins has been a lecturer at Elam School of Fine Arts, and in 1985 he was artist in residence at the Canberra School of Art. The following year he was awarded Australia's Transfield Art Prize. His work incorporates a variety of media, including etching, screenprinting, watercolour, acrylic and oil painting.

Rohan Wealleans was born in Invercargill in 1977 and graduated from Elam School of Fine Arts with a BFA in 2000, and gained an MFA in 2003. In 2005 he won the Waikato Art Award and was the Frances Hodgkins Fellow at the University of Otago; in 2006 he won the Paramount Prize at the Wallace Art Awards, and in 2010 his work appeared in the 17th Biennale of

Sydney. Curator Robert Leonard has described Wealleans' work, which combines the figurative and the abstract in striking and often startling ways, as 'pornographic abstraction'.

John Weeks (1886–1965) was born in Devonshire, England, and came to New Zealand in 1892. He studied under Archibald Nicoll at Elam School of Fine Arts between 1908 and 1911, and later at Canterbury College School of Art, and spent time at the Royal Scottish Academy of Painting, Sculpture and Architecture, and André Lhote's Academy in Paris. He travelled widely in France, Italy and North Africa before returning to New Zealand in 1929 and settling in Auckland. Weeks was to become influential both as an artist and as a teacher, known for his cubist-influenced style and strong sense of design and colour.

Nugent Welch (1881–1970) was born in Akaroa, although he moved to Wellington when quite young. He studied briefly at the Canterbury School of Art and Wellington Technical College, but was essentially a self-taught artist. After working as a clerk he became a full-time painter in 1907, and was an official war artist for a time during the First World War. Later, after returning to Wellington, he became a successful landscape and marine artist. He was an active member of the New Zealand Academy of Fine Arts, and a member of the management committee of the National Art Gallery from 1936 to 1964.

Grant Whibley gained a Diploma in Figurative Studies from the Whitecliffe Art School, Auckland in 1984, and later studied at Elam, graduating with a BFA in 1994 and an MFA (First Class Honours) in 1997. He has exhibited throughout New Zealand since the 1990s and has won a number of awards, including the Emerging Artist Award at the James Wallace Awards in 2002, the Premier Award in the Norsewear Art Awards in 2003, and the Molly Morpeth Canaday Award in 2004. Whibley was born in Tokoroa and grew up in Whakatane.

Freeman White is best known for his portraits, although he is also an accomplished landscape painter. He was born in Hawke's Bay in 1979, and studied at the Learning Connexion in Wellington. In 2006 he won the Adam Portraiture Award and was invited to undertake a residency at the National Portrait Gallery of Scotland. Following this he undertook a residency at the Staffelter Hoff winery in Germany's Mosel Valley, and in 2009 he was artist in residence and exhibited at The Studios of Key West, Florida. A number of his works are held in the New Zealand Portrait Gallery.

Brendon Wilkinson was born in Masterton in 1974. He studied at Elam School of Fine Arts, graduating BFA in 1998. Working as a model-maker and painter, he produces works that reflect his interest in surrealism and science fiction, using a range of media. He remains Masterton-based.

Emily Wolfe was born in Auckland and studied at Elam from 1993–1996, graduating with a BFA. In 1998 she began studies at the Slade School of Fine Art in London, winning a Ryoichi Sasakawa Scholarship from Massey University in 1999, and completing her Master's degree in 2000. She continues to be based in London, exhibiting throughout England, in Belgium and in New Zealand, and she travels between this country and the northern hemisphere frequently.

Toss Woollaston (1910–1998) was one of New Zealand's foremost landscape painters, and the first New Zealand artist to be knighted in recognition of his services to art. He grew up in

Taranaki, later moving to the South Island where he spent a year at the Canterbury School of Art before moving to Dunedin where he studied with Robert Field. In 1934 he moved to Mapua, near Nelson, and in 1949 to Greymouth. In 1968 he moved back to the Nelson region, and it is his landscapes of this area, with their characteristic ochre colours and free brushwork, for which he is best known today.

Image Credits

Page 11 image courtesy of the Auckland Art Gallery Toi o Tāmaki (gift of the Friends of the Auckland Art Gallery, 1964) and permission courtesy of the Colin McCahon Research and Publication Trust; **page 13** author's own image; **page 15** image courtesy of Archives New Zealand Te Rua Mahara o te Kawanatanga Wellington Office (reference number: AAAC 898 NCWA 15) and permission courtesy of Simon McIntyre; **page 17** image courtesy of the Christchurch Art Gallery Te Puna o Waiwhetu (presented by the Christchurch City Council in memory of former Town Clerk, Mr H S Feast OBE, 1961) and permission courtesy of the AA Deans Art Trust; **page 19** image courtesy of Museum of New Zealand Te Papa Tongarewa (purchased 1951, registration number: 1951-0005-1) and permission courtesy of The Bridgeman Art Library Limited; **page 20** author's own image *Tiger Tim's Annual*, 1926; **page 21** author's own image, *A Book of Ships*, Blackie & Son, 1954; **page 23** image courtesy of the Auckland War Memorial Museum; **page 24** author's own image, *New Zealand Flowers and Birds*, New Zealand Tourist and Publicity Dept.; **page 25** image courtesy of Museum of New Zealand Te Papa Tongarewa (gift of Sir Henry Kelliher, 1957, registration number: 1957-0022-1); **page 29** image courtesy of the collection of the Hawke's Bay Museums Trust, Hawke's Bay Museum and Art Gallery (reference number: 6793); **page 31** image courtesy of the collection of the Hawke's Bay Museums Trust, Hawke's Bay Museum and Art Gallery (reference number: L89/5/2); **page 33** image courtesy of Simon McIntyre; **page 35** image courtesy of the Christchurch Art Gallery Te Puna o Waiwhetu (purchased, 2007) and permission courtesy of the artist; **page 37** image courtesy of Museum of New Zealand Te Papa Tongarewa (gift of the New Zealand Academy of Fine Arts, 1947) and permission courtesy of the Christchurch Art Gallery Te Puna o Waiwhetu; **page 39** author's own image; **page 41** image courtesy of the Christchurch Art Gallery Te Puna o Waiwhetu (69/148) and permission courtesy of Rosalie Archer; **page 43** image courtesy of Museum of New Zealand Te Papa Tongarewa (purchased 1995 with Dugald Henderson Bequest funds) and permission courtesy of Robert Lee-Johnson, Eric Lee-Johnson Limited; **page 45** image courtesy of the Auckland Art Gallery Toi o Tāmaki (on loan from The Fletcher Trust) and permission courtesy of the Fletcher Trust Collection; **page 47** courtesy of the Museum of New Zealand Te Papa Tongarewa (purchased 2003, registration number: 2003-0038-1) and permission courtesy of the artist; **page 49** image courtesy of the Christchurch Art Gallery Te Puna o Waiwhetu (gifted by Henry Charles Drury van Asch, 1932); **page 51** image courtesy of the Museum of New Zealand Te Papa Tongarewa (gift of the New Zealand Academy of Fine Arts, 1936, registration number: 1936-0012-273) and permission courtesy of Robin George Alexander Nicoll; **page 53** image courtesy of the Collection of The Suter Art Gallery Te Aratoi o Whakatu (presented by The Suter Art Society in 1904); **page 55** image courtesy of the Christchurch Art Gallery Te Puna o Waiwhetu (purchased 1955) and image courtesy of Patrick T Holland for the Doris Lusk Estate; **page 57** image courtesy of the Auckland Art Gallery Toi o Tāmaki (purchased 1967) and permission courtesy of Rachel Wren; **page 59** image courtesy of the Chartwell Collection, Auckland Art Gallery Toi o Tāmaki (1977) and permission courtesy of the Guardian Trust as Trustee of the Estate of Margot L Philips; **page 61** image courtesy of collection of The Suter Art Gallery Te Aratoi o Whakatu, presented by The Suter Art Society in 1904; **page 63** image courtesy of Museum of New Zealand Te Papa Tongarewa (purchased 1996 with New Zealand Lottery Grants Board funds, registration number: 1996-0022-1) and licensed by Viscopy 2011, © Patrick Hayman/DACS; **page 65** image courtesy of Auckland Art Gallery Toi o Tāmaki (purchased with funds from the William James Jobson Trust, 1982); **page 67** image courtesy of Auckland Art Gallery Toi o Tā maki (purchased 1976); **page 69** image courtesy of Webb's; **Page 71** image courtesy of Auckland Art Gallery Toi o Tāmaki (purchased 1957) and permission courtesy of The Estate of Rita Angus; **page 73** image courtesy of Museum of New Zealand Te Papa Tongarewa (purchased 1984 with New Zealand Lottery Board funds, registration number: 1984-

0066-1) and permission courtesy of the artist; **page 75** image courtesy of the collection of the Sarjeant Gallery Te Whare O Rehua, Whanganui (commissioned by the Sarjeant Gallery Te Whare O Rehua, Whanganui, 1930, reference number: 1930/5/1); **page 77** image courtesy of the owner (photographed by Patrick Reynolds); **page 79** image courtesy of the Hanly Family Trust; **page 81** image courtesy of Auckland Art Gallery Toi o Tāmaki (purchased 1959) and permission courtesy of Philip Woollaston as Trustee of The Toss Woollaston Trust; **page 83** image courtesy of Auckland Art Gallery Toi o Tāmaki (on loan from a Private Collection) and permission courtesy of the Colin McCahon Research and Publication Trust; **page 85** image courtesy of Milford Galleries, Dunedin (photographed by Glenn Frei); **page 87** image courtesy of Auckland Art Gallery Toi o Tāmaki (gift of Margaret Orbell, 2002) and permission courtesy of Gregg Schneideman as Trustee of the Gordon Walters Estate; **page 89** image courtesy of the owner (photographed by Patrick Reynolds); **page 91** image courtesy of Auckland Art Gallery Toi o Tāmaki (purchased 1969) and permission courtesy of the artist; **page 93** image courtesy of the BNZ Art Collection; **page 95** image courtesy of the owner; **page 97** image courtesy of the owner; **page 99** image courtesy of the owner (photographed by Patrick Reynolds); **page 101** image courtesy of Museum of New Zealand Te Papa Tongarewa (purchased 1978 with Ellen Eames Collection funds, registration number: 1978-0031-39) and permission courtesy of Rachel Power; **page 103** image courtesy of the BNZ Art Collection and permission courtesy of Mary Fomison; **page 105** image courtesy of owners Ross and Bev Christoffersen (photographed by Ross Coombes); **page 107** image courtesy of Bett Gallery; **page 109** image courtesy of Ron Sang Publications and permission courtesy of the artist; **page 111** image courtesy of the artist; **page 113** image courtesy of Brian Culy; **page 115** image courtesy of the artist; **page 117** image courtesy of the artist; **page 119** image courtesy of the collection of the Tom Kreisler Estate (photographed by Kreisler Photography); **page 121** image courtesy of Bath Street Gallery and permission courtesy of the artist; **page 123** image courtesy of ART+OBJECT and permission courtesy of the artist; **page 125** image courtesy of the artist; **page 127** image courtesy of Gow Langsford Gallery and permission courtesy of the artist; **page 129** image courtesy of Christchurch Art Gallery Te Puna o Waiwhetu (photographed by Brendam Lee) and permission courtesy of the artist; **page 131** image courtesy of Hamish McKay Gallery; **page 133** image courtesy of Museum of New Zealand Te Papa Tongarewa (purchased 1998 with New Zealand Lottery Grants Board funds, registration number: 1999-0014-1) and permission courtesy of the artist; **page 135** image courtesy of the artist; **page 137** image courtesy of Auckland Art Gallery Toi o Tāmaki (gift of the Patrons of the Auckland Art Gallery, 1996) and permission courtesy of Marie Shannon on behalf of the Julian Dashper Estate; **page 139** image courtesy of Hamish McKay Gallery; **page 141** image courtesy of Bowen Galleries and permission courtesy of the artist; **page 143** image courtesy of John Leech Gallery and the artist; **page 145** image courtesy of Michael Lett, Auckland and permission courtesy of the artist; **page 147** image courtesy of Sue Crockford Gallery and permission courtesy of the artist; **page 149** image courtesy of Gow Langsford Gallery and permission courtesy of the artist; **page 151** image courtesy of Gow Langsford Gallery and permission courtesy of the artist; **page 153** image courtesy of Gow Langsford Gallery and permission courtesy of the artist; **page 155** image courtesy of the collection of Te Manawa Art Society Inc. and permission courtesy of the artist and Te Manawa Museums Trust; **page 157** image courtesy of the artist; **page 159** image courtesy of Christchurch Art Gallery Te Puna o Waiwhetu (purchased 2001) and permission courtesy of the artist; **page 161** image courtesy of owner (photographed by Patrick Reynolds); **page 163** image courtesy of PAULNACHE (photographed by Tom Teutenberg); **page 165** image courtesy of OREXART and permission courtesy of the artist; **page 167** image courtesy of the artist; **page 169** image courtesy of Fox/Jensen Gallery, Auckland and Jensen Gallery, Sydney; **page 171** image courtesy of Gow Langsford Gallery and permission courtesy of the artist; **page 173** image courtesy of Mark Hutchins Gallery and permission courtesy of the artist; **page 175** image courtesy of Jane Sanders Art Agent (photographed by Studio La Gonda); **page 177** image courtesy of Ivan Anthony Gallery and permission courtesy of the artist; **page 179** image courtesy of Ivan Anthony Gallery and permission courtesy of the artist; **page 181** image courtesy of Ivan Anthony Gallery and permission courtesy of the artist; **page 183** image courtesy of Ivan Anthony Gallery and permission courtesy of the artist; **page 185** image courtesy of Ivan Anthony Gallery and permission courtesy of the artist; **page 187** image courtesy of Mark Hutchins Gallery, Wellington and permission courtesy of the artist; **page 189** image courtesy of Melanie Roger Gallery, Auckland; **page 191** image courtesy of the owner (photographed by Patrick Reynolds); **page 193** image courtesy of Gow Langsford Gallery; **page 195** image courtesy of Ivan Anthony Gallery; **page 197** image courtesy of the artist; **page 199** image courtesy of Gow Langsford Gallery (photographed by Tobias Kraus) and permission courtesy of the artist; **page 201** image courtesy of the Gow Langsford Gallery; **page 203** image courtesy of the artist; **page 205** image courtesy of Melanie Roger Gallery, Auckland (from the collection of the Queensland Art Gallery, Australia) and permission courtesy of the artist; **page 207** image courtesy of Melanie Roger Gallery, Auckland (from a private collection) and permission courtesy of the artist; **Page 209** image courtesy of Melanie Roger Gallery, Auckland and permission courtesy of the artist; **Page 211** image courtesy of Melanie Roger Gallery, Auckland and permission courtesy of the artist; **Page 213** image courtesy of Melanie Roger Gallery (from the Wallace Trust Collection, Winner of the Park Lane Wallace Trust Development Award in the 2008 Wallace Art Awards) and permission courtesy of the artist; **page 215** image courtesy of Melanie Roger Gallery, Auckland (from a private collection) and permission courtesy of the artist; **page 217** image courtesy of the artist; **page 219** image courtesy of Antoinette Godkin Gallery and permission courtesy of the artist; **page 221** image courtesy of Brett McDowell Gallery and permission courtesy of the artist; **page 223** image courtesy of the owners (photographed by Chris Coad); **page 225** image courtesy of the artist; **page 227** image courtesy of Melanie Roger Gallery, Auckland (from a private collection) and permission courtesy of the artist; **page 229** image courtesy of Sanderson Contemporary Art and permission courtesy of the artist; **page 231** image courtesy of the artist; **page 233** image courtesy of the artist; **page 235** image courtesy of Christchurch Art Gallery Te Puna o Waiwhetu (Lawrence Baigent / Robert Erwin bequest, 2003) and permission courtesy of Cathy Harrington.

Index

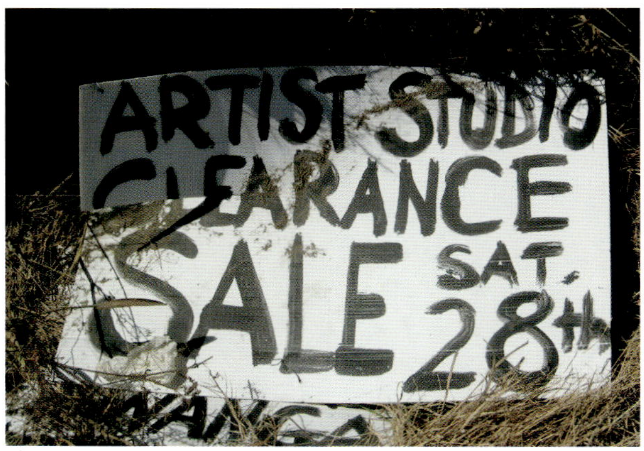
ARTIST STUDIO
CLEARANCE
SALE SAT.
28th

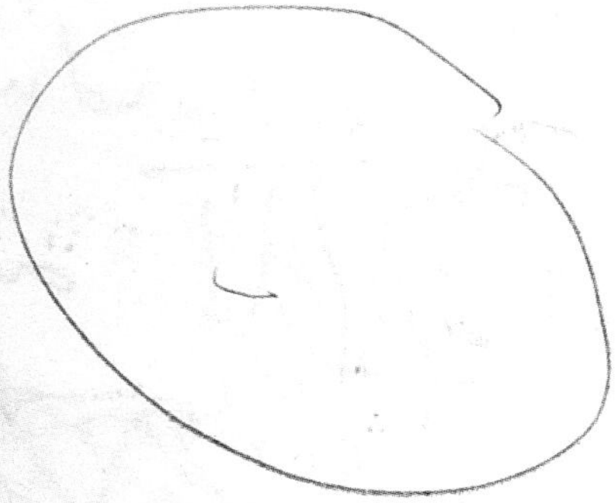

Candle in a dark room
does is it for me — the elevation
of the crude + the comic to
a statement of the best that
can be.

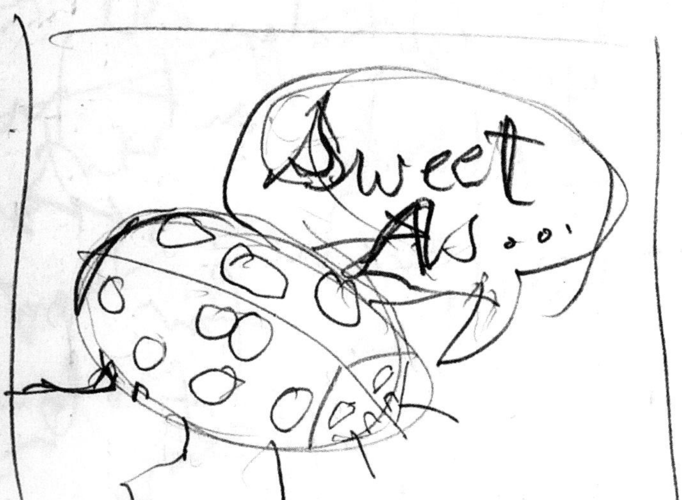

a millimetre of wrongness